Overcoming Al

'Dr Farren's achievement is ~~~~~~ ~~~~~uent. He has succeeded in writing a book that combi~~~ ~~ the stories of real people with the latest in scientific research. This book will, without doubt, become indispensable to those with alcohol-related problems and to their families.'

Professor Patricia Casey
University College Dublin

'A highly readable and accessible book on the topic of alcoholism. The cases in the book reflect the challenges faced by real people but also show how those with an alcohol problem can find real solutions.'

Dr Muiris Houston
Irish Times columnist and health analyst

'Dr Farren mixes elements of education, coaching, motivation and compassion to help those who are suffering as the result of alcohol-related disorders. This is a book that will help many people in need.'

Professor Roger D. Weiss
Harvard Medical School

'This is a comprehensive and humane book that should be an essential companion to those in recovery from alcohol dependence. It provides a thorough description of the nuts and bolts of treatment, recovery and relapse prevention, and provides a valuable description of AA and how to work with AA. Partners and families will find a lot of help and support here also.'

Professor Michael Farrell
Institute of Psychiatry, UK

'Dr Farren is uniquely qualified as a clinician researcher, patient advocate and author to provide a medical overview of addiction that reaches out with science and hope to patients and their families.'

Dr Mark A. Frye
Mayo Clinic, US

'A most excellent and timely book written by a leader in the field.'

Professor Bankole Johnson
University of Virginia

'A practical and comprehensive guide to help individuals and their families educate themselves about the disease of alcoholism, available treatment options, and the process of recovery.'

Sherry McKee, Ph.D
Yale University School of Medicine

'Dr Farren not only talks to us about alcoholism. It is clear that he has walked with many sufferers and their families....He has known many to recover, and he points the way to recovery, recognising that the way may differ for each person. His experience as a psychiatrist helps us understand the part that emotions, especially anxiety and loneliness, can play. I hope this book will be read by many....Here is learning, wisdom and humanity.'

Professor Jonathan Chick
Chief Editor, *Alcohol and Alcoholism*

'Concise and clearly written. A most valuable source for people with alcohol problems, their families and friends.'

Professor Karl Mann
Central Institute of Mental Health
University of Heidelberg

'An excellent read. A great guide for both the problem drinker and their families, with useful information for the professional carer as well.'

Dr Eugene Cotter, GP
Killorglin, Co. Kerry

Overcoming Alcohol Misuse

A 28-Day Guide

Conor Farren

KITE BOOKS

Published by Kite Books
an imprint of Blackhall Publishing
Lonsdale House
Avoca Avenue
Blackrock
Co. Dublin
Ireland

e-mail: info@blackhallpublishing.com
www.blackhallpublishing.com

ISBN: 978-1-84218-213-0

A catalogue record for this book is available from the British Library.

Printed in Ireland by Colorman Ltd.

Preface

This book is based on my experience as a treating psychiatrist for addictions and on the best and most up-to-date treatment research. Some of the material in this book is derived from teaching material I have developed for academics, medical students and psychiatrists, and also from the multiple presentations I have given to lay audiences of sufferers and their families, as well as members of the general public, over many years.

My experience as a treating physician, a teacher and a researcher has taught me that there is a tremendous need for material that can help those with alcohol addiction to gain understanding of their own problems. The partners and families of sufferers from alcohol addiction also need to gain that understanding, and to learn how to help their loved ones to start on the journey into recovery.

Addiction is a very lonely place, for those suffering from it and for those around them. This book is intended to show that there is no need for the experience to be so lonely and that a vital part of the alcohol misuser's journey into recovery is the ending of that loneliness, both for them and their loved ones. A vital component of making the journey into recovery a success is for the alcohol misuser to reach out for help and support. Loved ones cannot bear the burden alone and they too must reach out for vital support.

About the Author

Conor Farren, MB, Ph.D, ABPN (Dip.), FRCPI, MRCPsych, is a consultant psychiatrist at St Patrick's University Hospital and a clinical senior lecturer at Trinity College Dublin (TCD).

He graduated in Medicine from University College Dublin (UCD) in 1985 and trained in Psychiatry at St Patrick's Hospital, Dublin. He studied Addiction Psychiatry at Yale University, New Haven, Connecticut, and conducted research into new treatments for alcohol misuse. He took charge of the addiction psychiatry section of Mount Sinai School of Medicine and the Bronx Veterans Hospital, New York for a number of years, where he continued his research and founded the dual diagnosis treatment programme. He returned to Dublin to establish the dual diagnosis programme at St Patrick's University Hospital.

As well as having written numerous scientific articles on the subjects of addiction and mental health, he has also written extensively for newspapers and popular journals, and has spoken on radio and television on the same topics.

He is married with three children, and lives in Dublin. This is his first book.

This book is dedicated to my wife Anne, my children Ciara, Anne-marie and Lucas, and to my parents Andy and the late Moya Farren. It is also dedicated to those who I have met and tried to treat over the years but who did not live to complete their journey.

Note on Terminology

The primary term for those addicted to alcohol is the word 'alcoholic' and I could have chosen to use that term throughout this book. However, that word can have many negative associations for some individuals, and thus my preference is for the term 'alcohol misuser'. This term is close to the new term 'alcohol use disorder', which the largest psychiatric association in the world, the American Psychiatric Association, will endorse in the near future. This term will replace the terms 'alcohol dependence' and 'alcohol abuse', which will be consigned to the dustbin. It is important to get the terminology right, but it is more important not to pay too much attention to the issue and to get the information right. Occasionally other terms like 'alcoholic' creep into the book, and that's okay too. The point is to gain an understanding of the way the terminology is used and not to get caught up in it.

Acknowledgements

Many people have played a direct and indirect part in the genesis and development of this book, and I am grateful for the opportunity to thank them for their support and encouragement over the years.

First, I owe a debt of gratitude to the late Professor Anthony Clare for inspiring and encouraging me at various stages in my career, and to my many mentors, including Professor Ted Dinan of University College Cork, Professor Keith Tipton of Trinity College Dublin and Professor Stephanie O'Malley of Yale University. I would also like to thank my numerous colleagues at St Patrick's University Hospital, Dublin, Trinity College Dublin, the Connecticut Mental Health Centre and Yale University, and the Bronx Veterans Hospital and Mount Sinai School of Medicine, who I worked with over different stages of my psychiatric career and from whom I learned so much.

I acknowledge with gratitude the many addiction counsellors and therapists at the above institutions from whom I learned about the nature and the treatment of addictive problems. I have also learned a tremendous amount from the thousands of sufferers from addictive problems and their loved ones, who I have had the privilege of tending to and hopefully guiding over the years.

I would like to thank addiction psychiatrists Dr Matt Murphy and Dr Gerardine O'Keeffe for reading the first draft of the book and providing such useful guidance. I am immensely grateful to Elizabeth Brennan and all of the team at Blackhall Publishing for their interest, their dedication and their skill in bringing this book to publication.

I would like to thank my loving and encouraging wife Anne for all her support and affection over many years, and my wonderful children Ciara, Annemarie and Lucas, who make it all worthwhile.

Contents

Contents

Introduction

How to Use this Book

This book provides a clear step-by-step guide to achieving sobriety. It looks at all the important issues associated with that achievement, and aims to do so in a caring and accessible way.

I have spent many years trying to understand just how an ordinary person can develop an addiction to alcohol. My years in the field of psychiatry have taught me that alcohol misusers are among the most 'normal' of people to suffer from mental health issues, and yet they do the most damage to themselves, their lives and the lives of those around them. I have asked hundreds of alcohol misusers over the years how they developed alcohol dependence and the most common answer is that they just drifted into it. A series of tiny changes in habit and attitude to alcohol over years can produce full alcohol addiction. So, a significant part of the book deals with the question: 'Where am I and how did I get here?'

The next important question is, 'Now that I am here, and it's not a good place, how do I get out?' I have asked thousands of sufferers who have made the steps into recovery how they have done it and none of them have been able to give me a simple answer. However, they have told me about the steps they took that were helpful to them. The rest of the book deals with the possible steps that may be beneficial to individuals.

Introduction

This book is a series of pointers, guidelines and principles learned from people who have entered recovery, from my own observations of the numerous sufferers I have treated and from research carried out by the best minds in the recovery field. I have been conscious of including information on treatments and techniques that actually work. I have tried to make sure that the principles and guidelines I advocate are not just theories, but are proven methods that are effective.

The book contains twenty-eight chapters, to reflect the standard care plan of twenty-eight days in rehabilitation. The chapters provide background information and deal with the various issues that an alcohol misuser entering rehabilitation might face over the course of the 28-day period. The chapter points at the beginning of each chapter set out the theme of the chapter. The learning points at the end of each chapter indicate what I want the reader to get out of the chapter.

At the close of each chapter I've included a case study. The case studies, in most instances, are based on people I have met and helped to treat for their addiction. I've also included a couple of cases relating the recovery from addiction of people in the public eye. Each chapter contains an installment of 'Joe's Story', which relates the day-to-day experiences of one person as he journeys from alcohol misuse into sobriety over those first crucial twenty-eight days. Joe's experiences show just how complex and individual that journey can be. He is not based on any particular individual, but aspects of his journey do reflect the experiences of different people I have come across in my work.

The book is divided into three sections; however, the sections are not self-contained and feed into each other. The first section (Chapters 1–10) provides basic information about alcohol addiction, including the causes of alcoholism; the effects of alcohol on the body; the effects of alcoholism on all aspects of your life, including family, work and friends; associated problems such as depression; important information on 'types' of drinkers; and the importance of treatment. This is useful information for alcohol misusers, their concerned loved ones and interested professionals.

The second section deals with the bridge between alcohol addiction and recovery – that period of change and the beginning of sobriety. Chapters 11–16 look at how the alcohol misuser can be drawn into the recovery process through becoming aware of the damage the addiction is causing to themselves and those around them. A key concept here is insight. Once the alcohol misuser has achieved some insight into their condition, this can be worked on by a professional therapist or counsellor to help them into long-term sobriety. A concerned loved one may find this section interesting from the perspective of gaining insight into the mind of the alcohol misuser and the various forces that influence it, including those related to withdrawal and anxiety.

The third section (Chapters 17–27) provides information about the various techniques that are helpful in the recovery process, giving balanced information about different treatments and allowing alcohol misusers to choose what suits them best. This section is also valuable for the family member or friend standing by during the recovery period as it provides insight into what the stages of recovery entail for the alcohol misuser. This section would also be of use to a treating professional, since it outlines the positive and negative elements of each treatment technique and provides an update on the latest treatment research.

Chapter 28 provides a summary of the most important principles in treatment, for both the alcohol misuser and their loved ones. Information is provided in the Appendix on professional organisations that can help in guiding someone through his or her recovery process. Like all of the methods described in this book, not all of the organisations work for everybody, but sometimes a range need to be tried out for the alcohol misuser to find what is effective for him or her. It is important to remember that recovery is a work in progress and not a destination.

The book can be read one chapter at a time, one day at a time. It can be dipped into at any stage in the recovery process. As each person's recovery journey is individual, different issues need to be dealt with at different times. So, some parts of the book may be more relevant than others at any one time. The principles, guidelines, instructions and observations can be used on and off, according to an individual's needs. The chapters are intentionally brief and the topics dealt with cover all aspects of alcohol misuse and recovery. I wish to reach the largest number of sufferers and their families. I hope that such a broad approach will increase the chances of individuals landing on a treatment that works for them or coming across a story of alcohol abuse and recovery that will resonate with them.

I

What You Need to Know about Alcohol Misuse

1

Alcohol Misuse – What Is It?

> 1. Alcoholism and addiction can be a matter of life and death.
> 2. Alcoholism is avoidance.

What does the term 'alcoholic' mean? How can you tell if someone is an alcohol misuser? There can be no perfect definition that covers everyone, since each person's pathway into addiction is absolutely individual. However, it is true that, once an individual has reached an addictive state, this is obvious to everyone around them, if not actually to that person. Everyone knows that the red line has been crossed and the evidence is the terrible toll that alcohol addiction takes on the individual, their health, their family, their workmates and on society as a whole.

The importance of having a clear definition of 'alcoholic' or 'alcohol misuser' comes to the fore when there is a debate about whether someone has actually become an addict or not, or when an individual doesn't believe they are an addict but everyone around them is convinced otherwise. When there is some degree of doubt, either in the potential addict's mind or in the minds of those around them, it is vital to be clear about what constitutes an addiction to alcohol. It took many years of debate for the definition of alcohol dependence as 'clearly defined alcoholism' to be reached and, even now, forty years after the first discussion of alcohol dependence, there is still some debate in the treatment community about what the syndrome is.

Essentially alcoholism is a state of being. There is no simple single factor that determines whether someone is an alcohol misuser. Almost all aspects of a person's life have to be taken into account to determine if he or she is an alcohol misuser or not.

How many people have an alcohol problem? The trite answer to this question is, 'How long is a piece of string?' You can say that the answer is dependent on how you define the question. Using the term 'alcohol dependence' in place of 'alcohol problem', the answer is quite precise: in Western Europe, according to the World Health Organization (WHO), the figure is about 4 per cent of the adult population at any one time, with a further percentage abusing alcohol but not quite dependent. The figure for the US is similar, and the estimation is that 12.5 per cent of the US population develops alcohol dependence at some stage over the course of a lifetime. Unfortunately one of the most distressing associated figures is that only 20 per cent* of those with alcohol dependence are seeking help for it at any one time, and a smaller percentage are engaged in an effective therapeutic programme (Hasin et al., 2007). This leaves a lot of undiagnosed alcohol misusers out there, and a lot of misery going untreated.

Alcoholism, alcohol dependence, alcohol misuse or alcohol addiction is characterised by two things:

- A person's life is centered around alcohol, and

- Alcohol plays a harmful role in that person's life

---

* This is the figure for the US, but it is probably more or less the same in Europe.

What Is a Life Centered around Alcohol?

If a person's life is centred around alcohol, that life does not necessarily have to be falling apart. It is possible for a person to hold down a job, keep a marriage or relationship together, survive financially and still have alcohol as a major part of their lives. A life centred around alcohol is a matter of focus and priorities. It is a matter of prioritising alcohol above just about everything else. It is a matter of thinking about alcohol first thing in the morning, planning how to keep going until that first drink and trying to schedule the day around it. It may be a matter of resisting starting drinking until a certain time of the day or until after certain tasks are completed. It may be a matter of recovering from the previous day's drinking by taking alcohol early in the day. It can involve making plans to hide the day's drinking from someone – a spouse, child or work colleague. It may be calculating how to get as much alcohol as possible for as little money as possible. It may involve looking around for the cheapest alcohol and considering how to make the money stretch as far as possible. It may involve calculating how to avoid other responsibilities that could distract from drinking alcohol. It may involve deliberately inventing excuses to avoid work or family obligations. It may involve provoking others into a fruitless argument or confrontation to create an excuse to drink. It may involve making promises to faithfully attend some function or other, only to break those promises at the last minute in order to go drinking. It may involve fooling everyone and fooling no one. It may involve even fooling yourself, if you are the drinker. But eventually it involves everybody and everything else, because everybody and everything else is secondary to alcohol.

Alcohol does not play a positive role in an alcohol misuser's life. It may well have played an enjoyable role previously; it may have been the gateway to good times. A person many have used alcohol to get past shyness or social anxiety and to allow him or her to mix with others. It may even have played a part in the development of a significant relationship. Alcohol may have allowed a person to relax at the end of the day or week, and signalled the change from work life to social life. It may have been long associated with enjoying life, and that association can remain so strong that no other method of enjoyment seems possible.

What Is Harm from Alcohol?

Eventually alcohol can cross over from being a pleasure to being a necessity in a person's life. It moves from being a desire to being a need, from being a choice to being a compulsion. Pleasant thoughts about wanting to have a drink become decided urges to want that drink, and then become outright cravings for alcohol. And along with those urges and cravings come the negative consequences associated with drinking: the physical drain on energy and focus; the emotional toll of dealing with a disgruntled family member or spouse; the financial toll of spending too much money on alcohol; and the problems associated with not spending enough time in or effort on work. Ultimatums are delivered by increasingly upset family members, spouses, and sometimes work colleagues and supervisors. A propensity to miss appointments, targets and deadlines eventually leads to others changing their allegiances and moving away. Increasingly, life becomes filled with negativity and strife. The anger of surrounding family, friends and colleagues eventually wins out, and the individual becomes increasingly isolated as support whittles away. Eventually health consequences get in the way. Accidents, falls and visits to the hospital become more frequent. Specific medical problems such as those related to the pancreas, liver, brain or heart become established. Forgetfulness and memory loss become a way of life.

How Does a Person Become an Alcohol Misuser?

It may take thirty years to reach the stage of true dependence on alcohol. However, it can take just thirty days to enter recovery, if everything goes smoothly. One thing can be guaranteed: the course of true addiction never runs smoothly.

Addiction is, by and large, something that a person drifts into over a significant period of time, and is not 'achieved' instantly. Of course, some people feel an instant draw towards alcohol and report an almost instantaneous love affair upon first tasting it, leading to addiction. This group, however, represents the minority of alcohol misusers and not the majority. There is no Nobel Prize for becoming a misuser of alcohol in the shortest period of time. There is also no limitation on how long it can take to develop an addiction. It is a process that could take years rather than months. There is no single factor that marks the passing of a person from social drinking into alcoholic drinking. Most people who end up in an addictive state are perfectly capable of stating in all honesty, 'How did I get here?' It is not something anybody sets out to achieve.

The drift into alcohol addiction is an individual one. However, the process of loss of control over alcohol can be marked by a number of stages:

1. Enjoyment of alcohol in a social and positive manner

2. Increase in frequency of alcohol consumption to daily, or a shift to a regular binge drinking pattern

3. Significant narrowing of daily activity to include alcohol. Alcohol becomes a primary focus in life

4. Negative consequences on personal relationships, work, emotions, social life, finances and health

5. Drastic consequences: ending of personal relationships; loss of employment; financial disorder; downgrading of living circumstances; major psychiatric disorder; severe liver, pancreas, brain, heart difficulties; and hospitalisation

6. Early death

There are many grey areas between these stages. Negative consequences of a life dependent on alcohol may come in no particular order; such consequences may appear at the same time as the narrowing of daily activity. Some alcohol misusers can die denying that alcohol has become a major factor in their lives. There are those who might claim that alcohol has had no negative consequences in their lives at all. But the above stages are recognisable to all professionals working with alcohol misusers, the family and friends of addicts, and the vast majority of addicts, if they are honest.

It is true to say that not all people with an alcohol addiction inevitably go through stages one to six. Everyone has their own trajectory, and, theoretically, a person can stop at any one of the stages and not progress from there. But the majority of those addicted to alcohol who do little or nothing about it (and that is the majority of alcohol misusers) will work their way through the stages and suffer dreadful consequences.

A State of Unawareness

An alternative title for this book could be *Sobriety for the Accidental Alcoholic*, because addiction is a process that creeps up on an individual unawares. The addiction is usually recognised by the addict retrospectively, not as it is occurring. The process of descent into addiction may or may not be recognised by others; it may be a slow or a long process; it may have immediate negative consequences or it may not.

If the pathway to alcoholism is lit by avoidance, it is shadowed by denial. That unique inability to see what is happening to you as it is actually happening is one of the defining characteristics of the alcohol misuser. Psychologists have euphemistically named this state 'pre-contemplation'. Alcoholism is akin to a numbed state of post-traumatic stress. The alcohol misuser is simply unable to believe their eyes, ears and senses, and is also unwilling to comprehend what is happening to them. This state of incomprehension can be almost total, no matter how unbelievable this is to an outsider.

Alcoholism Means Avoidance

Alcoholism and avoidance are part of the same problem. If there is a major life crisis to be faced up to and dealt with, the alcohol misuser can be trusted to miss the opportunity completely. No problem is too large to be ignored and no issue present that cannot be dealt with by sticking the head in the sand. As mentioned, some alcohol misusers, at least in the early stages, can carry on most of the normal functions of life. However, what they are not capable of doing is dealing with emotional reality. All major issues, such as the loss of a loved one, financial difficulties, relationship stresses, child-rearing problems and the difficult stuff of life in general, are dealt with in the same manner. The only coping mechanism is alcohol, and damn the consequences. The negative fallout from drinking itself is dealt with by the same mentality of denial. Drink becomes the universal cure and a complete way of life. It is this denial that enables an alcohol misuser's shameless descent through the stages of addiction, while refusing to acknowledge alcohol's influence on his or her life, however astonishing this may be to others.

However, denial is not absolute, and the alcohol misuser, at some level or in some tiny way, understands that something is not quite right. It is this small gap in the alcohol misuser's armour that therapists, family and friends, and, ultimately, the addict themselves must recognise, explore and expand on if there is to be any hope of recovery. It is the job of those around the alcohol misuser to focus on the chinks in his or her armour, and the alcohol misuser must be receptive to that exploration. It may even be necessary to create that gap where it did not previously exist. A person's way back from the descent into the last stages of alcoholism can only be achieved by, first, acknowledging the existence of a significant problem in their life and, second, acknowledging addiction to alcohol as its origin.

Recovery Means Acceptance

Just as the descent through the stages of alcohol addiction is characterised by partial denial, so the process of recovery relies on gradual acceptance, albeit also partial. Just as denial is never absolute, and some quiet admission of the problem is always present, so recovery is never fully complete, but is a process of continuously hard-won partial acceptance. The acceptance that sustains the recovery process must be fed and strengthened regularly for recovery to continue.

Ownership of the problem is the first step on the journey towards recovery. If the alcohol misuser learns to 'own' their problem, they eventually take responsibility for the problem. One very important point an addict needs to acknowledge is that he or she may actually want to continue drinking alcohol and may not want to give it up at all, no matter what the consequences are. Every alcohol misuser wants just one last drink to see off the addiction or to show they are not addicted. That desire, or idea, never fully leaves the misuser, and it can lead to an addict taking a drink after five, ten or even twenty years of sobriety, potentially leading to a full relapse.

The American abolitionist Wendell Phillips said, 'Eternal vigilance is the price of liberty', and so it must be for the recovering alcohol misuser. Eternal vigilance, eternal doubt and eternal effort will maintain sobriety, and the day the alcohol misuser declares himself cured is the day he relapses and has to start all over again.

Make the problem yours, and eventually you will become responsible for it.

Case Study: The Reluctant Alcohol Misuser

Maria grew up in a small town where everyone knew each other and each other's business. Her family was tight-knit, with a hard-working father, a mother who worked in a part-time job and two sisters. She was the eldest, and felt she had to shoulder the responsibility of looking after the other girls.

She was quite bright in school, and developed a flair for art and design. Being shy, she found it difficult to meet other people socially. When she was fourteen, she began to take a drink from her father's drinks cabinet before going out to meet other people socially. She didn't want to take alcohol; she didn't even like the taste. Eventually this grew into a need to go out and get drunk while socialising.

Drink began to interfere with her school work and, when she left school, with her course work in the local community college she attended. Around this time she began to take Valium and Xanax tablets from her mother, and then on prescription from a local doctor. This habit grew until she was getting tablets from three different local doctors.

She entered rehabilitation for the first time at the age of twenty-one, and went through a torrid time withdrawing from both the alcohol and tablets. She achieved sobriety after leaving hospital, and began to attend AA. She resumed her studies in the local college. She would get so far into her sobriety and then relapse to a combination of drink and tablets. Her mood would deteriorate also and she could get significant panic and anxiety attacks. She had to restart her college course while all her friends graduated and moved on to careers. She became increasingly isolated and found it difficult to function in daily life.

Her panic and then depression gradually got the better of her. She relapsed to alcohol again shortly after her third admission to rehabilitation in a local hospital. She found it increasingly difficult to function and ended up going back to doctors asking for the same addictive tablets she had such trouble getting off two years' previously. She spent an increasing amount of her time at home in her room, unable to go back to her course, and emerging only for her meals and for a foray into town to get drunk in the local pub.

She died after a significant binge of medication and alcohol finally took its toll on her overstrained body. No one knows if the final binge was a suicide attempt, a cry for help or simply a major relapse to addiction. She was twenty-three years old.

Joe's Story: Day 1

Joe woke up on a Sunday morning. His head ached, his stomach hurt, his hands were shaking and he had just spent a jumbled, restless night. He had been awake for most of it.

His wife came into the bedroom, took one look at him and went out again. Joe had been married for seven years. From the look on his wife's face he wasn't sure if he was going to be married for another seven days.

He had been drinking the previous day for most of the afternoon and evening. He lost count of the number of pints he had; it might have been twelve or maybe fourteen. It had been an all-too-familiar story: he went out for just one drink and ended up drinking way too many. He did not come home at the time he said he would and he had missed his Saturday evening date with his wife. She wouldn't be pleased about that.

Maybe he should do something about his drinking; it had really gotten out of hand recently. Maybe, if he was honest, it had been out of hand for at least a few months, maybe even a year or two. Things just didn't seem to be going right at all. He thought he should probably do something about it. But what?

2

Do You Have a Problem with Alcohol?

Every person's pathway into addiction is unique and different.

The 'X Factor'

When you ask a person, 'Are you an alcoholic?' the simplest and most common answer is an emphatic 'No!' If you ask for more of an explanation, the most frequent answer is, 'I know I'm not an alcoholic because of X.' 'X' represents any manner of explanation that an alcohol misuser can use to convince themselves and others that all is fine. This is the real X factor.

Examples of the X factor include:

- Because I'm still holding down a job

- Because I'm still married

- Because I don't drink as much as someone else and nobody is accusing them of being an alcoholic

- Because I have always been able to hold my drink

- Because I just want to enjoy myself

- Because I only drink to cope with my problems

- Because, if it wasn't for that person (spouse, boss, relative), I wouldn't need to drink at all

- Because I used to have a problem, but I am able to control it now

- Because I simply am not an alcoholic and that's all there is to it!

How to Evaluate if You Are an Alcohol Misuser

However, the very fact that someone has asked you the question 'Are you an alcoholic?' means that it is a point for discussion and worthy of attention. It leads to the important question – how do you evaluate if you are an alcohol misuser? There are a number of ways of finding out whether a person has a problem with alcohol. No one method is foolproof.

One method is to ask yourself a series of seven questions:

1. *Is Alcohol* Central *to Your Life?*

The answer to this is yes if you spend a significant amount of time getting alcohol, drinking it or recovering from its effects; a prominent part of your day or your week revolves around alcohol; and it is a dominant focus of your thoughts.

2. *Has Alcohol Caused* Harm *in Your Life?*

The way you evaluate if alcohol has caused harm in your life is to examine four major areas of your life and to do an assessment of those areas, reasonably objectively. For example:

A. Relationship with Loved Ones

If your spouse or a loved one has mentioned alcohol to you in a negative way, if it has caused arguments between you, if you have split temporarily from him or her, or if you have split up and alcohol played any role in that split, then that is, by definition, harm.

B. Work or Primary Occupation

If your boss has mentioned your alcohol consumption to you or if you have missed days off work because of alcohol, this constitutes harm to your work. If you have your own business and you have missed deadlines with your clients because of alcohol, this is work-related harm. If you are a housewife and have neglected the house or the children, that also constitutes harm to your work life. Even if you don't miss days at work and are not in trouble with your boss, but are underperforming according to your own standards because of alcohol or recovering from it, then that is harm.

C. Social and Family Harm

If you have given up various social activities, physical activities or hobbies because of alcohol, that constitutes harm to your social life. If you avoid going out because it interferes with drinking time, that is social harm. And if other family members mention alcohol to you as being a problem, that is also evidence of harm.

D. Health Harm

Your health has been harmed if you have been hospitalised because of alcohol, say, for pancreatitis, gastritis, liver trouble, heart trouble or brain disorder due to alcohol. If your doctor has warned you to cut down your alcohol intake, that is health harm. If blood tests have come back indicating excessive alcohol intake, that is harm. And if you have been injured in a car accident, fight or assault in which your alcohol consumption played a role, these are also cases of health harm. A hangover or a headache from the previous night's drinking does not constitute harm from a health perspective.

3. *What about Your Alcohol* Withdrawal?

Severe withdrawal from alcohol is not hard to diagnose. Some people might suffer from shakes, excessive sweating, severe anxiety and jumpiness, bad nausea and vomiting, and, at an extreme, hallucinations, which can involve hearing voices, seeing frightening things like rats and reptiles, and even feeling things crawling on your skin. Some people actually get epileptic fits as part of withdrawal, but may not ascribe these to alcohol if they occur two or three days after they stop drinking. If, as part of withdrawal from alcohol, you go through minor shakes (tremors), sweating or a feeling of being hot at night, anxiety, desire to escape from current surroundings or even a general sense of anxiety that could easily be treated with just one drink, then that is withdrawal and is not just about missing the booze.

Alcohol withdrawal can be dangerous and sometimes even fatal. It tends to get worse as the years go by, and those who get some withdrawal symptoms on ceasing to drink alcohol can eventually end up with a severe withdrawal pattern. The treatment for alcohol withdrawal, including seizures, is abstinence. Severe withdrawal needs to be dealt with in hospital because of the associated medical dangers. Moderate withdrawal should have medical attention, and a doctor should decide if hospital admission or withdrawal medication is necessary or not. Mild withdrawal is generally treated with quietness, fluids and food, and is finished with in a number of days. Severe withdrawal lasts five to seven days, but I have seen withdrawal lasting up to twelve days in very unusual cases. Chapters 15 and 16 deal with alcohol withdrawal in more detail.

4. Is there Evidence of a Change in Your Tolerance?

Tolerance is the medical term given to the ability to hold one's drink. If your ability to hold your drink is unchanged and if it takes the same amount of alcohol to get you intoxicated as it did a number of years ago, then your tolerance for alcohol has not changed. If, however, it now takes more drinks to get you drunk relative to years ago, then your tolerance for alcohol has gone up, and that change in tolerance is another pointer towards alcohol dependence.

Some longstanding drinkers find that their tolerance for alcohol goes down and not up as they grow older. They find that they can't hold their liquor and that they have all the signs of drunkenness – slurred speech, a woozy feeling in the head and even an alteration in their mood – with a relatively small quantity of alcohol. This alteration downwards in tolerance is also a sign of dependence on alcohol. It may be that the brain is beginning to suffer from long-term damage from alcohol and that is why it exhibits the decrease in tolerance. Some people have gotten to the extreme situation where they can appear drunk to other people even when they have no alcohol on board at all. This is rare and, not surprisingly, is not a good sign overall, indicating quite significant brain damage.

5. *Do You Have a Desire to* Cut Down or Control *Your Alcohol Use? Have You Made a Number of Unsuccessful Efforts to Do This?*

Recurrent efforts to cut down or control alcohol use often indicate a stopping-and-starting addictive pattern and is common in various parts of the world, mainly the US, the northern half of Western Europe, Russia and most of Asia. The idea of binge drinking, having a break and then going on 'the tear' for a number of days or even weeks is classically associated with alcohol dependence. Some people have it built into their year, giving it up after Christmas, giving it up in the summer, but allowing themselves to drink at other times.

In the southern part of Europe, largely the wine-producing areas, in the wine-producing areas of the western US and the wine-producing areas of South America, the pattern of problematic drinking is different. In these areas, people with drinking problems and dependence tend to drink continuously, and don't go on binges. Theoretically, this pattern is less problematic. A continuous moderate intake leads, in general, to less social problems and less obvious personal consequences. There is less social disruption and less obvious family distress. However, there are a lot of liver problems in these areas and, although some of the facets of alcohol dependence may not be as prominent, early death is just as big a problem. A lot of alcohol misusers try to cut down and control alcohol use, but this inevitably leads to another break-out or an increase in intake until they are back to the same level as before.

6. *Do You often Take Alcohol in* Larger Amounts *or over* Longer Periods *than Intended?*

This can mean you have difficulty ceasing drinking at any one particular time. If you find it difficult to stop drinking at closing time or if you find it hard to refrain from finishing every bottle of wine you open or from finishing the bottle of spirits before going to bed, this is a definite pointer towards dependence and is a significant marker on the descent into addiction.

7. *Do You* Persist *in Drinking Despite Your Awareness of a Problem?*

If you know there are some issues associated with your drinking, but you keep on drinking anyway, that persistence is a sure sign of a problem. Only one person can make that judgment because, no matter how strongly you protest that you don't have an issue with alcohol and how little it influences your life, the personal cold judgment alone in the dead of night may suggest otherwise. It's not that you have to state to others that you are an alcoholic or even admit it to yourself, but you have to believe that alcohol may be causing some problems in your life.

The above questions signify the seven deadly sins, and the astonishing thing is that a person only needs to answer yes to *three* of them before they can be judged alcohol dependent. What these questions show is that there is no one diagnostic pointer for alcoholism – a number of seemingly unconnected factors makes up the syndrome.

Within the category of dependence it can be argued that there are those who are severely dependent and those who are mildly dependent, and that those who have six or seven signs of dependence are in a different category to those who have three or four only. There may be some truth in that statement. But the important thing is whether the line in the sand has been crossed or not, and that line in the sand is determined by a personal assessment in the context of each of the above seven diagnostic pointers. While the assessment is best carried out by a professional in the area of addiction, since they can ask the right questions and sidestep the evasive answers, in truth, the questions are fairly basic and can be effectively answered in a self-evaluation.

However, alcohol dependence is not something that needs to be declared by an addiction therapist; it needs to be declared by the individual involved. The main trick for any person evaluating themselves is not to fool themselves in answering the questions.

CAGE Questionnaire

One of the most common 'quickie' guides to discovering whether you have a problem with alcohol is the CAGE questionnaire.* This asks four questions:

1. Have you tried to *cut down* your alcohol consumption? This really asks about your own concerns about your alcohol consumption. In other words, have you been so concerned about your alcohol consumption that you have not only thought about it but you have made genuine attempts to decrease your alcohol consumption over a period of time? If the answer is yes, strike one

2. Do you get *annoyed* when people talk to you about alcohol? This question really asks two things: have people around you – family, coworkers or friends – actually spoken to you about alcohol, and have you had a bad reaction to those concerns or comments? Thus, the question implies that people

---

* An internationally used assessment instrument for identifying problems with alcohol, developed by Dr John Ewing. 'CAGE' is an acronym formed from the italicised letters in the questionnaire (cut-annoyed-guilty-eye).

around you have been concerned, and then concerned enough to risk transgressing normal social etiquette to ask you about alcohol. If you have reacted defensively, getting annoyed or even upset about the question and its implications, this could indicate an element of denial on your part

3. Do you feel *guilty* about your drinking? This gets to the heart of the assessment. Are you in some form of denial, and does this denial cause upset feelings or guilt when you are thinking about it by yourself? At the end of the day, it is not someone else's feelings about your drinking that are important, but your own, and this question asks about those feelings

4. Do you have an *'eye-opener'* in the mornings? This is a simple question about drinking pattern: do you have a drink in the mornings? The obvious implication is that someone who drinks in the morning is more likely to have a problem than someone who drinks only in the afternoon or evening

Answering positively to one of the four questions may mean that a problem is brewing for the future. Answering two questions in the positive may mean that there is a current problem and it should be taken to the next level of intervention. The wonderful advantage of this questionnaire is that it is quick, simple and brutally clear.

> **In order to find out if you have a problem, it is necessary to be brutally honest, if not with others then at least with yourself.**

Case Study: The Anxious Alcohol Misuser

Serena came for help with significant anxiety and shyness problems, as well as alcohol addiction. She had a problem for years whereby she felt afraid to go out and meet people. She suffered from panic attacks and from significant social phobia, and tended to stay indoors rather than engage with others. She was married, with four grown up children, and she began to drink secretly to cope with the stress and anxiety.

She had been raised in a small rural community by a strict father and a timid mother, and she had suffered physical abuse at the hands of her father when he drank too much. She married a kind and hardworking man, but he was generally too busy running a large farm to give her the attention and comfort she needed. She drank wine in the evenings with her main meals, but she also drank vodka by herself in the afternoons. She thought no one would find out about it.

While the drink proved mildly helpful in the short term, she found herself drinking almost every day of the week. She would sometimes be woozy and a bit drunk when sitting down to her evening meal with the family. Eventually they persuaded her to seek help and she came to a psychiatrist for treatment.

After a series of successful interventions, she settled down to maintaining sobriety and fighting her anxiety through a combination of medication, therapy and self-help. Unfortunately, her husband suffered a heart attack soon afterwards and, after a very tough month in hospital, had a second heart attack and died. She did surprisingly well for six months or so, and then gradually succumbed to bouts of anxiety and began drinking again in the afternoons. The alcohol tended to mask the symptoms for a few hours or so, but then would make her anxiety and depression worse for the next few days.

It required a further series of interventions to help her back to sobriety and reasonably good mental health. She found it difficult because of her anxiety to attend groups like AA and preferred to try and do things for herself, by herself. That allowed her to stop focusing on her tendency to use alcohol as an avoidance technique. It took a combination of effective medication, continued support from a group and a therapist, and gentle but persistent family pressure to keep her well.

A number of years after her first brush with treatment and her husband's death, she still struggles with her sobriety but wins most of the time. Her life has slowly improved overall and she is forging a new social circle for herself.

Joe's Story: Day 2

His wife had had enough. She had given him an ultimatum: 'It's alcohol or me.' Joe decided to take things into his own hands and he called his GP.

Joe's GP listened to his story for a minute and made a strong, simple suggestion. Joe should go into rehabilitation. Joe was very reluctant. Wasn't that for alcoholics? What did he want to be sent in there for? He might have a bit of a problem and might have gotten into trouble on a few occasions, but he wasn't an alcoholic. He still had his job (though the boss was quite ropey with him after he missed two days in a row the previous week) and he still had his marriage (although his wife was quite upset with him at the moment).

Joe and his wife agreed that they should give the treatment centre a call and then see what happened. Joe thought about having a few pints to help him along to his impending treatment but he wasn't sure he would get away with it.

3

Causes of Alcohol Dependence – Family, Genes and Environment

> The main causes of alcohol dependence are genetics and environment.

Most alcohol misusers do not set out to become so. A person in this situation might ask, 'Well, how did I get here?' and 'Am I really responsible?' The answer to the latter question is, yes, the drinker is ultimately responsible, but a number of factors may have caused him or her to become dependent on alcohol. There are two major reasons for becoming alcohol dependent: genes and environment.

Genes

Let's not underestimate genes. Alcohol dependence is not solely a genetic disorder, but it is about 50 per cent genetic. It runs in families, in relation to the fact that family history has a significant effect on the origin of dependence. However, whether the origin of dependence is genetic or not has no effect on the clinical outcome of dependence or on recovery.

A lot of the original genetic research on alcoholism was carried out in the 1970s, and it was based on Swedish and Danish adoption data. The researchers found that, if you were the son of an alcoholic and you were adopted away and raised in a non-alcoholic family, you were three times more likely to become an alcoholic than if you were the son of a non-alcoholic and adopted away to be raised in a non-alcoholic family. Women are two and a half times more likely to develop alcoholism if they come from an alcoholic family and are adopted away to a non-alcoholic family.

Numerous studies over the last thirty years agree with those findings: alcoholism is genetic. And not only is it genetic but evidence is emerging that there are a number of elements related to developing alcoholism that are transmitted in the genes. For example, a researcher named Marc Schuckit (2009) found that sons of alcoholics are likely to have an increased initial tolerance for alcohol, and increased hormone levels related to stress and to the neurotransmitter serotonin. This suggests that it is not a great thing to be able to drink your friends under the table at the age of eighteen; this innate high tolerance may signify a predisposition to alcohol problems later on.

Another researcher, Robert Cloninger (1987), found that alcoholism is a disease of personality components and alcoholics have three major personality components: a high degree of 'novelty seeking', a high degree of 'reward dependence' and a low degree of 'harm avoidance'. He suggested that this triad of personality traits was passed on within alcoholic families, and that each of these three components was associated with an abnormality in a specific brain chemical transmitter. These characteristics make up the portrait of a person who is more adventurous than average (high degree of novelty seeking), likes getting the benefits of that adventurous spirit (high reward dependence), but is not great at learning the life lessons when something goes wrong (poor harm avoidance). This is a wonderful set of characteristics if you are a fun-seeking adolescent, but they are not so good if you are an adult with responsibilities. Of course, these traits can also be applied to other groups of people such as extreme sports enthusiasts, and so they don't necessarily signify that a person is or will become an alcoholic.

Nothing is entirely predetermined. Not everyone with a strong family history or with fun-seeking characteristics becomes an alcoholic. Indeed, the distinct majority of people with a strong family history of alcoholism do not become alcoholics. However, not surprisingly, if you have a strong family history of alcoholism, you are more likely than the average person to become addicted to alcohol. For research purposes, a strong family history of alcoholism means a first degree relative (parent, sibling or child) with alcoholism, or two second degree relatives (grandparent, aunt, uncle, niece, nephew or first cousin) with alcoholism. As about one-third of us have some relative or other with alcoholism, this means that a lot of the population is actually at risk.

Researchers are seeking to identify the gene that is associated with alcoholism, that is, the actual piece of DNA that causes it. However, because alcohol dependence has so many aspects and so many causes, it is highly unlikely that there is any one single gene that causes it. It is likely that there are multiple causes for alcoholism, and multiple genes that are likely to cause it or at least predispose someone to developing it. That unfortunately means that it is less likely that a single 'cure' for alcoholism exists, but it does increase the potential for developing a medication that is likely to help at least a subset of alcoholics. The exciting developments in that area will be dealt with in Chapter 19.

Environment

Why we drink and why we drink excessively are complex issues. No man is an island and we are tremendously affected by prevailing attitudes, even if we like to think of ourselves as independent-minded individuals. We can't help but be affected by the attitudes to drinking around us, in both the family environment and the wider cultural environment.

If we come from a family where drinking is acceptable and where people tend to consume alcohol frequently and heavily, we gain permission to do it. Children learn from the adults around them, and far more by example than by words. No matter what the adults say, the children pick up the 'appropriate' behaviour from what the adults do, especially regarding alcohol. If the adults feel it is appropriate to have a glass of wine with every meal, the children will feel it is appropriate. If the adults feel it is acceptable to get drunk a few times per week, then, even if the children see the negative effects of this, they are getting the message at some level that it is okay. If the children are brought to a pub as teenagers and observe the adults drinking, they will regard it as normal and aspire to do it themselves. Basically, research shows that, if parental drinking is heavy, more than any other factor this makes it more likely that the youngsters' drinking will be heavy. If parental drinking is social, then in all probability the adolescents' drinking will be social. If we don't educate our children about the dangers of alcohol and the dangers of addiction, they simply won't know anything about it.

Outside the family, the particular cultural environment around drinking alcohol has an enormous effect on the consumption of alcohol by individuals in a society. If we grow up in a culture that is permissive regarding alcohol – such as Russia, where alcohol consumption and even binge alcohol consumption is regarded as a mark of adulthood – it massively influences our personal consumption. If we are raised in a culture that forbids or frowns on alcohol consumption, such as most Muslim cultures or Orthodox Jewish cultures, then our individual consumption of alcohol is likely to be minimal. Of course, there are rebels in every culture, and there are many alcoholics who are Muslims or Orthodox Jews. But the fact is, if we grow up in a culture that permits and encourages heavy regular alcohol consumption, such as in the wine-growing regions of Europe (France, Spain and Italy), we are more likely to become regular heavy consumers of alcohol.

In Ireland we have a pro-alcohol culture and, as a consequence, we have among the highest levels of alcohol consumption in Europe and the world. We seem incapable of having any social gathering in this country without alcohol being involved, and most evenings out either begin or end with alcohol consumption. We have become so accustomed to alcohol being an integral part of Irish life, it seems hard to believe that over 100 years ago we were the temperance leaders of Europe, and that at one stage the Temperance Movement could bring 100,000 people to the streets to march against alcohol. How times change!

Altering Drinking Culture

A vital point that both history and research show us is that culture and environment are not written in stone and can be altered, especially regarding alcohol. In the era of prohibition in the US, from 1920 to 1933, there were significant shifts in attitudes to alcohol in US society. When prohibition of alcohol was introduced, this produced a massive reduction in alcohol consumption and a massive falloff in alcohol-related disorders like cirrhosis of the liver. However, with the advent of the speakeasy (a place where alcohol was sold illegally in this period), the smuggling of alcohol in from abroad and the rise of the bootlegger or illicit maker of alcohol, alcohol consumption began to rise and so did the incidence of alcohol-related disorders. People began to feel that the restrictive measures went too far and began to regularly break the law in order to drink. This led to the repeal of the prohibition laws in 1933 and the 'normalisation' of drinking in the US in the 1930s.

A similar large shift in attitudes to alcohol happened in Sweden, though in reverse. Due to the previous liberalisation of drinking laws, Sweden become notorious for heavy drinking and became the country with the highest level of alcohol consumption in Europe in the nineteenth century. In the early twentieth century, the Swedish Government decided to restrict access to alcohol and to make alcohol expensive and tightly controlled, but did not prohibit it altogether. As a result, Sweden became the role model for other countries in terms of how to manage an alcohol problem. Today, Sweden has the lowest level of alcohol consumption in Europe, which is one-third the level of consumption in Ireland.

These examples show that, through controlling the laws and the culture associated with alcohol, it is possible to control alcohol consumption and to change dominating attitudes to alcohol within a society over time.

Age at which You Start Drinking

A major influence on whether a person is going to develop an alcohol problem or not is the age at which they start drinking alcohol. If you start drinking alcohol at the age of twelve or thirteen, you are up to nine times more likely to develop a drink problem than if you start drinking at the age nineteen or twenty. That is a significant difference.

The earlier you begin drinking, the earlier problems occur, if they are going to. There is an ongoing debate in the research community about the significance of developing a problem with alcohol from an early age. Many researchers believe that those who develop a problem with alcohol before the age of twenty-five represent a separate group of alcoholics that need and may respond to special treatment interventions such as medication. The person who develops problems with alcohol before the age of twenty-five may also have a greater chance of having psychiatric problems and a strong family history than the person who develops problems after the age of twenty-five.

Despite all the influences around us – genetic, familial, environmental and cultural – we still determine our own destinies. We are ultimately responsible for ourselves and our actions, and, in the case of alcohol, for our own recovery. Even a person with the strongest family history of alcoholism, who is submerged in the most pro-alcohol of cultures, is not predestined to either drink or become an alcoholic. It is one of the great ironies of addiction research that Ireland has the highest degree of alcohol consumption in the world and also the highest proportion of teetotalers. Thus, a large group of Irish men and women are capable of ignoring the pro-alcohol culture in Ireland and abstain completely from alcohol. Nothing is written in stone; nothing is predestined.

An important piece of information to be aware of is that, in all studies into recovery from alcoholism, the results have shown that family history does not determine success. Those who have a strong family history of alcoholism have exactly the same chance of recovery or non-recovery as those who have no family history of alcoholism at all. So we may blame our family history and our culture for helping to make us dependent on alcohol in the first place, but we can't blame our failure to recover on anyone but ourselves.

> **'Alcohol dependence may be a disease, but I am still responsible for my own recovery.'**

Case Study: The Enthusiastic Alcohol Misuser

Peter was a bit of a wild child. He was constantly moving, doing things, getting into mischief. He got into mild trouble at school, missed a few classes, missed a few days and played the class clown at times. His problems began when he was fourteen, when some of the friends he hung around with began to go out drinking. He tried it and found almost instantly that he enjoyed getting drunk and the feeling of being intoxicated.

He began to drink quite seriously at the age of fifteen and, by seventeen, he had developed a significant drinking problem. He would binge drink at weekends and even into the week. He would drink almost anything – wine, beer, spirits – and he began to spend most of his time drinking or recovering from it. He dabbled in some drugs, but found he didn't enjoy them as much as alcohol.

He got into significant trouble at home, and was asked to leave the house on a few occasions. He dropped out of school and did odd jobs around the place to earn bits of cash. He got into trouble with the law for minor offences like being drunk and disorderly, and spent a few nights in police cells, sobering up. He eventually got into serious trouble by breaking up his parents' living room and then assaulting the police who came to quell the disturbance.

He came into treatment very reluctantly at the age of twenty-one, and took a long time to detoxify and to stabilise his agitated mood. He eventually settled, with the use of calming medication, and was able to focus on the seriousness of his alcohol addiction. He completed his rehabilitation, but relapsed seriously to alcohol within two months of discharge from the programme.

He then came into treatment a second time and this seemed to have more effect. He was discharged back to his parents, and he remained sober with the combined help of AA meetings and calming medication, with regular doctors' appointments. He has broken out on a few occasions, but remains committed to trying to turn his life around.

Joe's Story: Day 3

Joe ended up agreeing with the very nice and reasonable person on the phone that there was no harm in visiting the treatment centre, and then deciding to stay if he liked it. So, he packed a few night clothes into a hold-all bag and he got into the car.

His wife drove him there. She looked less and less agreeable the longer she was in the car with him. She downright refused to talk to him, and she was really angry and tight-lipped by the time they got to the centre. She practically dumped him on the doorstep, and only stayed long enough to give his details to the receptionist.

They were very nice people in reception, and they assured him that he wouldn't be locked up or mishandled in any way. He was beginning to feel a little ropey – he hadn't slept well the previous night – but overall he felt okay about the whole thing.

He got through the admission procedure quickly enough. The admission nurse was quite sharp in her questioning of his drinking, especially in relation to what he drank recently. The doctor prescribed some medication and some vitamins, and then he was led up to his bed. By now he was feeling more than a little irritated by the whole rigmarole and would have been okay with going home, but no one was offering that as an option.

He accepted a few pills and went off to bed in a six-bed observation unit. He didn't want to be there at all.

4

The Effects of Alcohol on the Body

Alcohol can severely damage every organ system in the body.

We can be fooled that alcohol is a safe product. It is not. Alcohol causes a vast number of harmful disorders – sixty significant ones at least – to the body and mind, and is the sole cause of many diseases known to man. If alcohol was presented today to a regulatory authority, such as the Food and Drug Administration (FDA), it would never gain approval as either a drug or a food. It has some pleasant effects, such as mild intoxication and a decrease in social anxiety for some people. In very small quantities it can have protective effects on the heart and the cardiovascular system. However, it has a vast array of dreadful effects.

Just how harmful alcohol is to the body is not fully appreciated by the majority of the population for many reasons, some of which are listed below:

• Alcohol has been around for millennia

• A lot of people, including governments, make substantial amounts of money from alcohol

- Not a lot of people know just how dangerous it is

For many years it was not known how alcohol caused damage to the body. For example, it was thought that the reason alcohol misusers suffered from liver damage and eventually cirrhosis of the liver was because they were poorly nourished and the cirrhosis was caused by starvation of the body. It was only in the 1970s that the truth of alcohol damage to the body began to emerge.

With this understanding, a whole new set of disorders and health problems associated with alcohol were discovered. Fetal Alcohol Syndrome (FAS) was only recognised in the 1980s; it was initially known as a major syndrome but was considered rare. In the twenty-first century it is now recognised that FAS represents a large spectrum of disorders in the newborn. There can also be signs of significant conditions in babies with FAS that previously were unidentified and not associated with alcohol. And so, alcohol-induced health disorders can be largely hidden (until it is too late) and they can be unassociated with alcohol. There are also a lot more of these disorders than the ones generally known (even by most doctors).

Women and Drinking

There is a difference between men and women in the way they process alcohol. Women are generally more sensitive to the effects of alcohol and they suffer proportionally more health consequences from alcohol than men. Why this is so is not known at present. It is quite possible for a woman to develop cirrhosis of the liver from an amount of alcohol that would do almost no damage to a man. Some women can die from a degree of alcohol abuse that neither they nor their families knew was a problem. There is a big shift taking place in the way women drink, and their pattern of consumption is beginning to resemble that of men. With the significant increase in female consumption of alcohol over the last twenty years, more and more women have to deal with the health consequences of drinking.

In the past, women who developed problems with alcohol drank in two distinct ways. They drank in the company of, and under the influence of, a heavily drinking male partner or husband. A woman could develop a drink problem along with her husband. In these situations, it was not unheard of that the man might overcome his drinking problem and then leave his partner. A related fact is that women can often tolerate a significant degree of alcohol abuse in their male partner, but men, by and large, are not as tolerant of female drinking. The other pattern of female drinking was for a woman to start drinking in a non-social context and alone, and to develop a pattern of abuse that would go virtually undetected, by the nature of its secrecy. The stereotypical scenario of a single, separated or widowed woman buying wine or liquor in an off-licence and drinking alone actually corresponds to an established pattern of female drinking that was prevalent for many years.

Over the last forty years, it has become permissible for women to drink sociably and publicly. Women can now be seen drunk in public without as much social scandal as previously. Women can drink together, without a man present, and it is not regarded as odd. But this loosening of social rules and the establishment of social equality comes at a price. This price is the percentage of women who go on to develop addiction problems. If you take into account the relative increase in female alcoholism across the Western World and you add to this the sensitivity of the female body to alcohol, you've got your reason for the rapid increase in alcohol-related deaths among women.

The Major Alcohol-Induced Diseases

Here is a list of some of the major alcohol-induced diseases, working from head to toe:

- Brain damage: dementia, delirium, short-term memory loss, seizures

- Head and neck problems: carcinoma of the oesophagus, throat and face

- Heart damage: cardiomyopathy

- Stomach damage: gastritis, duodenal ulcer, chronic pancreatitis

- Liver damage: cirrhosis, alcoholic hepatitis, hepatoma (liver cancer)

- Nerve damage: neuropathy, severe hand and foot pain, staggering gait

- Joint damage: gout, arthritis

- Muscle weakness: alcoholic myopathy

- Reproductive problems: impotence, infertility

- Skin problems: blood vessels under the skin, bulbous nose, acne, thinning skin

- Obesity

- Psychiatric disorders: depression, anxiety, psychosis, bipolar disorder (see Chapter 8)

In order to comprehend just how toxic alcohol is, it is important to look at some of these disorders and examine how alcohol damages vital organs.

The Liver

The liver's main function is to weed out and break down harmful substances taken into the bloodstream, and also to manufacture essential products (proteins and enzymes) for the body. About 80 per cent of all alcohol absorbed into the body is broken down in the liver. It is not surprising, then, that liver disease is the physical problem most classically associated with alcohol, and that a significant number of alcohol misusers eventually get liver disease. Cirrhosis of the liver is by far the worst kind of liver disease.

In response to the excessive alcohol intake of the alcohol misuser, the liver increases its capacity to absorb and deal with the alcohol, and indeed the body can increase its tolerance for alcohol. Alcohol can make the surrounding membranes of liver cells a bit leaky, and allow them to release their proteins and enzymes from liver cells into the bloodstream. These liver enzymes can then rise in the bloodstream and this can be detected with blood tests. Therefore, a rise in liver enzymes can be a sign of liver damage.

As the liver tries to cope with excessive amounts of alcohol being processed, it initially increases in size. This increase in size is associated with the deposition of fat-like substances in the liver and is labeled as fatty infiltration of the liver. This can be detected by either a physical examination of the abdomen, whereby the enlarged liver can be felt, or by an ultrasound or CT scan of the abdomen, which can detect the fat deposits in the liver.

As the liver tries to cope with increasing amounts of alcohol, the fat-like deposits in the liver are replaced with fibrous or connective tissue. This fibrous tissue is less bulky than the fatty tissue and, as it replaces the fatty material, the liver shrinks. As it shrinks, its functions begin to break down. Since the liver is no longer effectively ridding the body of harmful substances, the level of such substances begins to rise in the body and cause problems, and some of the manufactured essential proteins and enzymes begin to be missed by the body. Eventually the liver shuts down completely, and the body cannot survive. This is called total liver failure, and there is only one treatment: liver transplantation.

Once cirrhosis of the liver gets established, it is very difficult to reverse. It gathers momentum by itself and the liver begins to fail, even if alcohol intake is stopped. As part of that liver failure, there can be a multitude of physical problems, including jaundice or yellowing of the skin; bleeding problems due to a lack of coagulation enzymes manufactured by the liver;

oesopheageal varices, where there can be a swelling or even a bursting of blood vessels in the gut; and hepatic encephalopathy, which is confusion and drowsiness caused by the excess of liver toxins in the bloodstream.

As treatment goes, liver transplantation is pretty severe. It is a 'last gasp' treatment and a majority of patients don't make it as far as obtaining a new liver. A liver transplant is a massive operation and requires the expertise of a dedicated team of doctors, surgeons, nurses and transplant coordinators, who run the procedure. After the transplant is done, and the operation may take a large number of hours and require many units of blood, the patient may have to spend weeks recovering in hospital. They will have to go onto rejection suppression medication* for life. They run the risk of a significant number of complications after surgery, including their body rejecting the new liver, the new liver rejecting the body, complications with the medication (which affects the immune system), infections, bleeds and many other problems. The tragedy is that up to one-third of alcohol misusers who receive a new liver and survive the transplant go back to drinking alcohol, and so increase the chances of the transplant failing. Overall, it a risky procedure with many complications and it is far better to prevent liver failure rather than to try and treat it with a liver transplant.

One of the unfortunate things about alcohol-induced liver damage is that you can be drinking less alcohol than people around you and still develop liver damage. As mentioned, women are much more likely to get cirrhosis than men. They can get it with a lower level of alcohol consumption and earlier in their drinking career. It is very difficult to know what to say to a young woman in her thirties or forties who has developed cirrhosis from alcohol abuse and is likely to die from it, but who never believed she actually had a problem with alcohol as she drank less than the men around her. It is also true that certain

---

* Medication that suppresses rejection of the new liver by the body's immune system.

individuals are more vulnerable to alcoholic cirrhosis than others and may have a genetic vulnerability to alcohol liver damage. This vulnerability can be in men as well as women, and may help explain why some people can drink significant quantities over years and 'get away with it', while others succumb to cirrhosis at a much earlier stage in their drinking career.

Alcohol liver damage can be significantly accelerated by infection with liver toxic viruses such as Hepatitis C and HIV disorder (AIDS). It appears that the damage caused by one toxin to the liver makes the liver more prone to damage by another toxin. It can take much less alcohol to cause cirrhosis in someone with Hepatitis C than someone without it, and thus it can happen at a much earlier age. Indeed, such is the vulnerability of the liver in Hepatitis C cases that the only safe quantity of alcohol that can be consumed is absolutely nothing. Another unfortunate problem that can arise in the liver due to alcoholic cirrhosis, and particularly in those with Hepatitis C, is a liver cancer called a hepatoma, which is a dreadful disorder and frequently quickly fatal.

By and large, however, alcohol liver damage reflects a large quantity of alcohol consumed over years. The older the drinker gets, the more likely it is that he or she will develop liver damage. Cirrhosis of the liver tends to occur in the middle aged and the elderly, so it appears that the most important factor in the development of cirrhosis is the cumulative effects of alcohol consumed over time.

The Brain

Alcohol causes significant brain damage. Most importantly, it causes alcoholic dementia where the brain shrinks due to alcohol damage and is left permanently and progressively disabled. Prior to causing full dementia, alcohol can cause various toxic brain syndromes.

First, alcohol can cause blackouts. These are episodes of short-term memory loss that may or may not be due to actual brain damage. Generally these episodes are associated with acute intoxication (drunkenness), and generally they consist of the alcohol misuser getting drunk and not recalling the next day the various incidents that took place while he or she was intoxicated. As intoxication interferes with attention and concentration, it obviously interferes with registration and memory. So blackouts may simply indicate gross intoxication and not represent actual damage. However, if blackouts are frequent and memory loss is total rather than partial, blackouts can represent the thin end of alcohol-induced brain damage. Frequent blackouts are associated with a downward spiral into full alcohol dependence, and it can be difficult to ascertain if there is genuine brain damage present or whether a person is so frequently intoxicated that he or she does not have enough sober time in which to make a judgment.

There are a variety of medical disorders that come before full dementia. These include Korsakoff's psychosis, hepatic enceph-alopathy and transient short-term memory loss. There are also other rare ones that relate to damage to various specific areas of the brain.

The main disorder of the brain caused by alcohol is alco-holic dementia. Just how alcohol causes the damage is not clear, but there is no doubt about the damage that alcohol can do. A significant percentage of alcohol misusers, perhaps 10 per cent, get full alcoholic dementia. This results firstly in transient memory loss, then permanent short-term memory loss, and then complete short- and long-term memory loss. There is a tendency to confabulate or cover-up the memory loss through exaggera-tion or denial. The disorder can progress to produce behavioural changes, including irritability and disinhibition.** Eventually the disorder progresses to a full dementia, with deterioration in personality function, decline in personal self-care and lack of recognition of family members. It is, of course, a terminal disor-der and one that can span years rather than months.

** A term used in psychology to describe a lack of restraint and can include ignoring social conventions, taking risks and general impulsivity.

The chance of developing alcoholic dementia generally increases as a person gets older and is more likely in the elderly, although of course it occurs in middle age as well. Its existence and its progress is directly associated with the quantity of alcohol consumed, so it gets worse the more you drink. After it has become established, it progresses even if drinking has stopped altogether. It causes a general shrinkage of the brain that can be detected on a brain scan. It can cause a particular shrinkage of the frontal lobes of the brain, which are the areas associated with personality and self-control. Since these are the areas of the brain that would be needed to stop drinking, this 'frontal lobe' syndrome can make it more difficult for the sufferer to give up drinking. This syndrome is characteristic of alcoholic dementia. After a while, alcoholic dementia becomes indistinguishable from Alzheimer's disease.

The Pancreas

The pancreas, an organ in the middle of the abdomen, manufactures insulin among other hormones and is thus highly important in the regulation of blood sugar levels. The pancreas also manufactures enzymes that help absorb food into the body from the intestine, and is important in digestion as well.

Pancreatitis is an inflammation of the pancreas. Whether it is acute (short term) or chronic (long term), pancreatitis is one of the most painful conditions known to man. It is characterised by severe abdominal pain, which can last from a number of hours to a number of days or weeks. The pain is so intense that it can mimic a heart attack or severe ulcer pain. These attacks of pancreatitis can be brought on by a heavy bout of drinking or by heavy drinking over many years. Pancreatitis often requires hospitalisation and may require heavy painkiller medication to decrease the pain. Pancreatitis can be so severe that patients can die from it.

The most effective way to prevent alcohol-induced pancreatitis is to abstain from alcohol. Unfortunately, in some cases, once established, pancreatitis can become chronic and not require alcohol to precipitate an attack.

Eventually, long-term pancreatitis can cause diabetes, which may require either tablets or insulin injections. It may also cause severe food absorption problems which require a pancreatic enzyme supplement.

Other Disorders

Other disorders, including neuropathy, cardiomyopathy, myopathy and gout, are all caused by alcohol and may all progress even after consumption of alcohol has ceased. Abstinence from alcohol is the only effective cure and also the only way to prevent the progression of these diseases.

Sometimes the damage done by alcohol is irreversible.

Case Study: The Accidental Alcohol Misuser

June was forty-five when I got to meet her. She was referred to me from a local hospital, having been diagnosed with severe alcohol liver disease.

She came from a relatively normal middle-class background in a large city. Her father was an engineer and her mother a housewife. Her father's father was a known heavy drinker, but her own father was a teetotaler as a reaction to the negative experiences he had when he was growing up. She went to school locally, and was reasonably bright, well liked and excellent at sports. She left school and, after completing a secretarial course, got a job in the local higher education trust.

She met and married a secondary school teacher and after her second child was born she stopped working outside the home. She had a reasonably happy marriage, but found her life rather dull and unfulfilling. She got used to having a glass of wine with dinner in the evening, and then a second one before she went to bed.

After her eldest left school, she began to go to the gym a few times every week and to meet her friends for lunch on the other days. She would often have one or two glasses of wine with lunch as well as the wine in the evenings. She was stopped once by the police on her way home from lunch and was charged with drink driving, but she got off on a technicality and didn't lose her licence.

Although her husband was annoyed on occasions by her drinking, it never became a massive issue as she continued to keep up the house and not bother him too much. She embarrassed her daughters at her nephew's wedding where she got drunk and fell over late in the evening. Her school-going younger daughter mentioned her drinking to her a few times, but she was able to brush it under the carpet to some extent.

She began to experience severe fatigue, and vague aches and pains. She also noticed that she had a very good tan for the time of year. She went to her GP, and was surprised to be told that her liver enzymes were abnormal. She went for a few days to the liver unit at a large hospital, where a biopsy was performed. She was told that her liver was damaged and that she needed to give up alcohol. She found it more difficult than anticipated and she relapsed to alcohol within a month of her discharge from the hospital.

Six months later, she was re-admitted to the hospital with some bleeding into her stomach. After a liver biopsy she was shocked to be told that she had full cirrhosis of the liver. On discharge, she was immediately referred for treatment and completed a full four-week inpatient treatment programme. Her liver function stabilised, even improved, and she was discharged home to attend AA, go to an aftercare programme and to keep an eye on her liver's health.

Six months later she was still abstinent and moderately worried about the state of her liver, which appeared at that stage to be stable. She openly admitted that her main reason to change was her fear about her health, and she was still in some degree of disbelief that she had ended up with a dependence on alcohol and having liver damage. Her family was supportive, but a little less surprised than she was about her diagnosis.

Joe's Story: Day 4

At this stage Joe was not feeling well. He was sweating profusely, he had had a bad night's sleep and, to make matters worse, he had spilt half his coffee at breakfast. Not that he had had much breakfast, since he was quite nauseous, but the nurse was insistent that he have something in his stomach.

He was told to stay in his night clothes, even though they were somewhat damp from the night sweats. He was decidedly anxious, even panicky for most of the day, and he had a tremor in his arms and legs. The nurses were polite, but were taking no nonsense from him. They gave him a variety of pills to help with his withdrawal and to ease his anxiety, but these only went so far. He felt really awful and, worst of all, he knew a drink would ease his pain significantly. He talked to the doctor and all he was offered was another tranquilizing pill.

He began to regret coming into treatment. He would rather face his wife and his boss than deal with this kind of strain.

5

The Effects of Alcohol on the Family

> Alcoholism is a familial disease in terms of both cause and effect.

The focus of this book so far has been on alcoholism as a disorder that affects the individual. In fact, alcoholism affects families in many different ways. To begin with, alcoholism is genetically transmitted; it does not always occur in isolation. The genetics of alcoholism was explored in Chapter 3, and it is clear that the genetic influence on the commencement and the subsequent development of alcoholism is very strong. Alcoholism is one of the most genetic of medical and psychiatric disorders, and sometimes families have not one or two members who are in recovery, but maybe even three or four. Also, the family is the primary environment that influences any individual's behaviour and thus has a massive influence on whether or not any individual becomes an alcohol misuser.

Within an 'alcoholic' family there may be little recognition of the problems associated with very heavy drinking. Problems stemming from alcohol dependence may be ascribed by the family to individual personality characteristics and not to

excessive drinking. There may be a collective blinkered attitude to all drink-related negative activity because it is simply
accepted as normal. Such a family may be less likely to judge
the situation correctly and intervene to help the alcohol misuser.
An alcoholic family could suffer more direct and indirect consequences of an individual's alcoholism than a 'non-alcoholic'
family and still not try to force the alcohol misuser to change.
There can be a lot of misery in an alcoholic family that is directly
related to heavy drinking but blamed on other things.

Consequences of Alcoholic Family Drinking

Children, when growing up, are enormously vulnerable to
the consequences of heavy or alcoholic family drinking. Children of alcoholics may spend their entire childhood witnessing
drinking, its consequences and its fallout, and this may be what
informs the child about his or her relationship with alcohol. It
may be normal for a child to anticipate a parent drinking heavily every night. It may become normal for children to witness
inebriated conversations frequently, to see drunken behaviour,
to experience aggressive or even violent behaviour, or even to
be the victims of violence or abuse because of alcohol. Children
may spend years not bringing their friends back to their house
because of fear of what the friends might see. Children may be
forced to grow up early, to take on adult responsibilities, and
even to assume the role of the parent in the face of the parent's
refusal or inability to carry on normal parenting.

These negative experiences, coupled with the genetic possibility of becoming alcohol misusers themselves, can make the
lot of children of alcoholics very unpleasant. Theoretically, a
child experiencing a significant number of negative consequences of alcoholism should find everything about alcohol to
be negative. Theoretically, they should be in less danger than the
average child of developing a fondness for alcohol themselves.
However, while some children of alcohol misusers successfully
avoid becoming addicts, and maybe even become teetotalers
in response to their experiences, the incidence of alcoholism in

children of alcohol misusers is at least three times what it is in the general population.

What Do the Children of Alcohol Misusers Experience?

There is absolutely no positive aspect about being the child of an alcohol misuser. Most of those dependent on alcohol find it difficult to believe just how aware their children are of their drinking, and just how much it affects them and how much they hate it. Many alcohol misusers believe that if they do their drinking away from home, if they continue to maintain some sort of family income and if they don't come home too drunk, their children aren't aware of or aren't affected by their addiction. Many alcohol misusers feel that, because they don't think their drinking affects the family too much, the family shouldn't really have the right to be angry or upset at them. There can be an enormous mismatch between the alcohol misuser's perception of their own drinking and the family's perception of their drinking.

A child's life is their home. No one observes another human being like a child observes his or her parents. Every little foible is absorbed, every little characteristic noted, and every subtle shift in mood is noticed and adjusted to. This is at the best of times. At the worst of times, in situations of high stress, family illness or major aggravation, the child may suffer lifelong emotional scarring that affects their perception of the world and their interaction with other human beings until the day they die. If the child is in a situation of high stress, such as when an alcohol misuser is drinking, he or she is on guard for warning signs about what will happen next. 'Will he shout at my mum because he is drunk?' 'Will he shout at me?' 'Have I done anything that might irritate her and make her turn her attention to me?' 'Will she be irrationally irritable when she is drunk until she passes out from the alcohol?'

Every step in the progress of the addiction undermines the confidence of the child. Children crave security and certainty, and an alcohol misuser's drinking destroys that security and takes that certainty away. Most children of alcohol misusers are so insecure in their perception of the world that it colours everything they do. They may take fewer risks than the average person. They may seek out the choices in life that are determined by a need for security, and not make the best choices because of that need. They may seek out relationships with people based on their relationship with their alcoholic parent. They might seek out people who drink too much (because at least it is a familiar dynamic), they might seek out people who undermine their confidence in themselves (because at least that too is a familiar dynamic) or they might seek out people who they drive away through unstable behaviour (because they expect an unstable relationship and must create one even if their partner is stable). What they will not be able to do is to ignore their experiences of alcoholism as they make their way into a world away from the alcoholic parent. These experiences affect their evaluation and interaction with the world, and, more particularly, the people in it. Many children of alcohol misusers need a lot of help, and it can take a lifetime of support from such organisations as Adult Children of Alcoholics (ACA) (see Appendix) to enable them to break free from the yoke of their parents' alcoholism.

One of the most difficult aspects of family life due to alcoholism is the tendency to blame. As the alcohol misuser decides to hide from the consequences of their drinking, it becomes necessary for him or her to find a reason for things going wrong. It is necessary to blame someone or something for all the negative consequences of their alcoholism. That someone or something is almost always close at hand. At some stage in their disease, alcohol misusers often blame their family members for day-to-day upsets or even for their own drinking: 'You made me do it'; 'If you hadn't done that I wouldn't have picked up a drink again.'

Often the child willingly accepts the blame because their self-worth is so destroyed; they just accept the blame as accurate and appropriate. Children of a certain age blame themselves for everything, good and bad, that happens to them. Alcohol misusers, at the worst point in their disease, take advantage of that tendency, either consciously or unconsciously, because it allows them to continue drinking. At certain times, the alcohol misuser may even believe it and genuinely blame their children for their own drinking, bizarre as that might sound. This allows the alcohol misuser to control the household through a form of emotional blackmail, while continuing to drink. The child is caught between guilt and a sense of something being wrong with that guilt, and this inner conflict prevents them from confronting the situation in hand. As the child gets older and better able to judge the situation more accurately and to act independently of the alcoholic parent, they may still be unable to escape their younger patterns of thought and behaviour and can remain stuck in a state of helplessness.

Point of No Return

Children, no matter how loving or caring, can eventually reach a point of no return in their reaction to the alcohol misuser. This can come at any time; it can be early or late in the alcohol misuser's drinking career. It can come after a series of threats, such as, 'If you don't give it up, I will never talk to you again,' or it can come out of the blue with no warning. The child may have experienced a very happy childhood, with only a few years of drinking to cope with, and still end up enormously resentful and indeed unforgiving of the alcohol misuser. The opposite can occur, with the child being unreservedly supportive and enabling up to the end of the alcohol misuser's drinking career.

A significant factor in whether a child gives up on the addict or remains supportive is the amount of anger and abuse they have had to tolerate. If the alcoholic parent has been angry, bullying and aggressive when drunk, the child often gives up on the parent more quickly. If the child has been the particular focus of the alcoholic parent's anger, they might never forgive that parent, no matter how repentant the parent is later. Unfortunately, once a point of no return has been reached, there is no guarantee that the child will ever forgive the parent, even when a sustained recovery has been achieved. All the love and affection that the child naturally feels for the parent can be turned on its head, and can turn into anger and, indeed, hatred. At that point, there may be nothing an alcohol misuser can do to salvage the situation, and they have lost the most precious thing in life – their children's affection.

That point of no return is unpredictable and may vary from child to child, from situation to situation. But it does exist; no one has an infinite amount of patience and tolerance. Unfortunately, either consciously or unconsciously, the alcohol misuser has an instinct about just how far to push the situation. They often know when they can no longer push the child into compliance or tolerance of drunken behaviour. So it often takes the child reaching the point of no return, reaching the point at which they actually break off relations, something they may have been threatening for years without any real intention of carrying it out, to make the alcohol misuser sit up and take notice. At this point, the power in the relationship shifts and the child becomes the one in control. The ultimate power in a relationship is the power to walk away from that relationship, and it then becomes the child's right to exercise that power when they want.

The alcohol misuser may or may not pick up on the change, but it is real and often irreversible. The child may do any number of things: stop talking to the parent, leave home, stop visiting the home, avoid any contact at all or just treat the parent in a cold and distant manner. It is the ultimate tragedy that it takes the destruction of the relationship between the alcohol misuser and their family for them to truly see just how destructive their drinking behaviour is to those around them. Clearly the trick is for the alcohol misuser to change their perception in advance of their children reaching this point.

Children will go through three basic emotional reactions to a parent's drinking:

1.   Upset, anxiety, guilt and depression

2. Anger and intolerance

3. Indifference

By and large, the first two stages lead directly into one another and can occur at the same time. The third, however, is generally complete in itself and separate, and is the stage when the child tries to let go of all the previous emotions. The child can cut off the parent for a lifetime, even after the parent has reformed and entered long-term recovery. After the power has shifted, the child can do with the relationship as they please; they can re-enter it or leave it to one side. The child can decide to wait for a number of months and see if recovery is sustained, or even longer to see if there is a genuine lifetime change. The child may have to wait themselves and see what happens to them emotionally, and judge over a period of time whether they want to re-enter a relationship with their parent or not.

The alcohol misuser has to be aware that it is not possible to change a relationship overnight, even in recovery. If they achieve long-term recovery, they must ensure they change their pattern of behaviour towards their children. They must recognise what they have been doing to their children, and be fearless in their own critique of themselves and their behaviour. It is very common for a recovering alcohol misuser to retain the same controlling or emotionally blackmailing attitude to their children, and to drive them away a second time.

It is the ultimate tragedy for the alcohol misuser to lose their children after they have entered recovery. The achievement of sobriety is but the first step towards recovery, and the recovery process is about much more than giving up drinking. If the alcohol misuser is to truly recover, they must learn to listen to their family and get past their own anger and refusal to accept the blame. Early recovery, when the alcohol misuser is attempting to gain true insight into the extent of their drinking and its effect on others, is the most delicate period of recovery from a family perspective. By and large, it is the alcohol misuser's preparedness to listen and to accept the perspective of others that determines what happens with his or her relationships, not the degree of damage that has gone before. The simple message to the alcohol misuser is this: shut up and listen, and don't say anything for about six months.

Family Recovery

Amazing as it sounds, most families where the alcohol misuser enters true recovery do very well. Most children are delighted to see their parent give up alcohol and are thrilled not to have alcoholism dominating their emotional lives. That relief and joy often translates into genuine affection for the alcoholic parent, and pride in their recovery. It is astounding the turnaround that can occur in the first six months of genuine recovery. Families that were torn apart can spend happy time together. Family occasions become enjoyable as opposed to torture. Children can end up more affectionate towards the parent and are able to state it openly. Lives can be utterly transformed and the addiction cycle that could get transmitted across generations can be broken.

Unfortunately, the addiction cycle may not be broken and family dynamics can revolve around addiction for many years and even across many generations. While most families do recover, some never truly enter into recovery and can remain scarred for years.

> **The effects of alcoholism can last through generations of a family.**

Case Study: The Cattle Trader's Family

Walter was a 49-year-old man who was involved in the cattle trade. He ran a large farm with his two sons and daughter. They farmed and traded cattle for the beef industry. He was easily the driving force behind the success of the business. Although his wife had been brought up on a farm, she allowed him to call the shots in the family business. He worked long hours, traveled extensively, and ate and drank cattle and farming all day long. Despite his family being around him, he was effectively a loner, taking the responsibility for major decisions about the business. It was he who determined what cattle to breed and what ones to sell, and how to make the profits.

His drinking escalated over the years, from a nightcap of a single whiskey every night to help him sleep up to three-quarters of a bottle of whiskey every night, together with best part of a bottle of wine at dinner most nights. He was still able to function, however, and the business kept going despite his drinking.

He began to lose money, and slowly he became more estranged from his wife and children, despite his business success. As he spent more time drinking and then recovering from the effects of alcohol, he began to spend less time on the business and began to lose his golden touch in his choice of cattle to buy and breed. His daughter moved away, and his son became a salesman to get away from him. His wife gave up on him and, as the children grew into adulthood, she spent more time with her friends and less time in the house.

He grew more angry and resentful, feeling that he had all the responsibility and no emotional return for his hard work. He lost his temper frequently and gradually all the family members became alienated from him, leaving him to his own devices.

It took steady pressure from each of the children at various different times to get him to seek help. He initially refused to accept all offers of intervention, falling back on relying on himself and his own judgment. It was when his youngest son, announcing that he was going to leave the family business, put it to him that he should enter treatment that he relented and went into rehabilitation. There were many acrimonious family meetings, and many threats and counter threats distributed among the family members. He eventually agreed to stay off alcohol for a period of three months, but *promised to go back on it after that time as he felt he had every right to drink if he wanted to.*

Fortunately, three months became six and, after a year, he made the decision to cease drinking altogether. When he was a few months into sobriety, he began to listen to his son and made provision in the business for his other son and his daughter again. His son and daughter returned to the family home and took up various roles in the business. His wife started doing the bookkeeping for the business, and he began to consult with the children about making day-to-day decisions.

One year into sobriety, family harmony had been restored. Although he still acted as a 'lone bull' a lot of the time, he felt he learned the lesson of compromise to keep the family peace and to keep him off alcohol. While the benefits were very palpable in the end, they were achieved over a considerable period of time.

Joe's Story: Day 5

Joe had slept the previous night, but he didn't feel fully rested. His stomach was a bit better, and he was eating a few bits and pieces for each meal. His anxiety was still strong, but his tremors were a bit less intense. He felt, at this stage, that he had put up with an awful lot.

He didn't want to talk to anyone, but people kept coming up and trying to make conversation with him. He was upset, but not enough to get into an argument with them. He called his wife and told her that the place was 'hell on earth', and insisted that she come in and take him home. She wasn't listening to him. She promised to come in the next day to see him, but not to take him home. He felt like signing himself out, but he knew that he wasn't wanted at home in his present state, and he didn't know if he had a job to return to.

His wife had said that his boss was understanding about his situation and wanted him to get treatment. He was too afraid of his boss's reaction to call him himself.

He had an appointment to see a counsellor the next day, for all the good that would do. But for the moment he would stay and see what happened.

6

When Alcohol Rules – Work and Friends

> Alcohol changes a career into a job, and a job into a distraction. Friendships that are based on alcohol are damaging.

Work

A job can be everything and nothing. It is, of course, the main means by which we support ourselves financially, and thus the source of everything material we acquire in life. It is often much more than that, with a career becoming a vital part of our identity, our self-worth, and our sense of purpose and achievement in life. We often spend a vast amount of time at work, thinking about it, recovering from it and figuring out how to make it better. Personalities and people from work often dominate our waking life and the finances accruing from work determine our financial future and, subsequently, our sense of status.

It takes qualifications, experience and a track record of excellence or repeated good work to gain a good reputation in any area. People earn a living by their reputation, by word of mouth and the impressions left in the back of people's minds. Just one or two whiffs of bad service, of minor scandal or inappropriate behaviour leads to a professional reputation being diminished or destroyed. This applies to any job in any walk of life.

Like everything else in an alcohol misuser's life, work is threatened by alcohol. Once work is placed second to alcohol, it begins to suffer, though it may take some time for this to be noticed. Depending on the nature of the work and on the stage of the alcohol misuser's deterioration, how addiction affects work, of course, varies. At an early stage, when there is no obvious sign of the addiction, an alcohol misuser's work colleagues or boss might not even be aware of anything being wrong at all. There might be no outward manifestations of a problem; the work might still get done, though perhaps not to the same standard. At this stage, the only person who might notice anything wrong is the alcohol misuser themselves, but, by and large, he or she is too preoccupied to care.

What happens next is variable. For some, there is the relentless decline, with poor performance at work eventually being discovered and called to attention. The alcohol misuser gets less done, misses days or occasionally turns up intoxicated, and this deterioration comes to the attention of their boss, their colleagues, or their customers or clients. Problems and complaints ensue, and the alcohol misuser is confronted and eventually censured, reprimanded or suspended because of the interference with performance.

Some alcohol misusers are able to hold it together at work. They underperform, but not to a crippling extent. They can lumber on for many years, not doing badly enough to get into trouble but gradually withdrawing their efforts as their addiction takes over and gains priority. It is staggering the number of alcohol misusers who keep work going and limp on towards eventual retirement. This is often the thread upon which denial is hung, with phrases like 'If I had a problem, sure I wouldn't be able to hold my job' being commonly used.

Of course, as mentioned, a job can be much more than just a job. Losing interest in work is much more than a symptom of deterioration due to addiction; it exemplifies what happens to your life if you are dependent on alcohol. The majority of people take justifiable pride in what they do, and try to do as good a job as possible. The alcohol misuser prioritises alcohol over almost everything, including their identity and self-worth.

This shift in priorities is not sudden; it takes place over years as the interest in alcohol grows. It is often in retrospect that the alcohol misuser is able to detail his or her mental shift from worker to alcohol-dependent worker. People around the alcohol misuser can notice the shift, while often not being aware of the causes. Work colleagues might notice the slight increase in their workloads as the alcohol misuser stops doing those little things that contribute to the larger tasks. After a while, employers may notice the reduced attention to detail in even routine tasks. Customers will feel just a little less well looked after, and may drift away to the competition. If an alcohol misuser is based in the home, children will eventually feel significantly neglected.

Signs that alcohol is taking over your job:

1. You miss Monday mornings, eventually on a regular basis

2. You turn up for work smelling of alcohol, either from the previous night's drinking or from the morning's drinking

3. You have accumulated a high number of absentee days for whatever reason

4. You have fatigue or drowsiness on the job

5. You have a reckless attitude to work, which contrasts with your previous attitude

6. Your appearance is deteriorating: you appear excessively casual or even disheveled

Deterioration at Work

The stages of deterioration in a work situation are varied. In extreme situations, on top of a diminishing reputation, the alcohol misuser can be repeatedly fired and/or refused promotion. A good reputation is rebuilt over twice the length of time as the first time around. While work may come someone's way in good times despite a bad reputation, it definitely dries up in an economic downturn. In harsher economic climates, people do not always give you a second chance, let alone a third, so a single poor performance related to alcohol can determine whether a customer stays or goes. It is rough out there, and economic success can turn on a sixpence into economic failure.

Occasionally, a boss at work can be a real support and help to an employee with alcohol dependence. Time and time again, I have heard reports of bosses who are understanding, helpful and willing to give time off and even financial support to aid an alcohol misuser in their recovery. Very often, those who are in recovery themselves or who are close to someone in recovery are the most supportive and helpful. Unfortunately, the vast majority of workplaces are unsupportive and even punishing in their attitude to an employee with an alcohol problem. Even when someone has entered recovery and is doing well, some employers are not willing to take risks of any sort and will not rehire or employ anyone with a reputation for alcoholism. Some customers or clients do not forget the missed order or the bad appearance one day, and shift their business elsewhere permanently.

Earning an employer's trust back is not an easy prospect for an employee. A person might decide that their addiction is going to be held against them, thus limiting their chances for advancement within that firm. It is not uncommon for an employee with an addiction to move on to another work setting. This can occur even when the boss or coworkers have gotten over the problems associated with the addiction and are happy to see their coworker restored to functioning good health. However, the effects of the alcoholism may have been so traumatic for all involved that the only way for people to move on is for the recovering alcohol misuser to leave the company, even on the best of terms.

If you, as a recovering alcohol misuser, decide to stay on, and are let remain, it can take a substantial period for you to regain the trust of your employer or customers. Since, at some stage, your employer could have lost money because of your addiction, it can take a long time for your employer to forget that loss. In general, however, if you do not lose your job because of your addiction, once you are recovering, things do return to normal. The whole thing is put down to an 'episode' and is essentially forgiven, if not forgotten.

Friends

Alcohol addiction dominates social life as well as work and family life. The friends we choose to spend time with often reflect who we are as people and what we spend our time doing. When our lives are dominated by alcohol, our choice of friends will reflect that, and the alcohol misuser often establishes a set of heavy-drinking companions to share their time with. Some alcohol misusers drink alone and no one knows they are drinking to excess, but the majority at least start off drinking in company. Drinkers tend to go to places where they can drink – pubs, clubs, bars, restaurants. It is easy for heavy drinkers to recognise one another and to gravitate towards each other. It is embarrassing, albeit mildly, for a heavy drinker to be constantly in the company of light drinkers because their heavy drinking is then much more apparent. Heavy drinkers find themselves buying an extra drink between rounds or pushing their companions to drink more to cover up their own excessive drinking. It is quite common for alcoholic drinkers to move around socially, and not to be seen constantly in the one place where their drinking pattern can be identified.

An alcohol misuser narrows his or her lifestyle to eliminate anything and anybody who does not support his or her drinking. Old pastimes that don't involve drinking are eventually given up, and those that do involve drinking are taken up or focused on with renewed vigour. Bridge is given up in favour of golf, since, with golf, there is a clubhouse where alcohol can be consumed before and after a round. Visiting friends for a cup of coffee is given up for meeting friends for lunch with a glass of wine. Watching football with the family on the TV is abandoned in favour of watching it in the pub while drinking with friends, or else drinking with friends at home. Going out to socialise in the evenings may be preceded by drinking alcohol, with or without friends. Conversations with other heavy drinkers can often turn to alcohol, what is liked and disliked, what the effects of drinking are, how work is avoided or affected, other people's reactions to drinking, and how good and enjoyable drinking is. Conversation at the end of an evening's drinking often turns to rather meaningless pedantry, and this is best indulged with other heavy, equally intoxicated drinkers.

If you, as an alcohol misuser, attempt sobriety, you can experience substantive pull and pressure from your former drinking friends to resume drinking. That pressure can be both overt and covert. It can range from friendly invitations to take part in drink-related activities and gentle questioning about altered drinking habits, to naked aggression and hostility towards your new-found sobriety. Drinking 'buddies' can feel threatened by one of their number achieving sobriety, and can place significant and persistent pressure on you until you resume drinking.

A lot of alcohol misusers find that it becomes either necessary or simply more pleasant to change their social circle while in recovery. It can be too challenging to be surrounded by drinking friends, excess alcohol and significant intoxication while suffering from the intense craving and deep desire for alcohol especially associated with early recovery. Some alcohol misusers feel that it is important to test themselves in these social circumstances, that it is important evidence of their cure that they can withstand the personal and social pressure by being surrounded by their former drinking companions. But there is no doubt that those who test themselves often fail, and that it is easier to withstand the pressure by avoiding these situations altogether.

It is also true to say that alcohol misusers often find a change in their outlook and social needs when in recovery. Things that were enjoyable when drinking are no longer enjoyable when sober. Company that was so entertaining or even necessary when drinking becomes less attractive and more superfluous when not drinking. The conversations with those drinking friends that seemed important and sensible when you were drinking can turn out to be repetitive and meandering when you are sober. There really isn't much to be learnt from drunken conversation. While, initially, an alcohol misuser in recovery can find themselves somewhat lost and missing their previous social life, this often turns out to be a blessing in disguise. The change that is brought about by the necessary avoidance of drink becomes more interesting and leads to a fuller, more satisfying social life.

It becomes a revelation to former drinkers that their old friends, their old way of life, their whole social existence was a false one. Friends who were really only drinking companions don't stay friends; hobbies and haunts that were so important were really only opportunities for drinking and drinking places. The alcohol misuser slowly realises that everything in his social life was built around drink and, without drink, he or she has no social life. Thus, one of the most important things about recovery is the reconstruction of a comprehensive non-drinking social and personal life (see Chapters 23, 25 and 26). This is, of course, very easy to say and a lot more difficult to do. It often takes many months or even years for a former drinker to discover themselves in different ways, to make genuine friendships without alcohol and to build a satisfying life without alcohol. But this is the way to a genuine recovery.

> A recovery involves the rediscovery of a vocation and the reconstruction of a social life.

Case Study: The Socially Anxious Drinker

Aoife was a 22-year-old college student. She had suffered from anxiety almost all her life and, although she had good friends, good social skills and a sharp sense of humour, she felt anxious and self-conscious in social groups. She began drinking at the age of seventeen, and felt she had found the solution to her social problems. She felt relaxed when drinking and could hold her own in a group of friends, even appearing outgoing and gregarious.

Things got a bit out of hand when she went to college. She began drinking almost every night of the week, at her house share as well as in the pub. While her friends tended to drink only with friends at the weekend, she found herself drinking alone as well as with her friends.

She found that she needed to drink even before facing into a normal student's day of lectures and tutorials. She particularly needed to drink before she went out to meet her friends as she got 'Dutch courage' from drinking. She even got some panic attacks before meeting people, and used alcohol to treat those attacks. She eventually found herself drinking for most of the day to treat her anxiety, as well as when she went out socially. She came in for treatment when she was unable to get out of the house to attend her college courses. She was brought in by her parents who simply could not believe that she might have a drink problem.

Aoife found it very hard to believe that she could have developed an addiction problem. She felt that her only problem was anxiety and that she only drank to deal with her anxiety. She was initially not interested in facing up to how much alcohol she was taking, and couldn't relate to other people with an alcohol addiction. Eventually, as she began to benefit from the anti-anxiety therapy and anti-anxiety medication, she admitted she felt her drinking was getting way out of hand. 'The cure became the problem,' as she said herself.

After a fairly intense course of therapy, she felt better able to tackle returning to college. She had a number of bouts of anxiety initially, but she put into practice the various anxiety-coping strategies she had learned and she got through them without drinking. After she gained confidence that her anxiety was manageable, she felt happy to put her drinking aside. She avoided social occasions that involved a lot of drinking, and she made do with a social life that concentrated on her close friends and a few hobbies rather than going to large parties where she knew nobody.

Six months into her sobriety, she declared that she had never been happier. She still had residual anxiety, and needed to keep on her anxiety medication and to see her anxiety therapist on occasions to help her manage. She felt she was a work in progress.

Joe's Story: Day 6

Joe was feeling a bit better today. He had slept well the previous night. He was back in his day clothes and he was eating a full three meals a day, with hot chocolate at night. His tremor had disappeared and his anxiety had diminished in intensity, although he felt quite wary of a lot of people. He had the freedom to move around the place and he found that it wasn't the worst place he'd ever stayed in.

He had met the counsellor and he was starting on his programme that afternoon. He talked to a few people about the programme, and there seemed to be a fairly straightforward approach to things. He knew that the programme involved a few groups, lectures and therapy sessions. He would also have to go to AA meetings, though he did not want to. He had heard about those meetings, and he was simply not interested in them.

The good news was that his wife visited and seemed marginally less grumpy than when she had dropped him off on the first day. That was something to feel grateful for.

7

Tolerate or Confront?
The Role of the Partner or Spouse

> The alcohol misuser's partner is faced with a stark choice: to tolerate or to confront.

The relationship with a spouse or partner is the most influential of most people's lives. Decisions on how to conduct this relationship can be among the most important over a lifetime. A personal primary relationship can be the most effective pathway to a happy life, and ruination of the relationship can cause deep unhappiness. It is possible to make the wrong choice regarding your partner. However, it is also possible to damage a good relationship over an extended period of time.

This is not news. However, it is worth stating because a person's primary relationship often gets lost in the context of alcoholism. The alcohol misuser loses track of his or her relationship in prioritising alcohol over everything else. The alcohol misuser's partner loses sight of the person he or she started the relationship with, in the haze of booze-related trouble. It is likely that the future of the relationship is determined by the alcohol misuser's relationship with alcohol and whether he or she eventually decides to choose the relationship over alcohol. Often, the partner plays a pivotal role in the outcome, either by helping the alcohol misuser to find a pathway out of addiction or else by ending the relationship. Relationships stand or fall on the outcome of the addiction.

No one signs up for alcoholism when they start a relationship. A lot of people enter into marriage with the vow, 'In sickness or in health, till death do us part.' Many people, if they think of it at all, think of sickness as being physical illness, not a psychiatric or addictive illness. They consider it as helping a partner through an illness by bringing them to visit a doctor or giving them emotional support through a painful physical illness such as arthritis or heart disease. The majority of people do not see themselves as having to support an intoxicated, ungrateful, angry, manipulative and emotionally draining partner.

In the past, when divorce wasn't legal, the option of leaving an alcoholic spouse was not often present. So, tolerance, sweeping it under the carpet, not talking about it and sticking it out to the bitter end was the name of the game. In the twenty-first century, however, with a significant number of couples living together without getting married and the option of divorce readily available for married couples, there is much less pressure on a couple to stay together no matter what, and much less need for the partner of an alcohol misuser to stay if he or she doesn't want to.

As the alcohol misuser eventually exhausts the emotional fund available to them from their partner, so the partner can choose to stay or go according to their own desires and needs. If a partner stays, it is a choice and not a necessity. More and more couples are splitting up because of one person's alcoholism and the other person's tolerance and patience wearing out. Couples are now splitting up after a few years, sometimes in their twenties, because of addiction. That is bad news for couples, and certainly bad news for alcohol misusers.

Two Drinkers

Couples can get together and have a relationship that is primarily based around alcohol. They can meet while intoxicated, and can have an entire social and personal life centred around alcohol. Alcohol can be used to advance a relationship in its early stages, breaking down barriers and allowing the couple to become intimate quickly. It is not uncommon for two heavy drinkers to get together or for a lighter drinker to rise to the level of his or her partner's alcohol consumption over the course of the relationship. Unfortunately, it is common for a woman to rise to her male partner's level of alcohol consumption and to go on to develop an addiction, while he remains a social drinker.

If both people in a relationship are heavy drinkers, and one person develops a problem with alcohol, the other person may not see the problem for a significant period. The shared history of going out and drinking together means that the bar is set high for tolerance of heavy drinking in that couple's universe. Signs of abuse or dependence in one partner might simply not be noticed by the other. However, as the dependence develops and the problems mount, the alcohol dependent partner will find it more difficult to give up their addiction than if they had a light-drinking partner. A light-drinking partner is more likely to call 'Stop!' earlier, and it is easier to cease an addiction if it has been going on for a shorter time.

In the majority of cases, one partner (Partner 1) clearly drinks more heavily than the other (Partner 2) and develops alcohol dependence, which negatively affects the relationship. As the development of dependence is generally slow and insidious, so the realisation of the existence of Partner 1's problem comes gradually to Partner 2. In the meantime, Partner 2 can largely tolerate Partner 1's behaviour, including missed dates and late homecomings. Partner 2 has to step up to the plate in terms of child rearing and the general duties that make a family and relationship work. Partner 2's resentment can grow slowly, and, while there might be an occasional argument about it, by and large the couple can function much the same as previously.

The Realisation

Often it is a single incident or series of incidents that opens a person's eyes to their partner's drinking problem: an embarrassing episode of intoxication, an increasing financial problem, a particularly unhelpful neglect of family duties, or incidents of anger, aggression or violence. I recall one woman reporting that her husband got very upset when she slumped, drunk, against the front door on Christmas Eve and prevented the children from getting into the house after school during a snowstorm. That was certainly enough for the husband to realise that his wife had a problem, and his response was to threaten to throw her out of the house.

It is true that it is always the addict's spouse or partner who makes the discovery about the addiction first. I am still waiting for my first couple where the alcohol misuser reveals their addiction to alcohol to a disbelieving and surprised partner. This sudden realisation about a life partner's addiction can be a devastating blow, and not all people have the same reaction.

Once you have discovered your partner's addiction, what you choose to do about it is very important. Your first reaction would probably be to question and explore the situation, and not to push too much. Often evidence is gathered to absolutely confirm the problem. This is generally not difficult to find. The patterns of addictive behaviour become quite obvious once the possibility of addiction is perceived.

You would perhaps look for hiding places for empty bottles; you might question your partner's work colleagues about what your partner is doing with his or her time; and you could check your finances to see if money is being spent on alcohol in different settings.

Once you have gathered the evidence, you will be left with a very common dilemma: to confront your partner or to continue to tolerate the situation.

Confront or Tolerate?

It is very easy for the partner of an alcohol misuser to slip into what is termed an 'enabling relationship'. The partner enters a kind of denial and lives in a state of unrealistic hope that change will take place spontaneously. He or she can also live in a state of fear about confronting the alcohol misuser. This partner may not realise that they have entered into a silent pact with the addict for the latter to continue drinking while they tolerate it. The negative consequences of the alcohol misuser's drinking are not expressed openly; the partner just puts up with it or gives out about it with no intention of confronting the alcohol misuser. Often what is unspoken is more powerful than what is expressed, and this silent collusion can have quite a hold on a relationship.

The decision to tolerate or confront the addict is not necessarily made immediately. Like many major decisions, it can be reached either actively or passively over a period of time. The partner can decide to either go with the situation to a certain level to see what happens or to confront the alcohol misuser with any evidence they have about the addiction. Such a decision has consequences, and it will either help the situation or it will make it worse.

There is no golden rule for how a partner should deal with their loved one's alcoholism. The basic premise for any rule is that, if it succeeds, it is a good rule; if it does not succeed then it is a bad rule. The rules might change over time: what works at one stage might not work at a later date, and what fails at one stage may be helpful at another. The rules should be based on outcomes, not principles. One thing is fairly certain: if there is no attempt at change, things will not change. An addiction rarely goes away all by itself. Dependence on alcohol is a powerful force and it takes real effort by the alcohol misuser and his or her partner to enter into battle with it. Neglecting or ignoring it often makes an addiction worse.

Dos and Don'ts for the Partner of an Alcohol Misuser

Dos:

1. Engage in a self-help group for partners such as Al-Anon (see Appendix)

2. Regard the problem as a behavioural one; the alcohol misuser's behaviour must be encouraged to change

3. Continue to express affection for the person, and dislike for the disease

4. Analyse the situation and gain an understanding of what is taking place

5. Gather evidence about the extent of the problem

6. Maintain a critical eye on your own behaviour: 'Am I supportive or am I enabling?' 'Am I just venting my anger, or I am trying to effect change?'

7. Gently confront the alcohol misuser about the consequences of their drinking, but only when they are sober

8. Formulate a plan of action that you intend to follow

9. Establish a series of escalating negative consequences for the alcohol misuser if they don't seek help or cease drinking

10. Establish an appropriate time frame in which the alcohol misuser must seek help or do something about their drinking

Don'ts:

1. Avoid screaming, shouting and throwing abuse at the alcohol misuser; it is counterproductive

2. Don't confront them when they have been drinking or are

drunk; they will not be able to listen and probably won't remember what you've said

3. Don't hate the alcohol misuser; the problem may not be their fault, but the cure is certainly their responsibility

4. Don't say one thing and then do another

5. Don't use the children as bargaining chips, but do point out how they might be suffering as a result of the alcoholism

6. Don't enter into a Faustian pact: 'I'll let you drink, if you let me sleep around/spend your money/beat you up/or do something nasty to you in revenge'

The ultimate power is 'nuclear' power, the option to 'go nuclear' and end the relationship. That can take the form of throwing the alcohol misuser out of the home, perhaps refusing to see them or talk to them again. There are no rules about the nuclear option; advice cannot be given about when to merely threaten or, indeed, when to exercise it. However, the threat to go nuclear should not be made in the heat of the moment, in the middle of an argument or when either party has been drinking. It should only be made if there has been a series of escalating threats preceding it, and those threats have been carried out. The alcohol misuser has to be made fully aware that a threat will be followed by action if they do not comply with their partner's wishes. On the other hand, the alcohol misuser must also be made aware that, if they comply with the partner's wishes and go into treatment or cease drinking, the threat is removed. If the alcohol misuser feels that the relationship is lost no matter what they do, the incentive for them to change is diminished. If the alcohol misuser feels they will get away with another series of empty promises and their partner has no intention of carrying out any of the threats, that also diminishes the incentive to change.

The purpose of any action, intervention or threat is to help the alcohol misuser to change. The purpose should not be to just 'dump' on them or to make them feel rotten because they have made you, as their partner, suffer. However, gentle and persistent insistence is much more powerful than a single intense emotional outburst. The war against addiction is tough, with no guaranteed outcome at the end of it. It is a series of battles won daily, in a million different ways, and is not something that can be handled with a single knockout blow.

> **The therapeutic potential of a spouse or partner is nearly unlimited.**

Case Study: The Stockbroker and His Partner

Karl was a 45-year-old financial advisor. He was the head of an investment division in a bank and was in charge of a lot of money. He worked hard and was good at his job. He also partied hard. He drank with friends and colleagues from work, but they were not aware that he also drank alone before he went out with them and occasionally even before he came to work in the morning.

He had a daughter from his first marriage, and he felt in retrospect that his first wife eventually threw him out because of his drinking. His second marriage was entering difficulties, partly because of his drinking and partly related to his secrecy and his emotional distance from his wife.

He ended up losing his job at the bank because of his drinking. He moved to another bank and got into trouble at the second job, again partly because of his drinking.

He knew he had a problem, and he knew that keeping both his career and his marriage depended on his ability to get past drinking. He stopped drinking for a period of months and began a pattern of relapsing and remitting, lasting several months off the drink each time. He would often go to AA when sober, but got frustrated with it and antagonistic towards it when drinking. His daughter supported him in his sobriety, and he didn't want to lose her as well.

He eventually achieved a tentative but long-lasting sobriety through completing an inpatient rehabilitation, keeping active in AA, taking anti-craving medication, changing jobs to a less high-flying and less stressful financial consultancy, and dedicating himself to saving his second marriage and his relationship with his daughter.

Joe's Story: Day 7

Joe had come off all the medication at this stage and was happy to do so. The medication had helped a lot, but it eventually began to make him feel drowsy.

The programme had started and he had his first group therapy session. He hadn't said anything, although he had been welcomed and included. The others in the group were quite sharp with each other, but were civil to each other outside the session. They seemed to take a perverse kind of pleasure in sticking it to each other, but were not so keen at being on the receiving end.

Joe wondered if he could get away with doing the minimum of stuff on the programme and then make his way home quietly, with no fuss. He really didn't want to talk about everything that had been bothering him, and he didn't like the constant focus on drinking. A lot of people on the programme seemed to be worse than him. Some had lost their marriages and some had repeatedly lost jobs. He may not have been the most well-functioning person on the programme, but it was nice to know that he wasn't the worst either, by far.

8

Alcohol and Mood Disorders (Depression)

> A debilitating mood disorder can intensify the negative effects of alcoholism.

Alcohol is a depressant. It negatively affects drinkers' moods. However, the majority of light drinkers do not have any mood effects from alcohol at all, or, if they do, these more than likely relate to a pleasant feeling of mild intoxication.

A significant number of 'ordinary' drinkers experience negative moods triggered by alcohol, but get over them quickly. They might, for example, go out drinking with friends, end up going on a binge and feel quite depressed as well as hungover the next day. The depressive feeling may last for a few days, but not longer than that.

If someone suffers from a full depressive disorder, they probably find that alcohol makes their depression significantly worse, even if taken in relatively small quantities. The alcohol consumed might just be enough to trigger a full relapse to depression, and it might take weeks or even longer to overcome that bout of depression. Depression could continue even if there is no alcohol consumed afterwards.

If someone suffers from an alcohol addiction problem, they have approximately a one in two chance of also suffering from a significant degree of depression. Depression and alcohol dependence can have a complex and devastating interaction: one can feed off the other. Some people can go from a cycle of drinking into a cycle of depression or vice versa, until it becomes difficult to tell where addiction ends and depression begins. In order to understand this, we first have to look at the concept of depression itself.

Depression: What Is It?

Depression has many definitions. Just about everybody suffers from depressive symptoms at some stage or other in life, but most people do not suffer from a full depressive disorder. A full or major depression is more than a bad day; it can be a devastating psychiatric disorder that takes over a life as much as alcohol dependence can. Depression can be defined as a significant downturn in mood that lasts for at least fifteen days out of thirty. It has many associated symptoms, which are listed below. In order for someone to be seen as having depression, they must demonstrate some of the following symptoms:

- Loss of libido

- Poor concentration

- Poor memory, especially poor short-term memory

- Poor appetite; weight loss

- Anxiety

- Guilt

- Lack of sleep, especially due to waking early in the morning

- Inability to experience pleasure (anhedonia)

- Loss of motivation or interest
- Diurnal variation in mood (worse in morning)
- Feelings of being hopeless and helpless
- Pessimism
- Passive death wish; suicidal ideation or intent
- Hallucinations and delusions

An individual's depression may become apparent to those around them, such as family members. They can appear as lethargic, quiet, disinterested, lacking in energy, tearful, restless, self-critical and occasionally indecisive.

Depression affects a large number of people, women twice as much as men. Once it is recognised as being present, it may need expert medical attention, including that of a psychiatrist, in order for it to be treated successfully. The treatment may involve therapy, antidepressant medication or, in some situations, hospitalisation. In very difficult situations, where the patient is unresponsive to other treatments, even electric shock therapy can be useful.

There is no definitive cause of depression, but the following factors may have an influence:

- A recent major life event, for example, loss of employment or death of a family member
- Significant family history of depression
- Childhood trauma or abuse
- Loss of a parent early in life
- Giving birth (postnatal depression in women)
- Physical illness
- Substance abuse, including alcoholism

- Certain personality characteristics, for example, inflexibility or obsessiveness

- Certain medications, for example, steroids

Although depression may occur in childhood and the teenage years, the first depressive episode most commonly occurs in the twenties or thirties. Depression can occur, however, at any stage in life.

How Depression Interacts with Alcoholism

When a problem drinker goes drinking, they can get depressed as a result of the direct effects of alcohol. They can get depressed that evening, the next day or a few days later.

The amount of alcohol needed to make them depressed is variable. They can get depressed with just a few drinks, but this is not very likely. It is more common that they get depressed after a reasonable amount of alcohol, and particularly if they engage in a heavy amount of alcohol consumption or binge drinking. Some talk about only getting depressed if they drink spirits, but this may be because spirits contain such a large amount of concentrated alcohol.

The effects of alcohol on a person's mood can be quite variable, even idiosyncratic. An alcohol misuser can go drinking every weekend and drink the same amount. Yet, they might get depression only after every third or fourth occasion, for no apparent reason. The same amount of alcohol working on the same person with the same underlying mood can have a different effect at different times for no explicable reason.

Alcohol may not cause depression if the alcohol misuser is in good form when going drinking. If they are mildly down before drinking, alcohol may bring them to a moderate state of depression. However, if they are moderately down and go drinking, alcohol may cause them to become severely depressed or even suicidal.

Suicide and Alcoholism

Suicidal ideas can occur with depression and also with alcoholism. When the two conditions occur together, there is a significant increase in suicidal ideation, suicidal acts and completed suicide relative to either condition working alone.

Alcohol can act as a depressant on someone with a history of depression. Even a moderate amount of alcohol can bring someone down to a very black place. When someone begins to develop suicidal ideas because of depression, not only can alcohol make them more depressed and more suicidal, but it can allow them to act on the suicidal ideas when they become disinhibited.

Normally, when someone loses their inhibitions because of alcohol consumption, they laugh and talk more or they do something silly like dancing on the tables. If they are depressed and disinhibited, they are unlikely to do anything exuberant. If they are suicidally depressed, however, or if they are depressed and become suicidal because of the depressive effects of alcohol, they might change a suicidal plan into a suicidal action, or change a vague suicidal idea into a certain death. Overall, someone with alcoholism is at least three times more likely to die by suicide than someone without it.

Can an Alcohol Misuser Get Depressed, even When Sober?

The unfortunate answer is, yes, an alcohol misuser can get depressed even after having achieved sobriety. The incidence of depression in alcohol misusers with full sobriety is about two times the incidence in the general population. There are quite a few causes of depression in sober alcoholics, beyond the general causes of depression:

- Alcohol misusers can sometimes get depressed as part of alcohol withdrawal, during the first three to five days after their last drink

- Alcohol misusers can get bouts of craving, which can present as depression but really represent an underlying desire for drink

- Alcohol misusers can have a lot of problems to deal with in early sobriety, such as relationship problems, marital problems or job problems, which were either caused by drinking or ignored because of drinking. These problems can trigger depression

- Alcohol misusers can have poor or undeveloped coping skills. This can lead to bouts of depression as the sober alcoholic wrestles with problems and situations they haven't dealt with before, mainly because they were drinking

Fortunately, most alcohol misusers don't get bouts of depression when sober. Even if the occurrence of depression in sober alcoholics is more than in the general population, being sober greatly improves a person's chances of overcoming depression. When an alcohol misuser is drinking, they have between a 40 per cent and a 50 per cent chance of being depressed, but that falls off in the first weeks of sobriety to a 10 per cent chance, a very significant improvement.

It is true to say that, if a depressed alcohol misuser is successfully treated for depression but continues to drink, eventually the depression will kick in again because of the alcohol. The bottom line is that if there is a significant degree of depression present, it needs to be assessed and treated. The treatment of depression is different from the treatment of alcoholism, and thus it may require assessment and treatment by a professional such as a family practitioner, a therapist or a psychiatrist. If someone has a serious issue like depression then he or she needs to be seen by an expert and decisions taken after that. Depression is not something that should be messed about with or ignored.

Alcoholism and Bipolar Disorder

Bipolar disorder, previously known as manic depression, can also be associated with alcoholism. This disorder is character-ised by episodes of elation, which last for at least three days, followed by episodes of depression, also lasting anything from days to weeks.

This elevation in mood (mania) is associated with a list of symptoms:

- Increased energy
- Increased rate of speech
- Flight of ideas (jumping from idea to idea)
- Insomnia
- Racing thoughts
- Distractibility and poor concentration
- Poor memory
- Increased appetite; some weight loss
- Disinhibition
- Grandiose ideas
- Irritability and changeability of mood
- Indifference to problems
- Overspending
- Sexual indiscretion
- Lack of judgment
- Restlessness
- Dysphoria (feeling low despite increased energy)

These episodes of elevated mood can alternate with episodes of depression, each lasting at least a number of days or even weeks. The episodes of elation are generally noticeable, at least to loved ones or close friends who may see a significant number of the symptoms listed above. The person going through them may simply notice they feel incredibly well and have increased energy. At an extreme, an episode of elation can reach extremes of overwhelming inability to function, with lack of concentration, physical agitation, and even delusions and hallucinations.

The causes of bipolar disorder are the same as those of depression. There is an equal incidence of the illness among men and women, and there is probably a very significant genetic element to the disorder, with a large number of sufferers having some family history of bipolar disorder. It commonly begins in a person's twenties and it is unusual for it to begin after the mid-thirties. It can often present firstly as an episode of depression, with the bipolar element emerging later. Fortunately, bipolar disorder is less common than depression; however, up to 5 per cent of the adult population have significant symptoms.

There is increasing evidence that alcoholism can actually cause bipolar disorder in vulnerable people. Alcohol abuse can certainly trigger an episode of elation in someone with an established disorder, and alcohol consumption can make that episode more complex and more difficult to treat. People with bipolar disorder can end up requiring psychiatric hospitalisation more often if alcohol is in the mix.

It can be very difficult for an alcohol misuser with an undiagnosed bipolar disorder to achieve full sobriety. It is very hard, for example, for someone to concentrate on a recovery programme if their mind is racing, they are agitated and restless, they are overspending and disinhibited, and they can't focus on anything properly, let alone their recovery.

Unfortunately, alcohol misusers with bipolar disorder are twice as likely to attempt suicide as those with bipolar disorder alone. Like with depression, there is likely to be a number of causes of this, including the higher likelihood of depressive episodes, and the problem of disinhibition and impulsiveness while drunk.

Like with depression, a lot of symptoms of bipolar disorder that are present while someone is drinking can fade after a week or two of sobriety. That is why a diagnosis of bipolar disorder is best made during a period of sobriety, rather than when someone is currently drinking. Like with depression, once the diagnosis of bipolar disorder is made, it requires treatment above and beyond that of alcoholism alone. It should probably be treated by a psychiatrist and it is possible that medication such as a mood stabiliser would be required.

The good news is that, while a diagnosis such as bipolar disorder may frighten a sufferer initially, it is a disorder that tends to respond very effectively to the correct treatment. An undiagnosed bipolar disorder underlies a large amount of cases of difficult-to-treat alcoholism. If the disorder is diagnosed and treated in an alcohol misuser, this can allow him or her to obtain a long period of sobriety for the first time in years. If a person is an alcohol misuser and has bipolar disorder, both conditions need treatment for overall recovery.

> **If both alcoholism and a mood disorder are present, both need treatment.**

Case Study: The Depressed Alcohol Misuser's Story

Gabriel had an ordinary working-class background. He grew up in a hardworking household. He left home in his teens and spent a number of years in a seminary learning to see if he had a vocation, and he suffered abuse there at the hands of one of the priests.

He worked in various jobs, all the time pursuing his passion for the theatre and acting. He acted in a number of fringe theatre plays before being spotted by a TV producer and given a small part on a regular TV soap opera. Shortly afterwards, such was the audience response to the young, handsome, brooding actor with significant screen presence, he was given his own TV series, which was an outstanding success. He coped with the loss of his long-term girlfriend, who died early in life, and appeared to move on.

Hollywood beckoned and within a few years he was making a name for himself in the US as a hunk who could act. A few parts in respected high quality low budget movies led to him taking on the lead roles in a number of studio-backed big budget movies. At this time he met and married a beautiful American film star, and they had two children together. It was the textbook fairytale: looks, fame, money, and marital and family bliss.

The truth behind the headlines was less prosaic. Gabriel suffered from bouts of depression, despite everything positive in his life, and had recurrent doubts about his career, his talent and his success. He began to drink heavily and this exacerbated his depression massively. His drinking began to interfere with everything. His career stalled, and he failed to make it into the top tier of movie stars, though still constantly working. His marriage ran into difficulty, and he eventually split (amicably) from his wife, who went on to marry a billionaire. He stayed in the US to be close to his children, but did not marry again.

His drinking and depression became progressively worse. He refused to get any help, insisting that he did things his way. He would check into hotels and stay for days on end, depressed and drinking alone in his room. He said in an interview that he knew he had to do something about his drinking when he was pouring whiskey down his throat at the same time as he was vomiting up his stomach contents. He sought and obtained help for his depression, and entered treatment for his alcoholism. He hasn't drank alcohol since.

Since then, Gabriel Byrne has done very well, acting in theatre, doing film projects, and having the lead role in a successful TV series called, somewhat appropriately, In Treatment. *He still struggles at times, but keeps his eye on his demons and his head above water. He has revealed his past in remarkable detail and has been incredibly candid, without trying to exploit his own story. For his sins, he has recently been appointed as Ireland's International Cultural Ambassador, so he is certainly trying to give back to the community as part of his recovery. He is a testament to how outside appearances can differ from the real story, and how alcoholism and depression can take over the life of even the most apparently successful and fulfilled people.*

Joe's Story: Day 8

The weekend was turning out to be a bit of a drag, frankly. He had to get up and go to an AA meeting in the morning. That was reasonably diverting and he enjoyed chatting with the others afterwards. At times it felt a lot like a holiday camp, only for adults.

A lot of people had quite tough stories. One man described losing his wife because of alcohol, and another discussed job problems and a severe set of financial problems caused by alcohol abuse.

During the afternoon Joe tried to sit down and do some of the written work for the counsellor. He spent a fruitless hour in front of a blank page, writing little and thinking even less. He found out that he wasn't the only one with writing difficulties. It wasn't an easy task to write out memories of things he didn't want to recall, and to detail events that he wanted to let fade into the dust. This was neither pleasant nor effective, he thought.

They would be back to a more standardised programme the next day. Joe realised he was actually looking forward to it. Anything was better than sitting in a chair, thinking and writing.

9

Types of Drinkers and Treatment

> Different people drink for different reasons and in
> different ways.

There are numerous types of alcohol misusers. Researchers have come up with various theories for what distinguishes one type of alcohol misuser from another. Probably the most established theory divides alcohol misusers into the following two categories: early onset (addicted before the age of twenty-five) and late onset (addicted after the age of twenty-five). This theory suggests that early-onset alcohol misusers have a stronger family history, are mostly male, have a higher degree of associated problems such as depression and often have antisocial traits.

Effective new treatments for alcohol misusers have not emerged on the basis of this theory. In addition, no one theory is correct because there are as many types of alcohol misusers as there are alcohol misusers. No one is exactly the same; everyone's story is unique and follows a different pattern.

However, it is clear that, whatever the origin of an addiction, drinking patterns and reasons for drinking fall into a number of well-established categories. Knowledge of these categories is important because it can help a drinker understand the way in which they drink and some of the reasons for the particular drinking pattern that they have adopted.

There are five categories of drinking pattern:

1. The emotional drinking pattern

2. The social drinking pattern

3. The testing-personal-control drinking pattern

4. The interpersonal-conflict drinking pattern

5. The dedicated-drinker drinking pattern

1. The Emotional Drinking Pattern

This pattern is associated with stress-induced drinking. Drinking is seen primarily as an escape from other things, mainly negative emotions. The drinker takes alcohol when feeling angry with themselves, depressed, afraid or useless. They can feel empty and life can have little meaning for them. They can feel overwhelmed by panic and anxiety at times. Drinking may temporarily alleviate these feelings, which, in turn, encourages them to drink.

2. The Social Drinking Pattern

This pattern is common. The drinker feels a need to drink when feeling good about themselves and when in generally good form. They enjoy drinking and enjoy the company of others when drinking. They feel urges to drink when they have completed a significant task or even when they have got to the end of the working week without too much trouble. They feel that drinking can be a positive thing and that they have more fun when drinking. They can drift into a pattern of heavy drinking without noticing the change.

3. The Testing-Personal-Control Drinking Pattern

This pattern of drinking is associated with drinking alone. The drinker often feels that they can control their drinking and they want to test the boundaries of their ability. Socially, they will sometimes drink when offered a drink by others or when they see others drunk. Not drinking is a test of willpower, and whether or not to drink is a battle entered into frequently. Often they feel that people can act in a hostile manner towards them and this can drive them to alcohol.

4. The Interpersonal-Conflict Drinking Pattern

This pattern is associated with interpersonal stress. The drinker may feel jealous of others and may feel distant from them. They may drink after having an argument with someone at work or at home. They may have trouble communicating their feelings and can drink because of their frustration at this. They can feel unloved by others and have a sense of isolation. This type of drinker can drink alone or surrounded by people, but not feel part of the group.

5. The Dedicated-Drinker Drinking Pattern

This type of drinking pattern is associated with a feeling of power over drinking. The drinker feels that their drinking is not a problem and that they can control their drinking if they want to. They don't drink because of feelings of guilt or anxiety because they don't feel that way often. They feel they could stop drinking if they wanted to, but often they just don't want to. They don't believe they crave alcohol; they just want to drink. Sometimes they drink to prove they don't need to go into treatment for alcohol, that they are strong enough to control things themselves. By and large, this pattern is associated with a lack of feelings and is the result of a simple interest in obtaining drink.

The vast majority of drinkers relate to at least one of these drinking patterns, and they have some idea of what drives them to drink. Some people may find that their reasons for drinking straddle a few of these categories.

What use is it to categorise people according to their attitudes to and reasons for drinking? First, identifying an alcohol misuser's drinking pattern can increase their insight into their motivation to drink. Second, if an alcohol misuser gains insight into why they drink, they can use that insight to help address the problem. In other words, if a person's reasons for drinking are identified and categorised, this information can be used as part of the solution.

There is a central problem behind each type of drinking pattern:

- Type 1: the association between alcohol and negative feelings

- Type 2: the association between alcohol and social enjoyment

- Type 3: the association between alcohol and self-control

- Type 4: the association between alcohol and coping with others

- Type 5: the simple focus on alcohol above all other things

There is a form of inaccurate thinking associated with each of these types:

- Type 1: 'Alcohol allows me to deal with my emotions better'

- Type 2: 'I can calm my social anxiety with alcohol'

- Type 3: 'I am completely in control of my drinking'

- Type 4: 'It's other people's fault if I have a drink'

- Type 5: 'I deserve a drink to get through the day'

Fighting back against 'drinking thinking' is one of the methods of fighting against alcohol. Each type of drinker should examine their common drinking situations for examples of the thinking patterns indicated above. Each drinker must recognise their own particular thought pattern and then challenge it or contradict it with a self-generated 'control belief'.

Each type of drinker should fight against alcohol with the following control beliefs:

- Type 1: 'I don't need alcohol to deal with my emotions'
- Type 2: 'I don't need alcohol to deal with my anxiety'
- Type 3: 'I don't need to test if I can control my drinking'
- Type 4: 'My drinking is my responsibility, not the responsibility of others'
- Type 5: 'I don't need drink to get through my life'

Similarly, each drinking type is associated with a particular associated feeling that may occur before, during or after drinking. The most common feelings associated with each type are:

- Type 1: Low, useless, self-conscious
- Type 2: Anxious, awkward
- Type 3: Bored, agitated, isolated
- Type 4: Hopeless, desperate, angry
- Type 5: Emotionally numb, jittery, tired

It is very important for a drinker to recognise these feelings in themselves. Most drinkers do not realise that there are significant feelings around their drinking and a lot of people drink to numb those feelings. The only person who can identify exactly what the feelings are is the alcohol misuser themselves. Once an individual's feelings associated with drinking are identified, they can be explored and eventually dealt with. There are a number of ways to combat such feelings and each individual must find their own pathway to fighting them. Doing this involves three strategies:

1. A talking strategy: any talking strategy involves the drinker opening up to someone close to them, either in a personal or in a professional relationship. The drinker identifies and explores their feelings in the context of this relationship

2. A thinking strategy: any thinking strategy involves the drinker spending time, generally alone, working out for themselves exactly what their thoughts are around alcohol, particularly in relation to occasions at which alcohol is consumed. The drinker then tries to find a way to think differently, especially about alcohol

3. An action strategy: action strategies involve the drinker doing different things that distract them from drink-related thinking, that take them away from alcohol and allow them to engage in non-drink-related activity. This action strategy is something that the drinker themselves must decide on, and it should be relatively simple to put in place. It should be interesting enough for the drinker to make it relatively easy for them to choose to do it over drinking

Strategies like these can be employed in different ways in different situations. By and large, they work best when used consistently and over a significant period of time. These strategies have to be learnt and do not come naturally, especially if someone has been drinking heavily for some time and has developed a rigid way of thinking about their drinking. Often the best way to develop these techniques is with a professional addiction counsellor or therapist, through reading self-help books about addiction, such as this one, or using a computerised addiction therapy programme, such as www.onlinesobriety.com.

Computerised therapy programmes are designed to help an individual explore patterns of thinking, feeling and behaving that are associated with alcohol consumption, and to explore ways to change those patterns. They have been proven successful in a number of research experiments, but not in non-research settings as yet. Computerised addiction treatment is expected over the coming years to become a mainstay of addiction treatment, and to increase significantly the number of people with an addiction gaining access to effective and inexpensive treatment.

Overall, there is no one way to do these things; whatever method is successful for an individual is the best method. Some people have to try a number of methods to find one that works for them.

Understanding why you drink may help you to give it up.

Case Study: The Alcohol Misuser Who Started Young

Tom started drinking when he was thirteen. He hung out with his mates on a section of open ground not far from where he lived in a large estate. He initially drank at weekends, but over his teenage years he started drinking more frequently. By the time he was eighteen, he was drinking most nights of the week.

He had little parental supervision; his father worked nights as a factory supervisor and his mother was an alcoholic. In his last year at school he spent less than half of his school days in classes. He did not succeed in getting a finishing certificate. He also began to dabble in soft drugs like marijuana, but always returned to alcohol as his favourite escape. He found it hard to get employment, but had a series of temporary low-end jobs for a few years before giving up on the job scene altogether.

He lived on and off with his parents, and started living with his girlfriend after she got pregnant with his child. His drinking become more persistent and he started drinking spirits alone rather than going out with his friends and getting drunk with them.

He had a number of run-ins with the police and spent a short while in jail for an assault charge. At the age of twenty-four he decided that he had enough of his lifestyle and checked himself into rehabilitation to change his life around. His motivation was initially based on trying to avoid a further police charge, but he picked up enough of a message in rehabilitation to start going to AA on the outside.

He spent two years with a psychiatrist and an addiction counsellor trying to get past his addiction and depression problems. He had a significant number of relapses and failures to attend for appointments. His girlfriend began to put him under pressure at the same time as his mother achieved sobriety herself. This prompted him to make a further effort, and he began to attend his AA meetings, his aftercare with his counsellor and to take his antidepressant medication from his psychiatrist.

He maintained his sobriety through a further difficult two years. He finally settled down with his girlfriend and his son, and maintained a security job during that period.

He feels he is at significant risk of relapse and he takes nothing for granted.

Joe's Story: Day 9

This day meant a resumption of the full programme. Joe got stuck into the meetings and groups and was able to participate well. He tried hard to relate to the others on the programme. He offered words of comfort and advice to others in the groups. He made suggestions about just how bad their addictions were, about what they should do about their relationships and what they needed to do to turn their lives around. He was attentive to others and tried to bring the quiet ones into the discussions.

Even in the evening time, when the formal groups were finished, he was busy dispensing wisdom and advice. He was concerned, caring and balanced, and he felt his advice was very appropriate. Privately he thought he was doing an excellent job. His suggestions to the others were helpful. It seemed to him that some of these people really were a lot worse than he was and needed some sound advice about what to do with their lives. Indeed, if there was eventually a problem with his own career as a plumber, he thought that he would make a fine addiction counsellor. He was a natural at it.

10

What Happens if I Don't Get Treatment?

> Untreated, the prognosis for alcoholism is not good.

Research shows that, if alcoholism is untreated, 25 per cent of alcohol misusers drink themselves to death. Another 20 per cent drink quite dependently over many years, 25–30 per cent drift in and out of alcohol abuse over the course of a lifetime, while 20–25 per cent of alcohol misusers stop spontaneously. As stated in Chapter 1, only 20 per cent of alcohol misusers are in some form of treatment, including attending a counsellor, attending Alcoholics Anonymous (AA) or participation in a full rehabilitation programme. These are very daunting figures. If the majority of people with alcohol dependence are not in treatment, and remain so, then they are likely to do badly.

Alcohol misusers can lose up to ten years of life due to alcoholism; some lose a lot more. It is not an easy task as a doctor to have to deal with someone who has a terminal liver disease due to alcohol while still in their thirties. It's even worse if it is you who has the disease. The good news is that treatment works, and the significant majority of people who get treatment receive a lot of benefit from it. Obviously the trick is to get those who need treatment to see the benefits of treatment, and to engage in it.

Research also shows that successful abstinence maintained through groups like AA for a period of five years often means full abstinence in the future. Attempts by an alcohol misuser to return to controlled drinking generally leads to a full relapse to dependence. Thus, once alcohol dependence sets in, it really is a lifetime diagnosis. There was a movement a number of years ago called Moderation Management. It was founded on the basis of the idea that heavy drinkers could have an alternative to AA as a therapeutic support group. This movement aimed to control alcohol intake rather than to strive for abstinence from alcohol. The group developed a twelve-step programme modeled on the twelve-step programme of AA. While a lot of people in the treatment field might have felt that it was really an expression of group denial, the movement flourished for a number of years. However, it eventually faded from prominence when its founder, Audrey Kishline, was arrested in 2000 and charged with a drink-driving offence. She, in fact, drove the wrong way down a highway and crashed into a car, killing its two passengers. She served time in prison and adopted the AA recovery model. This really showed the flaws in the group's founding idea.

A Lifetime of Drinking

When research follows a group of alcoholics for a lifetime, it tells a startling tale. George Valliant studied a group of Harvard College graduates and a group of inner-city Boston men for over sixty years. He found that, by the age of sixty, between 18 per cent and 28 per cent of all the alcohol abusers were dead, the higher figure being for the inner-city alcohol misusers. The figures for early death suggest that the death rate for alcohol misusers is over 2.5 times the rate for non-alcohol misusers of the same age group. The causes of death are multiple: accidents and road traffic accidents, liver trouble, heart disease, cancer, dementia and even suicide. There is no one thing that causes an alcohol misuser to die early; it is an accumulation of multiple physical and mental causes, coupled with the ongoing effects of a dreadfully unhealthy lifestyle.

Certainly, some alcohol misusers seem to have the ability to continue drinking and generally abuse their bodies and minds for years, to the astonishment of observers. 'How can he last so well with what he is doing to himself?' This is a comment I hear often. It's true that some people can continue this way for years until eventually it gets too much and the body simply falls apart. I recall one chronic alcohol misuser in his forties who was admitted under my care in a general hospital. He presented with a dreadful chest infection, alcohol withdrawal and a generally appalling nutritional status. He was very well looked after by medical and nursing staff, but failed to respond to the combination of antibiotics, medical care and good nutrition. He died after thirteen days. For fear we had missed some serious disease like tuberculosis, we requested a postmortem. Nothing else was found beyond a bad chest infection. It was only when talking to his family that we gained an understanding of just how much he had been drinking, and just how much he had neglected himself over the course of the previous five years. So, eventually, for some, the alcohol does take its toll, and you can't assume that you can drink to high heaven and not suffer the physical consequences.

Treatment

It is a vital point to appreciate that treatment works. Just about every alcohol addiction treatment study ever done shows that treatment intervention is helpful. The style of treatment intervention varies enormously, from a few words of counselling from a nurse or doctor to a self-help-based, AA-style treatment programme, a full outpatient treatment including group and individual counselling, the use of medication to deal with craving for alcohol or, indeed, a full inpatient treatment pro-gramme including psychiatric assessment and an aftercare programme.

What constitutes successful intervention may vary for indi-viduals, and what works for one individual may simply not work for another. Indeed, what a particular individual needs on one occasion to overcome an addiction may not work a second time for the same person if he or she relapses to prob-lematic drinking, and a new style of intervention may be required. The success rates of treatment interventions are difficult to determine, and the few studies that have been completed are not of sufficient duration to be regarded as being in any way definitive. For example, a treatment inter-vention measured over twelve weeks, the standard period for treatment trials, simply may not determine a successful or unsuccessful outcome, but may just give a hint about true outcome. True outcome should be measured over a period of years because true recovery takes place over a number of years, not just the first twelve weeks.

Later on in the book (Chapters 17, 18 and 19), I will look at the specific effects of different types of treatment and what the most effective forms of treatment intervention are. How to choose what type of treatment intervention will be most help-ful to you or someone you know may well be a matter of trial and error. It is difficult to state at point of assessment just who will respond best to any particular type of treatment. Efforts to divide people into treatment responsive subtypes or groups are only now beginning to demonstrate effectiveness, and then only in terms of response to some medications. No research has successfully divided subjects into groups according to their response to types of psychological therapy. Indeed, the best research available has shown that alcohol addiction therapy is very helpful. However, this is not strictly because of the type of therapy, but more because of the quality of rapport that devel-ops between the therapist and the patient.

Studies of Treatment: What Works?

One of the challenges in doing any kind of research into the treatment of alcoholism is to try and design a study which can take into account the potential real difference between the 'active' treatment, for example, medication or a new type of therapy, and the 'placebo' or neutral treatment, for example, standard therapy and group sessions. The researcher wants to see if the addition of the active treatment really does benefit the patient more than standard therapy. If the researcher designs a high degree of standard therapy, for example, a large number of individual therapy sessions plus a number of weekly group sessions, the research is less likely to show a difference between standard therapy and the new therapy under research because of the high intensity of the standard therapy. So the standard therapy, at least for the purposes of the research, may have to be low key or less intense for the new therapy to have any chance of proving itself. An added complication is that most good researchers include a significant number of assessments or questionnaires in their research to help detail the differences between those who do well and those who don't. Questionnaires tend to take a long time, and often the administering of these questionnaires can lead to an understandable rapport developing between the research assistant administering the questionnaire and the patient. This rapport can be quite therapeutic, and may be just as powerful as the actual therapy administered by the study therapist. So the very act of completing a careful, well-designed and well-administered research study may lead to an inability to discover if the new therapy or treatment is in fact an additional benefit or not.

Almost any treatment intervention in cases of addiction is potentially helpful, but it has to be focused on addiction. Treatment intervention that is not addiction-focused doesn't work. General supportive therapy, where a therapist can be very helpful in a non-specific way and makes a patient feel better, doesn't work. Supportive therapy that is addiction focused does help.

So, it appears that if the patient gets a lot of attention from a therapist or even a research assistant, and that attention and focus is related to addiction-associated issues, then those interventions are all helpful.

Not everyone gets that hoped-for and expected benefit from treatment, but a distinct majority do. Even if someone doesn't get total benefit, in terms of complete abstinence from alcohol over a prolonged period of time, the vast majority experience a big decrease in the number of drinks they consume relative to when they began the treatment. And, seeing as drink-related health harm is directly associated with the number of drinks consumed by the individual, this could be a life-saving benefit, if not a total benefit.

Treatment works.

Case Study: The Attention-Seeking Alcohol Misuser

Mary grew up in the suburbs of a large city. Her family was conservative and she grew up somewhat smothered by three brothers, who were clearly given priority by her parents. She grew up rather wild and a bit of a tomboy.

When she left school and went to college, she embarked on a journey to make up for lost time. She began to drink with her basketball team and spend nights in the college bar. She became known for her flamboyant personality and her extroverted manner.

She got married to an auctioneer and, after a few years working in public relations, she chose to stay at home to look after her three children. She began to drink again in the late mornings and afternoons, between when her husband left for work and when the children got back from school. She drank wine initially and then graduated to spirits, including neat vodka, the effects of which she felt her husband and children wouldn't notice.

After a number of years of alcohol problems, she began to have marital difficulties and her husband left her to look after the children. She achieved sobriety through AA and got a lot of help from AA members in her sobriety. She began a passionate affair with a married AA member and through him got a job in his firm. This relationship led to her relapse to alcohol and eventually to a disastrous confrontation with her lover's wife, after which she was forced to quit her job.

She became depressed at this and eventually achieved sobriety again through a combination of AA group therapy, antidepressant medication and counselling. She maintained her extroverted personality, despite her setbacks. She always said she could get through her difficulties through sobriety and ongoing support.

Joe's Story: Day 10

This day did not go as planned. Just after breakfast, and after Joe had started the day with a distinctly positive attitude, he went to the group meeting of the day. In that meeting Joe received feedback from the counsellor. He was told in no uncertain terms that he was losing his focus, and that he needed to refocus on himself and his own recovery. He was told that he was spending too much time thinking about others and their recovery, and not enough time on his own situation.

Joe protested that he was only trying to help, that there were others on the programme who were sicker than he was and that it was only right that they should get the benefits of his insight. Besides, he thought the purpose of the programme was to share and to help each other so that no one would have to do their recovery all alone. Joe was upset at the counsellor's intervention. He said so, and walked out of the group.

Joe felt indignant and angry about the counsellor and her comments, and he said so to whoever would listen. He was even prepared to walk out of the programme, he felt so strongly on the issue.

He went to bed that night, but vowed to tell everyone just what he felt the next day – that, as far as he was concerned, these guys simply didn't know what they were doing.

II

Gaining Insight and
the Beginning of Sobriety

11

Realising the Need for Change

> Every alcohol misuser has a vulnerable point that can help them to realise their need to change.

When we decide to change anything significant in our lives, from changing a car to ending a relationship, we usually go through a process of evaluation of the reasons for the change, the arguments against it, the difficulties involved and whether we will be able to stick with that change.

When contemplating changing your drinking pattern to become a lighter drinker or a non-drinker, the same criteria apply. It is a serious decision, maybe life changing, and it deserves careful evaluation. But first the alcohol misuser must recognise that he or she has a problem.

Refusal to Acknowledge and Reluctance to Acknowledge

It is possible for an alcohol misuser to be in a state of precontemplation, denial or what I term RTA1: Refusal to Acknowledge. There really is no such thing as total denial, despite that term being used frequently in the field of addiction. No one goes through alcohol addiction without being partially aware of what is going on and of what alcohol is doing to them. Refusal to Acknowledge is not the same as complete unawareness and a total inability to see. Unless someone with alcohol dependence is severely brain damaged, he or she must have some level of awareness of the issue, albeit with a lack of appreciation of its extent. The use of the word 'refusal' signifies that it is important to recognise that this state is a voluntary one; it is the result of a choice. Most sufferers from addiction are in a state of proud RTA1.

If a person moves from the state of RTA1 to the state of Reluctance to Acknowledge or RTA2, then progress has been made. This stage is different from RTA1. It implies at least the possibility of change; it suggests that someone is prepared to consider the issue, albeit without making up their mind. The change from RTA1 to RTA2 is never a simple process, but the states are not too far apart. Most people who proudly proclaim that they are in RTA1 are partially in RTA2; they just don't say so. Their refusal is a public stance, an angry one, a determined one, but never a complete one. There is always an evaluation taking place at the back of the brain, there is always questioning and there is always an internal back-and-forth dialogue going on. Unless there is brain damage or continuous intoxication, there is always the possibility of acknowledgement, the possibility of change.

Outside pressure can be both helpful and counterproductive. Outside pressure is often required to encourage some people from the RTA1 to the RTA2 stage. However, outside pressure also allows some people to stay in a state of RTA1 because of their pride. Pride and obstinacy block the process of change. Most people with an addiction find swallowing their pride incredibly humiliating and difficult. Like an ageing dictator who refuses to believe that the time to step down has come, so the alcohol dependant clings to the last vestiges of the old system of self-belief and self-delusion. Acknowledging your difficulty with an addiction means letting go of what has become an entire way of life and an entire way of thinking, and puts paid to the belief, 'I am in charge and not the addiction.'

Facing Reality

Everyone has something of which they are proud – an achievement, a relationship, a talent or ability. Everyone has a plan, a desire to achieve in some way. Everyone has a dream, however farfetched it may seem to the outsider. The change from RTA1 to RTA2 involves not just acknowledging the addiction but admitting to reality. This means giving up the illusion and admitting to the sordid reality of day-to-day addicted life. It feels like giving up hope, to the alcohol misuser. It involves giving up a unique personal way of thinking.

Everyone, when growing up, creates a set of core beliefs about themselves that determine their life choices: 'I believe I am good looking; I believe that I am a talented artist; I believe that I am a good and kind person; I believe that I am intelligent; I believe that I am in control of my life.' We all build our lives on these beliefs about ourselves. You wouldn't become a model if you didn't think you were good looking. You wouldn't become a scientist if you didn't believe you were intelligent. You wouldn't strive to work as a carer if you didn't think you were kind. Some of our core beliefs are built on the idea that we differ from others in a particular way. We all want to excel at something and to set ourselves apart. We want to be acknowledged, loved and admired for that talent, ability or achievement. We all want to be different to those around us, to be proud of ourselves because of that uniqueness.

To an alcohol misuser, acknowledging their addiction means being humbled and acknowledging their sameness; it means giving up their core beliefs about themselves. Acknowledging your addiction involves a massive change in your dreams and goals. It means admitting that your core beliefs are wrong, and that your dreams and goals have to be changed. Everything you have built your life on has to be altered. It is like being reborn. You start off at the age of twenty, forty or fifty to try and reconfigure your future in some new and unattractive universe, while having to admit that a lot of the past ten or twenty years has been wasted time. Let's face it, that's a big ask. You might say that the alcohol misusers stuck in the RTA1 stage are akin to Wild West heroes, stubbornly refusing to change and sticking to their addictive guns despite everyone being against them. They will defend the 'small town' of their own core beliefs against the 'outlaws' of reality. But this attitude is ultimately destructive.

Moving from RTA1 to RTA2

Trying to get someone to move from RTA1 to RTA2 involves two things: identifying a consequence of that person's addictive behaviour or lifestyle that upsets him or her and, frankly, 'beating them up' about it. This vulnerability may be the fear of the personal health consequences, as outlined in Chapter 4; it may be the fear of losing a core relationship with a spouse or child; it may the shame of the damage being caused to loved ones; it may be the fear of a loss of status and finances due to potential job loss. It can be anything that the alcohol misuser cares about, and the trick is to make that potential loss or shame as real as possible. I discuss the point of vulnerability in more detail in Chapter 12.

Getting the alcohol misuser to commit to change involves showing an understanding and appreciation of just how difficult the change will be for them, and how much pride and self-belief are being destroyed, and offering the addict support as they make the transition. Because this duality of tasks is often too difficult for a close family member to do correctly, and because it involves being harsh at some times and supportive at other times, it is often best to have the help of a professional in order to achieve that balance. Most spouses or others close to the alcohol misuser either end up being too harsh or too supportive (enabling), simply because they are too close to the situation and its consequences to be emotionally objective.

The process of undergoing change involves a simple equation: when the pain gets too great for the alcohol misuser, therein lies the motivation to change. If there is no pain, or if the pain is too little, then there is no motivation, or at least not adequate motivation, to change. This implies that motivation to change will not come from minor stresses, but from major ones; it won't come from minor emotional upsets, but from significant emotional threats. The threat may or may not be real, but it is vital that the alcohol misuser perceives it as real. Since addicts are masters at reading the difference between a verbal threat and real intent, and it often takes real intent to force an addict to listen, benign goodwill will not do the trick.

What Are the Reasons to Continue Drinking?

Part of any process of change is to assess the reasons for and against a particular activity. In this case, it involves looking at reasons to drink and reasons not to drink.

Reasons to continue drinking:

- I like it

- It is not causing me any harm

- What else can I do with my time?

- I enjoy getting drunk; I get a thrill from it

- I can afford it

- It makes all my problems disappear, right now

- It really diminishes my anxiety and makes me more sociable

- It makes me forget my depression

- I really crave a drink

- I really need alcohol

- Nobody cares for me and so it doesn't matter

- I only take some every now and again so it doesn't matter if I drink or not

- It doesn't affect me so why shouldn't I?

- I have lost everything due to drink, so what does it matter if I do?

- I love drinking so much that I simply cannot do without it

The main thing to note about the above points is that the subject is consistently 'I' and 'me'. There is no reference to anyone outside of the individual, and so all the reasons to continue drinking are selfish. The pride of the drinker is a selfish pride. There is little room for others in the drinker's reasoning. Thus, the question to ask is: what about other people?

What Are the Reasons to Change?

This list of reasons to change is endless, and there is nothing on this list that applies to everyone. Everyone is different, and everyone has unique aspects of their lives and their relationship with alcohol that makes drawing up a sensitive and specific list for everyone impossible. However, perhaps some points might make sense to the individual alcohol misuser.

Reasons to stop drinking:

- My life is a mess and if I don't change I will have nothing

- I can aspire to better things

- I have hope that things can be better

- I will lose my marriage if I don't stop drinking

- I will lose my children if I don't stop drinking

- I will lose my job if I don't stop drinking

- My health is suffering due to drink and it will get worse if I don't stop

- I am disgusted with myself

- I want to be in control of my life and not under the influence of any stupid substance

- My life hasn't moved on since I started to drink heavily and I am stuck in the past

- I am so depressed and anxious, and drinking is making it worse

- I am only drinking to stop the effects of withdrawal

- I will die from drinking if I don't stop

The important thing about the motivation to change is that it is a journey from a dreadful place to a much better one. If the bad place isn't bad enough, there is no reason to move on. Equally, if there is no better place to move on to, there is also no reason to move on. As a sufferer moving towards getting help, you must revise your goals and change your ambitions. If you don't, you will not move on, no matter how horrible the current situation is.

What if There Is No Desire to Give Up Alcohol?

This is probably the most important question in this book. What can you, the relative or spouse, do if the addicted person has no expressed desire to actually give up alcohol? What can you, the alcohol misuser, do if you are drinking too much and yet you feel the task of giving up impossible? What if you, as the alcohol misuser or the concerned person, are banging your head against a brick wall again and again, and nothing is happening to change the pattern of alcohol misuse?

First, you will recall those three personality traits that the alcohol misuser may have (see Chapter 3): alcohol misusers can be more adventurous than other people; they continuously seek out pleasurable things; and they don't always learn from negative consequences. That particular combination of personality traits lends itself to the alcohol misuser not paying attention to outside circumstances and only responding to internal personal triggers. Thus, outside circumstances are going to have to be on a pretty large scale to register with the alcohol misuser.

Second, no one can take anything on board when they are intoxicated or in withdrawal from alcohol, and thus someone who is drinking heavily needs to have the alcohol out of their system before anything can register at all.

Third, there is no single factor that can be made register with the misuser of alcohol. An individual can only react to personal circumstances and pressures. In general, it is impossible to say what that individual's point of vulnerability is, but it is true to say that most people have at least one. The objective is to find the point of vulnerability and direct the alcohol misuser's focus to it. What an outsider thinks may register with the alcohol misuser may not register at all; he or she might have a completely different set of motivations from what would be expected by others.

Balance of Forces

As a relative or friend trying to encourage an alcohol misuser towards abstinence, ascertaining the balance of forces in that individual's mind may be helpful. That is, trying to understand the forces that are pulling the person towards drinking and trying to fathom the forces that are pulling the person towards sobriety. These forces are completely individual and cannot be predicted simply by guessing.

From the inside, an alcohol misuser needs to try and focus on the negative consequences of drinking in order to increase the pull of sobriety. In general, this means focusing on long-term goals and issues rather than short-term goals. Most of the benefits of sobriety are long term and most of the problems (even those caused by alcohol) are immediate, and alcohol may provide an easy escape route from current reality. Thus, moving the alcohol misuser's thought pattern from immediate benefits to negative consequences is vital, and needs to be an ongoing struggle. Short-term pain and long-term gain is a lot better than short-term gain and long-term pain.

The alcohol misuser may slowly realise that alcohol is the boss and that there is a need for change. Change may take time.

Things may get bad before they get better. Personally, I have seen the most appalling situations turn around with persistence and I have seen impossible situations resolved. If the intention is there, the situation will eventually be resolved.

Finally, motivation is not an unchangeable and unitary condition; it is composed of various competing forces and these forces can change over time. Motivation, one day, may be focused on getting rid of powerful anxiety symptoms associated with withdrawal (perhaps by drinking), and a few days later it could be focused on trying to avoid relapsing. One day's priority may be to remain sober and make up for the past; the next day, motivation may be affected by having to deal with strong cravings for alcohol. The particular reasons that got a person to stop drinking may need to be revised and reassessed daily to get that person to maintain abstinence.

If an alcohol misuser's suffering is their motivation for recovery, then it is vital that this suffering is put to good use and that a recovery journey is plotted for them to follow. It is vital that the alcohol misuser learns techniques to deal with the addiction so that their suffering is not in vain.

> **There are more reasons to give up alcohol than not.**

Case Study: The Famous Alcohol Misuser

Reginald was born into a small working-class family in the suburbs of a medium-sized town. His father deserted the family at a young age and, as he grew up, Reginald's mother was the mainstay of his life.

His passion was music and he listened to all sorts of music throughout his teenage years. He learned to play the piano, and started playing in banks to try and earn some sort of a living. He wasn't able to compose lyrics of any quality, but found he could compose songs if he had lyrics to compose to. He teamed up with a poet and lyricist and, after a few false starts, he starting writing and recording songs. He released a few songs that made no commercial impact, but attracted the interest of music critics. He finally released a successful song and it became a worldwide hit.

Over a period of ten years he released record after record, toured constantly and became famous. He knew from a young age that he was homosexual, or bisexual, but failed to acknowledge this fully to himself or to the public, and this led to a number of disastrous relationships, including a failed marriage.

As part of the endless cycle of performing and recovering, and partly to deal with his troubled personal life, he became addicted to alcohol and other drugs. He was addicted for the best part of twenty years, despite being recurrently and highly successful.

He met a young boy with AIDS named Ryan and the boy's loving mother, which changed his life. After the boy died and he observed the extraordinary courage and dedication of the boy's mother, who continued to campaign to raise funds to research AIDS after her son's death, he decided to admit to his problems and get help. In part, he empathised with his own mother's struggle to cope with his problems, and he understood the hurt he caused her. He also felt guilty because those problems were self-inflicted and the pain she suffered was caused by him.

He openly says that he felt worthless at that time, that his life was 'shit' and the only thing he had going for him was his career. He checked himself into rehab. He hasn't used alcohol or drugs since.

He is more commonly known as Elton John, but his fame and money didn't help him with his addiction. That was both a very common and a very personal struggle.

Joe's Story: Day 11

This was probably the worst day so far on the programme. Joe went to the group session and ended up getting suspended from the programme.

He had waited for the group to start and then took the floor. He expressed his outrage at the way things were turning out. Everything he was trying to do was being opposed by the counsellors and he felt their focus was entirely wrong. He stated that he felt wronged and slighted, and he demanded an apology from the counsellor for her behaviour.

The group reacted badly to his suggestion and baldly stated that he was in denial about his own drinking, and that he was trying to divert attention away from himself. He was selfish, lacked insight and had questionable motivation about getting cured or getting clean. Once again, Joe felt slighted and indignant, and threatened to walk out of the group. He was warned by the counsellor that walking out a second time would mean automatic suspension from the programme, but at this stage he just didn't care and he stalked out of the room.

He was informed later that he was indeed suspended from the programme. Joe was furious, and started to pack his clothes. How dare they suspend him simply because he was trying to help those less fortunate than himself on the programme!

He decided that he would meet the doctor in the morning and then leave. He was done with the stupid programme, and he would probably have a drink on the way home just to prove that he was in control and didn't need their bullshit advice. He was done.

12

Contemplation and Denial

> Denial is not a single, immovable entity; its extent can vary.

As mentioned, total denial doesn't really exist. The idea that an alcohol misuser, who drinks excessively and causes significant damage to themselves and to those around them, has absolutely no knowledge about what they are doing is nonsensical (unless there is significant brain damage). All alcohol misusers have some idea of what they are doing. All alcohol misusers have some degree of knowledge that they are drinking excessively, all have some idea that it is not good for them and all have some idea that it isn't good for those around them. Unfortunately, at the starting point of the journey into recovery, that degree of knowledge or insight is very limited.

At the initial stages of addiction, the alcohol misuser might be closer to delusion than denial. They trust their perspective over any other in relation to all things, including alcohol. They think in terms of 'I' and nothing encroaches upon that singular perspective. Everything negative that happens is blamed on things apart from drink, even though alcohol may be the unifying factor behind a litany of disasters.

Limits of Perspective

The alcohol misuser's insight into the damage that alcohol is doing to themselves and others is limited by a number of factors:

- They might have simply not suffered enough for the bubble of self-delusion to be pricked and burst. They might be in good health, still functioning in a job and still have a relationship or marriage. They may be just arriving at the point of dependence on alcohol

- They may not have received enough honest feedback from those around them to impinge on their consciousness. It often takes an enormous degree of courage from family and friends to speak honestly to the alcohol misuser about their problem

- Because the disease of addiction is often insidious and develops slowly, alcohol misusers may believe themselves less advanced on the pathway to addiction than they actually are. They often believe that they are just heavy drinkers, and not alcohol dependent. They believe that they are not overcome by the addiction and that they are in control

- They may believe they are not alcohol dependent because of one single hold-out factor, the X Factor, as described in Chapter 2: 'I know I'm not an alcoholic because I still have a job,' 'I don't actually crave alcohol,' 'I never drink in the morning' or 'Nobody has ever said anything to me'

- If a person suffers from a degree of depression, anxiety or agitation that is made worse by alcohol, it is very common for them to state, 'I know that alcohol isn't the real problem; the real problem is my depression or my mood.' It is often difficult to admit that there are two problems and not just one, or, indeed, that there is primarily one problem – alcohol

- The alcohol misuser's perspective on life in general may have been hard won and they may have learned to trust their own judgment on a lot of things. The simple admission that their perspective is wrong about alcohol may mean them giving up on a complete way of thinking about the world. Alcohol may be central to their lives in many different ways

- They might simply not want to give up alcohol because they desire or need alcohol so much. Thus, it is simpler to pretend they are in denial rather than to admit they have a problem and then face the pressure to do something about it

So the problem is not one of denial; the problem is one of a degree of denial. Nobody is fully ignorant about themselves, nobody is totally unaware of other people's reactions to them and nobody is totally immune to physical, mental or social pressure. It is important to remember that the alcohol misuser always has some modest degree of awareness of their problem, however unexplored, unacknowledged or unexpressed. And that is vital information when working with someone with an addiction. There is always some way to identify the alcohol misuser's point of vulnerability that will overcome the stalemate and begin the recovery.

The Chink in the Armour

One important component of the pathway to recovery is the idea that the alcohol misuser can begin to acknowledge that his or her hard-won perspective might actually be wrong. It is vital to get in there and attempt to break the armour of denial by finding the chink or point of vulnerability. For some, that weakest point might be a single emotional vulnerability, and for others it might be a number of different vulnerabilities. Attempting to find that weak point and planting that seed of insight may be the most important things a concerned person can do to help the alcohol misuser out of their defensive delusion.

As mentioned in Chapter 11, that point of vulnerability is very individual and can't be predicted for each individual. For some, it is a family issue: 'What do my children think of me? Will they reject me if I don't stop drinking?' For some, it is a social pressure issue: 'Will I be embarrassed if I am caught drink driving and people find out?' For some, it is a mood issue: 'If I give up drinking, will my depression and anxiety lift and will I feel better?' For some, it is a financial or work issue: 'Will I lose my job or destroy my career if I don't stop?' For others, it is a health issue: 'My liver will give out if I don't give it up; my doctor has warned me.'

For the majority, it is an accumulation of factors and not simply one factor alone that breaks through denial. As denial is built up slowly over years, so the crumbling of denial also takes place over time and is not instantaneous. While there may be a moment of clarity, when a certain degree of insight or a certain leap of understanding takes place, by and large it is a painstaking process.

Some individuals are lucky in their recovery. They can identify a single event or thought that was, for them, their moment of clarity and everything good flowed from that point. This may have been the result of an exasperated comment from a friend; it may have been a response to an emotional threat from a loved one. Many people cannot identify what the breaking point in their denial is, even when they have been successfully in recovery for years. 'I just finally decided' is the most common statement I hear. As the build-up of denial over the years is a conscious and unconscious process, so the breaking of denial is both a conscious and unconscious process.

An Unconscious Process

Unconscious forces are, by their nature, undetectable, but they are important and vital in understanding a large part of what goes on in the psychological battle against addiction. Aiming to reveal a little of what those forces are within an individual can lead to major progress.

You know there are unconscious forces at work when there is a big mismatch between someone's thoughts and behaviour. If someone is constantly stating that they wish to give up alcohol and yet they don't manage to do so, obviously a significant unconscious barrier is present.

As someone enters into the process of evaluating their alcohol abuse or dependence, various psychological forces come into play. The triggers for these forces can be feedback from relatives or friends, professional information and encouragement from counsellors or doctors, and, indeed, periods of careful evaluation and thinking time in which the person engages privately. At the same time, there are many unconscious forces that come into play around the idea of giving up drink and what that might mean. These unconscious forces may manifest themselves as fear and panicky feelings about the future, as episodes of craving for alcohol, as disturbed or drink-related dreams, episodes of tension and restlessness, periods of lost sleep or unexplained irritability.

The best way to deal with these forces is for the alcohol misuser to attempt to increase their awareness of them, to put in effort to evaluate what is going on beneath the surface and to spend time carefully thinking about them. Unconscious forces cannot be eliminated; they can only be guessed at, considered and hopefully dealt with over time.

Unconscious forces are also prominent in the development of alcohol craving (see Chapter 22). A large number of alcohol misusers who attempt recovery and who fail will state that they have no idea what led them to drinking again; they will have no explanation beyond the fact that they drank again. They will often deny any feelings of craving, any upset emotions or any psychological explanation for their relapse. They will state that it 'just happened'. Therefore, there must be some unconscious psychological forces at work that make them drink when they don't want to. Those forces are identifiable in some and hidden in others, but they are present in all alcohol misusers.

The most likely dominant psychological force present is a sheer desire to drink for the enjoyment of it or because of a need for it. The whole battle for recovery is a battle to acknowledge just how great that desire and need is, and its extent is often a massive revelation to the alcohol misuser. Most people are unable to believe that alcohol is so big an issue that it dominates their lives. Most persist in the belief that it is only a minor issue or it is a significant issue but not an overwhelming one, until the sheer mass of evidence pushes them into an admission.

If the evidence is never presented to an alcohol misuser, if it is only hinted at or if it presented only when they are intoxicated and at their most irritating, then it is less likely to register with the misuser and give them insight into the extent of their problem. Of course, a significant minority of alcohol misusers will understand the evidence themselves, enter into some sort of treatment themselves and give up alcohol by themselves, but these are very much the minority – approximately 20 per cent. Thus, for the majority of alcohol misusers, it is a long battle for them to gain insight and change their behaviour. Chapter 13 looks at getting beyond the point of insight, when a decision to stop drinking is made, to putting that insight into practice.

The choice not to drink can take place in an instant, but it may take a number of hours, days, weeks or even months to manifest itself as behaviour. Decisions can change from day to day. An alcohol misuser may make a decision to drink one day for a particular set of reasons and then decide to drink the next day for a whole other set of reasons. An alcohol misuser may decide to quit drinking today for one set of reasons and may decide to remain sober the next day for a new set of reasons. However, the decision to drink or not to drink is the crux of the matter, and all internal thoughts and dialogue must end in a choice that leads to particular behaviour.

An alcohol misuser who states, 'I'm going to stop drinking' to themselves or to others may be trying to make it real, but the words have to be backed up by actions. If he or she continues to drink, then no choice has been made at all or, in fact, a reverse choice has been made and he or she has made a decision to drink, even if stating the opposite. The statement 'I'm going to give up drinking' is a great starting point, and very few alcohol misusers start on the road to recovery without making that statement. However, clearly it is not the end point; it is an attempt to reach that end point.

> **Denial can be battled against in a number of different ways at the same time. The semi-constant various battles against denial are hugely significant in the war against addiction.**

Case Study: The Alcohol Misuser in Constant Denial

Frank was a 34-year-old salesman. He was employed by a drinks company that gave him a territory and told him to get on with the business of selling to bars and clubs in that area.

He traveled in his own car and had little supervision from his superiors in the company apart from them looking at his monthly targets. He quickly got bored and began to take a drink or two at each of his client's premises.

His alcohol intake grew over a period of three or four years, but he was not caught for drink driving because he drank a little constantly and never got grossly intoxicated. He began to get depressed at times, and his wife expressed concern for his inability to enjoy himself. After a number of years, he began to take days off. He drank heavily on those days off, generally spirits such as whiskey. This would produce severe bouts of depression and he sometimes felt suicidal.

He eventually went into hospital to treat his depression. In hospital, his drinking was noted and he was encouraged to seek treatment for it. He steadfastly refused, stating the only problem he had was his depression.

He initially returned to work after recovering from his depression, but gradually his drinking increased to the previous level and this produced a fall in his mood again: After a second stint in hospital, he took a few months off work to recover. This only exacerbated his drinking and he became unable to work at all.

His wife returned to work, and after a few years she left him because he was unable to face up to his drinking. He drifted away from treatment and eventually wouldn't go out of the house to get any food or household supplies. He used to have the drink delivered to his door so he wouldn't have to go out and get it.

He eventually died a few years afterwards. He drank himself into a coma and didn't have the physical strength to get out of it. He wasn't discovered for six days after he died. He was thirty-nine years old.

Joe's Story: Day 12

Joe started the day determined to leave the programme.

He went in to see the doctor and told him just what he thought about how he had been treated by the staff and fellow patients. The doctor listened, and then stated calmly that Joe was a voluntary participant in the programme and he could leave at any time. He reminded Joe of the contract he signed at the beginning of the programme, which was an agreement to attend all aspects of the programme and that he would not drink during the programme. By repeatedly walking out on groups, he was not attending the programme adequately. That was the reason for the suspension. If he calmed down, if he accepted that he had broken the rules of the programme, and agreed to accept the rules, he would be allowed back into it.

The doctor suggested that Joe think about the overall purpose of being in rehabilitation, and that he consider what the consequences would be for himself and for others if he were to leave in failure. He told Joe that it was very likely that Joe would resume drinking and that, as a consequence, he would likely lose his marriage and end up in the same situation as the 'hard cases' he had tried to distance himself from. He could indulge his temper, get the satisfaction of demonstrating his anger to the others, but end up shooting himself in the foot. If he really wanted to save his marriage, and probably his job, he had to stay the course, even if he disagreed with it.

The doctor ended by saying that it was up to Joe what he would do, but the suspension stood until he made up his mind what his long-term goals were. The doctor would accept whatever Joe's decision was, but Joe had to either accept the rules of the contract or leave. He had twenty-four hours to make his decision.

Joe left the session very angry, but aware that the stakes were high and that there would be serious consequences if he left the programme early.

13

Turning Insight into Action

> Insight, all by itself, is not enough for recovery to take place.

Words versus Actions

There are many stages in the recovery process and everyone progresses at a different pace. Each person is effectively on a different journey. A 'verbal recovery' is the term I apply to someone who says all the right things, but who has no intention of giving up alcohol and who returns to drinking very soon after treatment. An 'emotional recovery' is the term I apply to someone who is trying to make a full and deep commitment to recovery. A verbal recovery does not indicate a full recovery. AA focuses particularly on obtaining the verbal admission 'I am an alcoholic' from every attendee. If a continued and frequent verbal admission leads to an emotional admission, then this is a worthwhile process. However, if the use of the words is just another avoidance technique, the emotional admission may be some distance away. Needless to say, it is the emotional admission that is the most important and transforming component of true recovery.

How do you know if someone means what they say, and their verbal recovery indicates a true recovery? If someone makes a verbal admission that appears easy, it is not likely to represent a genuine emotional recovery. If the verbal admission is difficult, slow, agonised over and takes place over a period of time, it is more likely to be true.

A verbal promise to give up drinking can be a big step on the road to sobriety. However, it can also be used to deflect attention from the alcohol misuser's true intention, namely, to continue drinking. If an alcohol misuser makes a promise to stop drinking when they are intoxicated, if they have had any alcohol that day or when they are in withdrawal from alcohol, it is essentially very suspect. A verbal promise frequently repeated, without any change in behaviour, is not a promise at all; it is a passive–aggressive combative position, the indication of a battle to maintain drinking behaviour.

Recovery must be practical as well as verbal and emotional. The most heartfelt, difficult recovery process that is unaccompanied by a change in behaviour is unfortunately a wasted journey. If alcohol dependence is largely characterised by avoidance, particularly emotional avoidance, then recovery is about facing up to things, self-confrontation and an emotional journey to full sobriety.

Translating even a small bit of real intent into change is a very difficult task. Insight is not adequate to effect change all by itself. There are two processes that must take place for the real journey into recovery to begin. First, the modest degree of insight must be worked on, increased and reinforced. Second, the insight must be guided into an effective route for change and choices must be presented to the alcohol misuser regarding effective changes in lifestyle. These two processes are different and can take place simultaneously and in different environments.

Increasing Insight

How to plant the seed of insight was discussed in Chapters 11 and 12. There are numerous ways for this to happen and, in general, it means finding the alcohol misuser's point of vulnera-bilty. The most effective ways to increase the impact of insight is for the alcohol misuser to find a suitable forum for exploration of this insight into their problem and its effects, and for them to use it. This forum could be individual therapy with a counsel-lor, it could be involvement in group therapy with a counsellor, it could be in an inpatient treatment setting with multiple coun-sellors and groups, or it could be in a self-help setting with AA or a similar group.

A significant number of people choose none of the above and decide that the most effective way to increase their insight into their addiction is to educate themselves or simply to engage in periods of addiction-oriented thought. It is important to state that addiction-oriented education and introspection are useful tools in the fight against addiction, but are inadequate by them-selves in the majority of cases. There appears to be something significantly reinforcing about interaction with others, be they professionals or other people in recovery, making the effort to increase insight easier. The very acts of self-expression and listening to feedback about one's addiction seem to register the seriousness of the situation to a much greater extent than doing it all alone. This type of interaction helps the alcohol misuser to register the addiction at an emotional level and not just at an objective or intellectual level.

Insight needs reinforcement, it needs encouragement, and it needs practice to make it real, embedded and effective. In one sense, it is like religious faith – there may be a spark to begin with but it takes real work to deepen it over time.

Maintaining Insight

An alcohol misuser will never gain 100 per cent insight into their condition. Insight itself isn't really a permanent or whole state of being. It is a constant struggle, albeit under the sur-face. An addict in recovery for ten or twenty years is still in danger of relapse, though this is less likely than in the early stages of recovery. When an alcohol misuser tells me that they understand everything they need to know about alcoholism and they have full insight, I know that this is a danger point and that they don't understand the true nature of addiction at all. Addiction is a lifelong struggle, and it is a disease that can be very effectively managed but never cured.

Insight may also wax and wane at various times. It has a life of its own and, at times, through no fault of the alcohol misuser, it may be difficult to maintain. I have had alcoholics many years into successful recovery ask me, 'Am I really an alcoholic? I have been sober for five years. Surely that means I wasn't really one at all.' The maintenance of insight, in those who have made a successful behavioural change, is vital to long-term success.

If insight into an addiction is neglected, it will eventually fade. Various things can lead to a drop in insight over time. Mood shifts, especially depression, can decrease insight. Changes in an alcohol misuser's circumstances, particularly downward shifts in lifestyle, can threaten hard-won insight. Outside pressures, including social pressure to drink and exposure to other people drinking at special occasions, can lead to a drop in insight. These outside pressures, coupled with an alcohol misuser's desire, craving and need for alcohol, makes the maintenance of insight into an addiction a difficult business. Bouts of craving, either conscious or unconscious, are also problematic.

Effective Change

Understanding your various motivations to change, gaining insight, having an awareness of forces that pull you towards an addiction and those that pull you away from it – these are all useful at the start of an addiction recovery process. But there is no recovery until alcohol consumption is successfully stopped and all that insight is put to good use.

Like with the maintenance of insight, there are a number of ways of achieving a full remission. Indeed, there are as many ways of achieving it as there are individuals in recovery from alcoholism. Everyone must find their own way and no one method succeeds for all. Anyone who states that their method is the only way to succeed is doing a large number of alcohol misusers a disservice. It is very hard to identify what the particular method is that will succeed for a particular individual; often it is a matter of trial and error.

Many assessments have been done regarding specific treatments, their effectiveness and their success rates. One principle comes through in all the research projects, in whatever setting and relating to whatever type of addiction: treatment retention is treatment success. In terms of treatment success, treatment retention is more important than family history, age of onset of disorder, gender, duration of drinking, amount of drinking, number of previous rehabs or the existence of any extra addiction. Nothing else works as well. That is why the most successful programmes are often the most flexible and do almost anything to hold onto the patient, within obvious limits.

Even if treatment doesn't work initially, the vast majority of people who stick with it do well. Equally, a large number of those who drop out won't do well.

However, not everybody who completes a thirty-day programme, who attends an aftercare programme and who attends AA regularly succeeds, but the majority do. It is hard to make a sustained effort, to try and try again, and not have some degree of success in addiction treatment.

It is even possible for an addict to gain significant benefit from treatment without a significant gain in insight. If someone refuses to believe that they are an alcoholic, yet decides to give up alcohol and maintain their abstinence, then they have gained what I call 'practical insight', even if they maintain their state of denial. And this is more common than many therapists or counsellors would like to admit. Unfortunately many people also decide that they are not addicts and that everyone else is wrong, and they decide to return to drinking when they want. Interestingly, a significant number of these alcohol misusers cut down their drinking considerably as they contemplate the wisdom or otherwise of the advice they have received.

Some alcohol misusers even give up alcohol and maintain sobriety just to spite their therapist or doctor: 'You said that I would never be able to do it, so I did it to prove you wrong.' That, of course, is fine for a while at least, but often the steam runs out of the alcohol misuser's anger and they might relapse. But often they maintain their sobriety, even after their anger runs out, for another reason. That reason is another principle gained from multiple research projects, namely: the further an alcohol misuser is into recovery, the more likely they are to succeed in their recovery.

This can be put another way: most people who are going to relapse do so in the early stages of abstinence. If a group of people who complete an effective treatment programme are followed up over a period of months or years, the rate of relapse is highest in the first month, lower in the second month, lower than that in the third month and so on. Another way of putting it is that, with every day of recovery, an alcohol misuser is less likely to relapse than the previous day. This finding would seem to back up the famous mantra of AA: 'One day at a time.' However, the research findings are more encouraging than the reasoning behind that phrase. That phrase suggests that every day in recovery is Groundhog Day and the alcohol misuser must repeat every day in recovery just like the previous one in order to succeed. Research is not quite as pessimistic as that and states that every day of recovery is in fact progress. One researcher has estimated that, if an alcohol misuser has achieved recovery for a three- to four-year period, they are essentially cured. While there are many anecdotal examples of alcohol misusers relapsing after ten, fifteen or even twenty years of abstinence, this is fortunately not a common event.

It isn't necessary to hit rock bottom on the way to successful addiction treatment. Indeed, 20 per cent of alcohol misusers only need a health warning and some advice from a practice nurse to gain the necessary practical insight into their addiction. Sadly, often more intense interventions are required for success. Often the alcohol misuser, their family and their employer must suffer for a long time before they can begin to turn their addiction around. Of course, what denotes rock bottom for an individual varies. It might mean financial ruin, losing a marriage, losing access to children or loss of whatever structure the addiction had created in an individual's life.

In Section III, I will detail what the various treatment options are and compare them. The recovering alcohol misuser should make persistent attempts to find the recovery method or methods that most suit them, and persist with these over a prolonged period of time.

> **There is no point in having the greatest understanding of and insight into a problem without using that knowledge to effect change.**

Case Study: The Professional Alcohol Misuser

James was a 29-year-old doctor. He was a small, good-looking and neat man. He was intelligent, but succeeded in his studies through hard work and worry. He was obsessive about his work and his studies. He worked harder than his fellow medical students and eventually passed his final exams with high honours.

During his student years, he met and married an attractive nurse. In contrast to him, she was outgoing and loved to go out and have a good time. She drank more than him, and over the first years of their marriage he began to drink to keep up with her when they went out. Eventually he became accustomed to drinking and he began to drink at home at the end of a long day. He stopped going out and spent most evenings at home drinking, both with his wife and alone. His marriage began to deteriorate and eventually his wife left him because of his drinking.

He began to get into trouble at work, and was asked to leave one medical practice where he was a trainee because he turned up to work with the smell of alcohol on his breath. In his next job, he was reported to the Medical Council by a patient for appearing intoxicated and his medical licence was suspended.

He returned to live with his parents and began to look for academic or paramedical work that did not require a licence. He entered into a rehabilitation programme in order to obtain a favourable report for the Medical Council. He presented throughout his stay in the programme as pleasant, superficial and in complete denial about his alcohol dependence. He found it impossible to accept any of the negative changes that had taken place in his life. He said all the things that he thought would look good on a medical report, but lacked conviction when describing what he had to do for his own recovery.

He was eventually discharged from the programme without having made a proper treatment plan. He felt unable to enter into a full follow-up programme and he drifted away from treatment. He found it increasingly difficult to gain employment because of his lack of a medical licence, and he relapsed to drinking soon after being discharged.

Three years and another treatment programme later, he began to accept the extent of his problem and the necessity to start battling his addiction properly. He stated he felt that having an addiction wasn't part of the image of himself he had spent many years trying to cultivate. He could not accept the difference between what he wanted to be, what he had spent his entire life trying to achieve and what he had become in reality. His was a very difficult journey.

Joe's Story: Day 13

This was the big day – decision day. Joe hadn't slept well; he had tossed and turned all night trying to decide what to do. He still felt slighted and wronged, but he realised that the ultimate decision as to whether he would stay or go was his.

He could try another rehabilitation centre, but he was not sure if his marriage would outlive a treatment failure. He called his wife on the phone and told her that he was thinking of leaving because the staff were so unreasonable. He was met with a stony silence at the other end of the line and he could feel his wife bristling down the phone. He hung up before she could launch into a tirade. He was left in no doubt as to where he stood.

He decided there and then to eat humble pie and give it another go. He told the nurse on the ward, who conveyed the message to the therapist. The therapist asked him to return to the group that afternoon, and he gave it a go.

This time he didn't offer any advice and only spoke when spoken to. He was surprised that he was given such a warm welcome back from the counsellor and all of the group members, even those he had given out to. Maybe they were able to see the wisdom of his advice and see just how good his opinions were. He brightened up and began to take part in the meeting.

He took on board what the others were saying, and determined to try and listen more. He was again surprised at the advice he was given by other group members, and how accurately they identified how he was feeling over the past few days. Maybe this advice and insight thing was a two-way street.

He slept better that night.

14

Guilt and Shame – How to Use Them

> Guilt and shame should be part of the territory of addiction.

If you feel guilty, you generally have something to be guilty about. Feelings of guilt are distressing and personal. They form part of our innermost secrets and we don't like admitting to them, either to ourselves or to others.

We should all feel some degree of guilt about things, even things that are not related to addiction. There are many things we should feel guilty about: people we have offended, people we should be more thoughtful about, decisions that were wrong or selfish, times when we could have acted better. If a person states that he or she feels no guilt and no shame, and that they don't have anything to feel guilty or ashamed about, then they are not thinking deeply enough about themselves. If we are unaware of our mistakes then we cannot learn from the past, and we are thus condemned to repeat our mistakes in the future.

The very same applies regarding an addiction. The alcohol misuser must engage in introspection, and the purpose of that introspection is to develop a sense of guilt and shame. Trying to do this while drinking or intoxicated is not helpful.

An intoxicated emotion is, by and large, not sincere, or may be exaggerated or unreal. Even a sense of guilt while drinking is not that helpful; it is generally not a useful guilt.

The old phrase 'in vino vertias' means that people state the truth when drinking. Although this phrase has its origins two thousand years ago, it isn't really true. What is true is that people are disinhibited when drinking, but being disinhibited is not the same as being truthful, either to oneself or to others. Alcohol affects the frontal lobes of the brain first. The frontal lobes are the parts of the brain that deal with self-control, personality, learned behaviour and conscience. They are the areas of the brain that make the most important decisions in life, the balanced, thoughtful and socially considered decisions. If we knock out that part of the brain with alcohol, we are left with an intoxicated person with less consideration for social norms, with an inclination to act or say things on impulse and with less thought for consequences. An intoxicated person is much less likely to feel guilt or shame because these are emotions associated with a properly functioning frontal lobe. Intoxication, with a deadened frontal lobe, leads to unbalanced decisions, selfishness and impulsive behaviour, and these are the hallmarks of addiction as well.

Thus, in order to make a careful evaluation of where you are regarding an addiction, it is vital for you not to be drunk. In order to feel the appropriate emotions of guilt and shame, you must first stop drinking. In Chapters 15 and 16, I will deal with the effects of ceasing to drink and the manifestations of alcohol withdrawal.

There are two things that an alcohol misuser should feel guilty about: first, the numerous acts inevitably carried out by an addict that are embarrassing or downright hurtful; and, second, the very fact of becoming dependent on a substance in the first place, which in itself is shameful.

What do alcohol misusers do to themselves and others that is so shameful? The list is potentially endless and is, of course, individual to each alcohol misuser. Here is a sample list of things an alcohol misuser should feel guilt and shame about:

- Being arrested for drink driving or being drunk and disorderly

- Deliberately sabotaging family events or nights out with friends to punish them for some non-existent crime

- Picking arguments and fights with loved ones to have an excuse to go drinking

- Making family members or children avoid coming home so they don't have to face you drinking at home

- Drinking away the family money and letting others go without important things in their lives because you have used the money to buy drink

- Forcing family members to gear up to confront you about drinking

- Emotionally blackmailing your family to do things they don't want to do in return for you trying to give up drinking

- Being deliberately blind about the consequences of your drinking, so that family and friends enter into a state of collusion

- Losing your temper and shouting, or humiliating and even hitting others when drunk, and then not dealing with it afterwards

- Forcing others to gear their entire lives around your drinking or not drinking, instead of having a balance of priorities in the family

- Letting people down at work in numerous ways; letting personal standards drop at work. Counting down the time at work until the evening when you can go and drink

- The sheer amount of avoidance of personal responsibility in your relationships, work and social life

- Of course, getting addicted in the first place

The last point is worth exploring. Getting addicted to a substance is a massive humiliation in itself. There is a loss of self-control and self-esteem involved in getting addicted. While owning up to that is a major part of the journey into recovery, it is the journey into addiction that is the humiliation, not the journey into recovery. Like all human beings, it is really only when caught doing something wrong that we experience the full weight of guilt and shame. While we are getting away with it there is an element of risk and indifferent bravado ('Sure, what the hell') about continuing to drink.

Most guilt and shame about drinking can be avoided or at least postponed while the person continues to drink. That, in itself, is a major factor in continuing to drink: 'What will I go through if and when I stop?' It is only when the alcohol misuser has stopped drinking that he or she faces the consequences. Thus, it appears to be easier to continue drinking than to stop.

Loss of Control

Because the process of developing an addiction is a gradual one, the process of loss of control over alcohol is also gradual. The alcohol misuser is not fully aware that he or she is becoming addicted and is not aware about the priority shift in his or her life. It is often only with the benefit of hindsight that the alcohol misuser can assess the process of how the substance became king, and what the stages of the addiction are. These stages are often marked by a series of humiliating events. The alcohol misuser can detail, often in retrospect, not just the progress of the disorder, but the progress of the consequences of the disorder in humiliating detail.

We like to think that there is a positive trajectory to our lives, and that decisions taken, choices made and events that take place are all part of that great upwards trajectory. We like to assign a greater purpose to life. We like to think that there is meaning to even the tragedies that befall us, and that apparent disasters or difficulties can lead to some point of understanding or achievement that makes it all worthwhile. This may be great financial gain, recognition at work, raising your children to successful independence, or significant spiritual enlightenment. Part of the acceptance of the existence of addiction is the acknowledgement that, instead of moving forwards in life in some way, we may be moving sideways or moving backwards and, worse still, that we are responsible for it. Accepting that you are addicted to alcohol is also an acceptance that you have made mistakes and that you may not be able to achieve a dream or goal that you were aiming for in life.

Giving up the personal dream or goal, however distant and unreal that that dream might be, is an essential component of giving up the addiction. It is the intrusion of reality into the fantasy land of addiction that eventually helps an alcohol misuser to start the journey into recovery. A personal confession of guilt and shame, generally about drink-related activity, is both the entry pass into recovery and the first emotional consequence of embarking on the journey. Without any guilt or shame, there really is no journey. Many people have professed to me that they understand what recovery is all about, but are unable to elicit any sense of upset or personal humiliation about their drinking. While some of these people do eventually go into recovery, the majority end up going through the same process a second or even a third time before really getting it and continuing to long-term recovery.

It is only when guilt and shame are acknowledged and then put to good use in an effective recovery programme that dreams of the future can be reconstructed. They may be different dreams – they should be different dreams – and hopefully they are tempered by reality. Hopefully recovery and the maintenance of it are incorporated into that reconstructed future reality.

Shame Is the Guide and Guilt Is the Trip

Guilt and shame are the most useful emotions in the recovery journey because they provide the road map which the alcohol misuser must use to explore their addiction and motivation for recovery. It is necessary for the alcohol misuser to explore and detail the most shameful events of his or her alcohol-related past, and it is necessary for him or her to feel guilty about them for a full recovery to take place.

People often resist exploring guilt and shame, and that resistance is understandable. Selective amnesia also plays a part. The alcohol misuser does not wish to recall the shameful events that have taken place, and thus isn't always capable of remembering them. This process isn't totally conscious; it is helped by unconscious forces. At the various stages into recovery, this selective amnesia often breaks down and the alcohol misuser is better able to recall shameful events and episodes. It is impossible to be certain if this selective amnesia is purely a reflection of the alcohol misuser's state of denial or whether it is a reflection of actual neurological damage or blackouts. There is no doubt that an alcohol misuser can lose significant memory ability as a result of alcohol damage to the brain, either temporary or permanent.

It is also true to say that this selective amnesia is often too convenient to be totally based on brain damage. I have heard too many admissions, weeks or even months after the shameful events have taken place, to believe that alcohol misusers remember nothing the day afterwards. There appears to be two factors at work. The first is the genuine alcohol-related interference with memory and the second is the psychological factor of not wanting to recall shameful or guilt-inducing events. Probably both of these factors combined lead to amnesia. Most alcohol misusers are able to recall some events in a hazy or incomplete way, and that is enough to go on.

How to Use Shame and Not Drink Because of It

A major tendency for an alcohol misuser is to drink because he or she has been confronted with a stressful, shameful or guilt-inducing fact. It is far more attractive to re-enter the world of intoxication than to face down the emotional difficulty of confrontation with reality. This pattern of continuous avoidance, particularly of anything resembling emotional distress, is often entered into on a daily basis: 'I can't face the day; I can't face what happened yesterday, so I drink again.'

Feelings of intense negative emotion may be intensified by alcohol withdrawal. Alcohol withdrawal can produce a significant degree of anxiety and depression over a number of days. Because anxiety and depression need a focus, that focus is often drink-related activity. So, the intensity of guilt and shame, felt particularly the morning after drinking heavily, is likely to manifest itself physically as well as emotionally. It is important to note that alcohol withdrawal reduces significantly after a few days, so the negative feelings associated with it fall away after a while. Thus, those intense feelings of guilt and shame do fade away, and quickly.

There is an enormous difference between the emotions and feelings that emerge during withdrawal, and the emotions and feelings that lie beneath. These real feelings emerge once withdrawal has passed. They can be uncovered through self-reflection and therapy and are used to battle the addiction in the long term. The alcohol misuser must become aware of the difference between these two sets of feelings. Drinking on initial withdrawal-related feeling is the equivalent of taking a drink to combat 'the shakes'. It is a temporary cure that goes nowhere.

It is an advantage for the alcohol misuser to know and understand the stages that they must go through towards recovery. Knowing that the withdrawal feelings of anxiety, guilt and shame will pass may not be adequate to enable the alcohol misuser to cease drinking and battle through this stage, but it can be useful and make the process more tolerable. The reassurance that the intensity of these feelings will diminish over a short period of time can be enough to stop the alcohol misuser taking another drink immediately. For some people, the knowledge that withdrawal from alcohol brings on feelings of intense shame helps them to avoid alcohol in the future.

And as the days pass, and the feelings lose their intensity, the alcohol misuser can see that there will be a benefit to ceasing drinking altogether. Of course, the residual long-term feelings will remain and will have to be dealt with, but the immediate intense feelings of guilt and shame do pass.

> **Guilt and shame may be the most helpful emotions regarding facing up to an addiction.**

Case Study: The Long Recovery

Peter was a 42-year-old single man. He grew up in an alcoholic family, with his father drinking to excess and his mother suffering from depression. She was admitted to a psychiatric hospital at various stages in his childhood.

He left school and qualified as a fitter. He began to drink heavily in his twenties and became angry, disappointed at himself and bitter about his difficult childhood. He became depressed as well and the antidepressant he was prescribed was only partially successful. He didn't get married and various relationships ran into difficulty because of his drinking.

Eventually, at the age of forty, he decided to go into rehabilitation in the form of a four-week treatment programme. He achieved sobriety with some difficulty and did well over the subsequent two years, only having two minor lapses.

He adopted the AA model and found it very helpful. He felt, however, that he needed to get treatment for depression. He saw a psychiatrist and went on another antidepressant. He sometimes got flak for this at AA, but he felt it was important for him.

He was significantly less depressed on the medication and he began to enjoy life, getting involved in various sports and travelling. He found a Dual Recovery Anonymous (DRA) group (see

Appendix) where he lived and joined it, feeling that it was a better model for his problems than AA. He entered into an intimate relationship and he settled down.

He eventually got married and after a while adopted a child from Africa to help complete his family. He struggled at various times, but found that his marriage, his attendance at AA and DRA, and his antidepressant medication all kept him sober and well.

Joe's Story: Day 14

It was the weekend again, but Joe decided that he wasn't going to go home on leave just yet. He got up and had a restful and uneventful morning. In the afternoon, Joe's wife came to visit. From the moment she walked in the door of the ward, he knew he was in serious trouble. She sat down with him in his room and she paused before speaking. That was not a good sign; normally she would say what was on her mind without deliberation.

She then launched into a tirade about what she had been going through. She talked about how selfish he had been while he was drinking and just what she had to put up with, trying to keep the household going and looking after the children while he was drunk in the living room. She spoke of her pain at being deceived and lied to: 'I might be able to take the drinking, but I can't take the lies.' She spoke of the difficulties in balancing the finances while he used their money for drink.

Worryingly, she spoke in a calm and almost distant manner, as if this all had been rehearsed. She didn't lose her temper; she didn't shout at him. She was reserved, emotionless. He was flummoxed and didn't know how to respond. He didn't know how to deal with the calm emotionless person in front of him. He was more used to her emotional, weepy response to his drinking. He would often know just when to make an angry reply to her hysteria and storm off in a huff to go drinking.

Even worse, he knew there was a certain amount of truth in what she was saying. She might be exaggerating, but he couldn't disagree with the points she was putting before him. Eventually he couldn't take it any longer and he turned and shouted at her: 'Well, if it's so bad for you, I'll just have to find someone else then.' She stopped what she was saying, went pale, looked at him, and got up and left without another word.

Joe didn't sleep very well that night.

15

Symptoms of Withdrawal

> **Withdrawal from alcohol can produce significant, intense anxiety.**

Withdrawal from alcohol is a significant medical and psychiatric event. Alcohol withdrawal is common among the general population; many people go in and out of alcohol withdrawal during periods of drinking and are not even aware of it. Withdrawal from alcohol is caused by drinking significant amounts of alcohol and then stopping for a period before often starting again.

Alcohol withdrawal starts generally within a number of hours after you stop drinking, though it can start as late as twenty-four hours after your last drink. Typically, it lasts a few days, often up to five days, but it rarely lasts longer than that.

The symptoms of alcohol withdrawal vary from individual to individual, and depend on the quantity and duration of previous alcohol consumption. Obviously, alcohol withdrawal preceded by a few days of drinking a glass of wine per day is much less severe than alcohol withdrawal preceded by a three-month binge of a bottle of vodka per day. However, even a small quantity of alcohol can produce withdrawal. Alcohol, even in a quantity such as one to two glasses of wine, can produce sweating, anxiety and even sleep disturbance in light drinkers. Alcohol tends to help people to go to sleep but to make the later part of the night more wakeful and restless. This reflects the low tolerance that light drinkers have for alcohol, but also exemplifies just how significant an effect that alcohol, even in small quantities, has on the mind and body. Women can suffer from alcohol withdrawal symptoms, including anxiety, more frequently than men.

Withdrawal often does not occur over the first few years of alcohol abuse, unless the quantities of alcohol consumed are very significant. Some people believe that alcohol withdrawal is the only sign of dependence and that, if there is no withdrawal from alcohol, there is no alcohol dependence. Unfortunately, that is not true. It is possible to be dependent on alcohol and never suffer from alcohol withdrawal. Similarly, it is possible to suffer significant episodes of alcohol withdrawal at times and not be dependent on alcohol, although that is rare.

Withdrawal and Anxiety

The anxiety associated with alcohol withdrawal is a frequent phenomenon. It is commonly misdiagnosed, misunderstood and is often not associated with alcohol. The anxiety can range from a slight nervous tension or mild restlessness that the sufferer doesn't ascribe to anything, to significant constant worry and anxiety that increases in severity over a few days, through to a full series of panic attacks that can last for hours at a time and can take a week or two to settle.

Often the key to diagnosing the nature of anxiety is to consider its occurrence in relation to times of drinking. If the anxiety frequently occurs in the twelve to twenty-four hours after ceasing to drink alcohol, if it eventually fades over a significant period of time, during which no alcohol is consumed, and if it can disappear quickly once alcohol is taken, the likelihood is that this is anxiety induced by alcohol withdrawal.

At least 50 per cent of alcohol misusers suffer from with-drawal-associated anxiety, and that anxiety fades for the vast majority if no alcohol is consumed. The severity of this partic-ular anxiety varies from individual to individual. For a small number of individuals, the anxiety turns out to be independ-ent of alcohol and persists for weeks or even months after they cease to drink alcohol. That type of anxiety is beyond the scope of this book and should be dealt with by a professional, either a doctor or a qualified therapist.

Alcohol and anxiety can interact negatively with each other. A significant number of people get addicted to alcohol because of its anxiety-relieving properties. People who find social engage-ments stressful can discover that alcohol diminishes their social anxiety and makes social events tolerable, even pleasant. They find that shyness disappears when they drink and they can talk to others, even members of the opposite sex. Alcohol can make some people lose their inhibitions, and they can do things they wouldn't necessarily do without having taken alcohol. If, for example, they get together with someone of the opposite sex, get drunk and even sleep with them, alcohol can be seen as either a help in moving the romantic encounter along or an excuse for regrettable behaviour that has to be apologised for later.

Interestingly, in studies where subjects don't know if they are getting alcohol or a similar tasting non-alcoholic drink, both groups report an equal amount of 'intoxication' and both groups report a similar level of enjoyment and social relaxation. So, a significant amount of the intoxicating and relaxing effects of alcohol are actually down to peoples' expectations, as well as due to the actual effects of alcohol.

A significant number of alcohol misusers find themselves taking alcohol at a particular time of the day because of a certain desire or unease, or a craving for alcohol. Some alco-hol misusers take alcohol early in the day to recover from the shakes, sweats or severe withdrawal symptoms from the previ-ous night's drinking. A much larger group resume drinking because of more subtle and, indeed, anxiety-related withdrawal symptoms that start during the day after the last drink. These symptoms include:

- Irritability

- Anger

- Annoyance with people

- Tension

- Physical restlessness

- Depression

- A need to get out and change things

- A feeling of being trapped

- General unhappiness

These feeling are, of course, relieved by alcohol, but the majority of alcohol misusers would not ascribe these intense feelings to withdrawal from alcohol. Since they are not necessarily accompanied by severe symptoms of withdrawal like sweats and shakes, it is easy for the drinker to blame other things and other people for those feelings, but of course they are related to alcohol. A significant number of people experiencing these withdrawal-related feelings will relapse to alcohol very quickly, but will ascribe their relapse to the intensity of the feelings and not to a desire or need for alcohol.

The anxiety associated with withdrawal can have positive and negative aspects. One of the positives associated with anxiety is awareness: if you know what is going on, it makes the process much more bearable. Of course, awareness is inadequate in itself to completely treat the withdrawal-based anxiety, but it is an important way of decreasing 'fear of the unknown' anxiety, which can severely increase withdrawal-based anxiety. Fear that the anxiety will never go away also makes the anxiety or tension worse, and causes a significant number of alcohol misusers to cease the withdrawal process and resume drinking. This resumption is doubly dreadful: first, because a resumption of drinking can spark a significant overall downturn whereby the alcohol misuser may not try to give up drinking again for a period of months or even years, and, second, this resumption of drinking might have possibly been prevented with the appropriate information and treatment over a very short period of time.

In general, one of the most important messages to understand about withdrawal is that it will cease after a short period, generally a few days.

What Are the Symptoms of Significant Alcohol Withdrawal?

Full alcohol withdrawal is much more than a bout of significant anxiety. It is a grave medical condition that can result in death or severe disability if not properly treated. It can be more severe than withdrawal from heroin or other drugs of abuse, and needs to be recognised for the medical emergency it is. At its worst, it should be treated in a full medical or fully equipped psychiatric ward in a hospital, with supervision and monitoring by a team of nurses and doctors. At its most gentle, it still requires medical supervision in order to be safely managed.

We have already seen that alcohol withdrawal can cause mild anxiety and irritability, but that is only one category of withdrawal symptoms. Other effects of alcohol on the mind and body include:

- Nausea: this can lead to severe stomach upset and vomiting

- Tremor: this can range from a mild occasional shake to a full uncontrolled tremor in the arms and legs

- Epileptic seizure: a severe tremor can indicate a full epileptic seizure and loss of consciousness

- Sensitivity and 'jumpiness': the anxiety and paranoia associated with withdrawal can cause a person to be easily startled by any surrounding sounds, such as a door slamming

- Sweating: this can range from a barely noticeable sheen on the hands and forehead to a full sweating episode in which an individual can lose litres of fluid

- Hallucinations: full visual hallucinations (such as seeing rats and ghosts around the bed), tactile hallucinations (such as a crawling feeling under the skin) and auditory hallucinations (voices that call from around the place) can all accompany severe withdrawal

- Confusion: withdrawal can result in disorientation, sometimes leading to full delirium and total confusion

- Hypertension: severe withdrawal can result in a rise in blood pressure which can cause major physical problems

- Flushing: the face and other areas of the body can appear red and flushed

- Insomnia: there can be a severe loss of sleep as alcohol leaves the system, particularly in the early morning

Withdrawal from Drugs

Alcohol withdrawal can be made much worse if a person is also going through a drug or medication withdrawal at the same time. The most common medications that complicate alcohol withdrawal are benzodiazepines, namely, Valium, Librium, Xanax, Centrax and a few others. With this 'double' withdrawal, symptoms, particularly insomnia and anxiety, can extend into weeks rather than days and their intensity can run to an extreme level. The desire for more medication can be overwhelming during this period and that is another reason why alcohol withdrawal, particularly if combined with withdrawal from benzodiazepines, must be undertaken with medical supervision.

Since benzodiazepines work on the same receptors in the brain as alcohol, the symptoms of withdrawal from benzodiazepines are exactly the same as for alcohol, but they may be significantly more prolonged. Ironically, benzodiazepines can be used to treat alcohol withdrawal, and can also be used to treat benzodiazepine withdrawal in carefully measured, gradually tapering doses.

> **Alcohol withdrawal can last for a significant time after you cease to drink.**

Case Study: The Long Withdrawal

Michael was a 60-year-old architect. He had been drinking for many years, initially with friends, then on regular weekly golf outings, and also while having meals with his wife and family. He drank on average about one bottle of wine per day, with one or two double whiskeys at the end of a hard day's work. He never stopped drinking, and his intake would go up on holidays, when he would drink beer all day and then have wine with his evening meal at night.

He never regarded his intake as a problem because he was able to function reasonably well at his job, and he was never nasty or abusive to his wife and growing family. After thirty years of this style of drinking, he began to deteriorate, his job performance began to go down and his wife began to tire of all of the slurred drunken conversations she was forced to endure. She encouraged him to consider rehabilitation and he went in voluntarily to a detox centre to help his overall health.

He had not stopped drinking in thirty years, and so his withdrawal was protracted and difficult. His concentration and memory was affected, and he found that, not only did he have to deal with the stress of withdrawal over a two-week period, but he had to deal with significant cognitive disability associated with his alcoholism.

His recovery was difficult and slow. He had to change his alcohol-saturated lifestyle; he had to give up his favourite social outings to the golf club and to his friends' houses. He stopped going out to fancy restaurants and having boozy meals with friends or family. He took up healthy activities such as running and going to the gym. He even took up yoga and found it helpful. He cut down his working hours (his work had begun to dry up anyway). He took up mentally challenging games such as scrabble and bridge, and used these to help him on his return to mental fitness. He attended AA and, although he never liked their approach, he certainly saw the benefits of regular attendance.

After one year of sobriety, he was able to increase his work hours again, while still avoiding alcohol. His concentration and memory returned to normal, with all that effort, and he felt he had regained all his cognitive faculties. He denied having cravings for alcohol, but he continually struggled with the concept of being an alcoholic. He felt he wasn't one, but he absolutely acknowledged that alcohol was ruining his life and health. He also felt his marriage was restored because of his abstinence, and he daily vowed to keep away from alcohol.

He felt overall that he got a new lease on life, and he really appreciated that.

Joe's Story: Day 15

This was not a good day. Joe began to have an emotional reaction to his wife's visit the previous day. He began to think through what she had said and he got frightened and upset. He had never before seen her so determined and so emotionless. She was definitely taking steps away from him and that was a very unpleasant feeling.

Probably for the first time in his married life, he began to feel the ground shaking under his marriage. Sure, there had been threats and upsets before, but never a situation where he felt things could really fall apart. In fact, if he was honest, he was a master at knowing just how much he could push his wife and how much he could get away with, and he had always just managed to stay on the right side of trouble. This was different, however, and he felt the power in the relationship shifting from him to her. If truth be known, he always knew that she loved him despite the problems in his life, but now for the first time he felt her love slip away from him.

He missed going to the AA meeting during the day, he was so upset and preoccupied. He went to the dining room to get some food, but he could barely touch anything so he went back to his room and lay down. There was no contact from his wife, no texts, no messages – nothing. He felt desperately alone, and lonely, but he was too afraid to call up and see how things were. He felt that if he called he would get the same response as yesterday, and he couldn't take that.

16

Withdrawal and Treatment

> Full alcohol withdrawal is a severe medical condition, needing medical treatment.

The more frequently someone suffers from alcohol withdrawal symptoms, the more significant those symptoms become over time. This phenomenon is called kindling; it implies that the nerves in the brain become sensitised to alcohol withdrawal and so its effects get worse over time. Alcohol withdrawal symptoms can indicate a certain degree of alcohol-induced brain damage, and frequent severe withdrawals are associated with short-term memory loss and even eventual dementia.

It is difficult to predict the extent of the symptoms of alcohol withdrawal that an individual will go through. The extent of withdrawal is determined by a number of different factors, including:

- Quantity of alcohol recently consumed

- Duration of the most recent alcoholic binge

- Gender of the alcohol misuser

- Severity and duration of previous episodes of withdrawal

- General physical health

- Degree of hydration and nutrition during withdrawal

- The existence of any other drug problems such as a Valium or Xanax addiction (benzodiazepines)

- A previous history of withdrawal problems including seizures

- The degree of medical intervention during withdrawal

Because of the potential severity of alcohol withdrawal, it is not adequate to 'handle it yourself'. A plan to shut the doors for a week and see what happens or to cut alcohol consumption down slowly over a few days is not only likely to be ineffective, it could also be dangerous. This type of self-induced withdrawal is, of course, the most popular form of withdrawal treatment. Unfortunately it is the least safe, and people die from it commonly enough. Death can result from withdrawal-induced seizures or else because the person is not getting enough fluid and nutrition during the withdrawal process.

Thus, the treatment of alcohol withdrawal of any extent is actually medical. There are two methods of treatment: inpatient and outpatient. The first step is to approach a doctor, generally a family doctor, and obtain advice about the best treatment for alcohol withdrawal. If the doctor recommends inpatient treatment, then that is the best way to go. If the doctor suggests a trial of outpatient treatment, then that is worth considering. What is not a good idea is to go through a significant withdrawal with no medical input. That can be very risky, even though it is done daily by thousands of people, including ordinary drinkers who drink to excess every now and again whether they realise it or not.

The medical treatment of alcohol withdrawal is to first monitor the situation and intervene appropriately. Benzodiazepines, such as Librium or Valium, are commonly used to ease the severe symptoms of withdrawal, including sweating, insomnia and anxiety, and mainly to prevent any possibility of seizures. It is vital to provide adequate fluids and to encourage adequate nutrition during withdrawal. It is also important to perform the withdrawal treatment in a gentle, medically supervised and calm atmosphere. All of these measures diminish the medical risk associated with withdrawal and make it an easier time for the person involved.

The most dangerous period for an alcohol misuser is the period immediately after they stop drinking. Because the withdrawal feelings are often very intense, and often misdiagnosed by the alcohol misuser, friends and family, the alcohol misuser can relapse because of an absence of pressure to remain sober. But it is at precisely this point that the drinker should remain abstinent. It is quite possible that the significant benefit of inpatient rehabilitation programmes is due to the fact that they hold the alcohol misuser in an alcohol-free environment during this early withdrawal period, and allow them the space to listen to a message of rehabilitation after withdrawal.

When someone is going through the anxiety and irritability of the withdrawal phase, it is not easy for them to feel anything else. So, any therapeutic or rehabilitation communications during this initial phase can actually be counterproductive and can intensify what the alcohol misuser is going through. It is very hard for someone experiencing intense negative emotions to turn around and think about the long term or about the pain of changing their life around. They are purely focused on what they are going through at that time and with trying to relieve the negative feelings as soon as they can.

The majority do not believe that such deep anxiety and negativity are related to alcohol withdrawal, and they do not believe that these feelings can be eliminated with a bit of time and the correct medical treatment. It is only in retrospect, after the symptoms and their associated emotions have faded, that they can see that they were going through withdrawal. It is only with appropriate treatment, and then appropriate education, that this message sinks in: alcohol can make you feel rotten, and alcohol withdrawal is the cause of an awful lot of emotional pain.

Craving can return with a vengeance in the immediate post-withdrawal period. Craving is any set of feelings or emotions that lead someone back to alcohol after they have stopped drinking (see Chapter 22). It can be conscious or unconscious.

Conscious craving is an explicit desire for alcohol and it can be almost uncontrollably intense. It can last in bouts for hours at a time. It is most common in the early days and weeks after ceasing alcohol consumption. It can come out of the blue, with no precipitating factors at all. It can occur after a 'cue' of some sort relating to alcohol, for example, if someone is passing their favourite bar or if the mind and body seem to be attuned to consuming alcohol at a particular time of day. Craving can be induced by consciously thinking about drinking, by coming across things that bring alcohol and drinking to mind, and by touching, tasting, smelling, hearing or seeing anything to do with alcohol.

Unconscious craving can occur for all the same reasons, but is not associated with the drinker feeling a strong immediate desire to drink. However, unconscious craving can be just as powerful in driving someone back to drink.

Some researchers have the theory that withdrawal in fact lasts for weeks or months after a person ceases to drink alcohol. They believe that the brain takes a very long time to normalise after alcohol, and that it is the long-term adaption of the brain to being without alcohol that causes most people to relapse. Some medications to help prevent people relapsing to alcohol are designed to combat this prolonged withdrawal phenomenon. Some studies have suggested that this prolonged withdrawal can last for up to one year after a person ceases to drink alcohol. That seems rather a long time, and I would hope that someone quitting alcohol would have found other activities and distractions in their lives to replace alcohol over that time period.

> Alcohol withdrawal can cause a lot of emotional pain and can be a dangerous period for relapsing to alcohol.

Case Study:
The Pattern of Withdrawal and Relapse

James was a 60-year-old rural shopkeeper. He ran his business for 35 years, and he had incorporated groceries, hardware and, in times past, an undertaker service into the shop. He was a successful man by local standards and he was well respected.

He had a drink problem, which he kept secret from his customers and neighbours, but which was well known to his family. He would remain sober for months on end and then break out on a severe binge of drinking that would last a week. He would drink at least a bottle of whiskey per day, and sometimes more. He would be unable to function and the store would be taken over by another member of the family during those times. When he could drink no more, he would stop himself and go into withdrawal in his bedroom. He would emerge a few days later and resume his work.

He carried on this pattern for many years, and his wife and three sons get very worried with the passing years. Although generally a pleasant man, he was rude and irritable when drunk and became increasingly difficult to manage. He was eventually admitted to hospital after a very severe binge when his family feared for his life. He stayed long enough to allow the alcohol out of his system and then left the hospital against his doctor's wishes. He did this three times over the course of five years and each time his stay in hospital was longer. But his attitude remained the same. He was not inter-ested in any support or therapy for his drinking; he just wanted to leave the place and get on with his life.

Eventually his family threatened not to take him back after his last admission and he reluctantly began a course of rehabilitation. He began to see a pattern in his drinking and acknowledged that he might have a problem. He left after a few weeks of rehabilitation, moderately determined to quit alcohol or at least to cut out the severe binges. Unfortunately he didn't have the will power to sustain his intent and four months later he relapsed to a binge of alcohol. Once again, he only agreed to treatment for withdrawal and refused addiction treatment. Despite his family's encouragement, he did his few days and then left against medical advice.

He was not for turning. He resumed his destructive pattern of drinking and, after a number of years, his health began to deteriorate. He did not enter into treatment again.

Joe's Story: Day 16

By the time Monday came around again, Joe was not in good form. He felt abandoned by his wife and, if truth be known, he felt at various stages that he could do with a drink to cope with all that was going on.

Joe attended a session with his counsellor. He found her less than sympathetic when he admitted that he hadn't gone to an AA meeting at the weekend. He felt he was at the receiving end of another lecture from someone who was pissed off at him.

He hadn't slept well the previous night, he was off his food, and he felt low and miserable. By the time he was finished with his counsellor, his mood had sunk even further. He felt hopeless. Was he was going to lose everything? He went back to his room and found himself tearful for the first time in years.

In the afternoon Joe attended a group session and found himself barely able to communicate. He had no interest in attending in the first place and he had even less interest in sharing his thoughts. Even when others in the group inquired about his form and how things were with his wife, he felt unable to give a half decent answer. He removed himself mentally from what was going on around him and felt a disconnection with the world in general.

He finished the day by refusing to take his tea, going back to his room and spending the evening alone and increasingly despondent. If this was what sobriety was then he wanted nothing to do with it.

III

What You Need to Do about Alcohol Misuse

17

Different Types of Therapy

> Various types of therapy are effective treatments
> for alcoholism.

Why does anybody need therapy for alcoholism? Is it necessary
to talk to somebody about the disorder in order to get 'cured'?
The simple answer is that some people can get effective treatment by themselves and may not need any form of therapy.
However, significantly more people get sober through engaging in some form of therapy than not. Therapy significantly
enhances any individual's chances of recovery. Anything that
works is worth trying.

So, what are the different types of therapy? You can get
group therapy or individual therapy. Group therapy involves
sitting in a room with a number of other alcohol misusers trying
to engage in recovery, with a therapist overseeing the group's
direction. Individual therapy is a process involving sitting
down with a single therapist alone for an agreed number of
sessions, anywhere between two and twenty-four, to examine
your addiction.

Most addiction therapists learn one or two types of therapy
and attempt to apply these in a consistent manner. The therapist

should be experienced in dealing with addiction – alcoholism in particular. Not everyone gets the same therapy from the same therapist. The interaction between alcohol misuser and therapist can be important for the potential outcome of the therapy. A therapist's warmth, support and positive regard for the alcohol misuser can greatly help in the treatment process.

Group versus Individual Therapy

Most research comparing types of therapy shows that group therapy is as effective as individual therapy. This is encouraging because obviously a lot more people can be reached through group therapy than individual therapy. However, a lot of people feel strange, at least initially, with the concept of group therapy and would prefer individual therapy.

In group therapy, each alcohol misuser can bring to the table their own experiences in struggling with their addiction and can share with the other members of the group what has and hasn't been helpful to them in their struggle. Group therapy also allows each alcohol misuser to confront the gaps and denials present in the thinking of other group members and, in the process, lay bare the gaps and flaws in their own thinking about alcoholism.

Many recovering alcohol misusers state that, although they liked individual therapy best, perhaps they gained more towards their recovery from group therapy sessions. In an ideal world, most alcohol misusers would have access to both group and individual therapy, but, apart from full inpatient rehabilitation programmes, this is often not possible.

Types of Therapy

There are many different types of addiction therapy. Some have been modeled on theories of addiction but have not been researched, and thus no opinion can be expressed about whether they work or not. A lot of therapists figure out themselves what works and apply that to each alcohol misuser with varying degrees of success. Most therapists adapt to the individual alcohol misuser and spend the most time on areas that are particularly relevant to that person, irrespective of the therapeutic model they are applying.

I describe below a number of different types of therapy, both group and individual, and give a description of how each is supposed to work. Each type of therapy has a full theory behind it as to why it should work. Afterwards, I will give some information as to what type of therapy in fact does work, as determined by careful research.

Relapse-Prevention Therapy

This type of therapy directly addresses the major challenge in recovery from alcoholism: how to prevent relapse. It is not based on exploring underlying reasons behind an addiction; it does not focus on personal and family stresses related to alcoholism; it does not address the stages of development of alcoholism over the years. Based on the cognitive behavioural therapy model for treatment of depression, this type of therapy tries to identify thought patterns that underlie a relapse to drinking. Having identified those patterns, the therapy helps the alcohol misuser to change them to prevent relapse. It explores a number of areas as part of its goals:

1. Inaccurate thinking

2. Triggers to relapse

3. Emotions and behaviours leading to relapse

4. Dealing with craving

1. Inaccurate Thinking

An alcohol misuser has a set of beliefs about drinking which is unique to them. These beliefs have developed over many years and the alcohol misuser is likely unaware that they actually exist. They are generally inaccurate, overestimating the benefits of drinking and underestimating the problems associated with drinking.

In order to clarify the thought patterns behind drinking, each alcohol misuser is asked about their belief systems in relation to drinking, first, in relation to single drinking episodes and then in relation to the overall consequences of drinking for their relationships, their work, their health and their emotions, among other areas. Through a series of questions and answers, the alcohol misuser becomes more aware that drinking causes more harm than good, causes more damage than previously thought and is an issue worthy of significant attention, rather than a minor thing.

One way to help an alcohol misuser to face up to their underlying beliefs about their drinking, and one commonly used by therapists, is to ask them to switch roles with the therapist. In their new role they must persuade the therapist and try to make the therapist understand that he or she has a problem with drinking. As the alcohol misuser makes an effort to expose the therapist, they begin to see that, in fact, they themselves have a lot of misguided positive ideas about drinking and don't have enough appreciation of the problems associated with it.

2. Triggers to Relapse

Many causes of relapse relate to internal as well as external factors. Internal factors can include negative emotions like depression and sadness, positive emotions like satisfaction and relief, and a need to test personal control – 'I can go to the pub without having a drink.' External factors can include social pressure, social anxiety, and conflict with others and the stress associated with that. Getting the alcohol misuser to explore their own triggers to relapse makes them more aware of the danger they are in when reacting to various internal and external forces.

Part of the therapy involves placing the addict in a 'risky' situation and practising ways of saying no to drink in that situation. While that risky situation may be imaginary, getting the alcohol misuser to repeatedly refuse to drink allows them to build up refusal skills which can be put to use in real-life situations.

3. Emotions and Behaviours Leading to Relapse

As the alcohol misuser increases their own awareness of how their emotions play a major role in relapse, they are asked to identify those emotions. They are asked to engage in exercises that explore the causes of emotions like anger and frustration, and to find strategies that deal with these emotions before they become overwhelming.

This exercise involves getting the alcohol misuser to stop and think, consider the options, develop an action plan (that doesn't involve drinking), carry out that plan and evaluate the effects of the plan. The purpose is to get the alcohol misuser to see that there are other potential outcomes to stressful emotions and situations apart from alcohol.

4. Dealing with Craving

Intense craving for alcohol is one of the main reasons why people relapse. Alcohol craving can be conscious or, indeed, unconscious. Craving can be a powerful force that is most prominent early in abstinence and thankfully fades over time. However, it can cause havoc in a person's recovery. One major way to deal with craving is to identify any situation or mental state that sets off craving and to avoid that situation. Another way is to have a preplanned set of strategies to deal with craving, which can be put into action when craving occurs. Those plans could include seeking help from a supportive person, getting out of the craving situation, using any one of a number of distraction techniques, or using relaxation or calming exercises to allow the upsetting experience to pass away.

Overall relapse prevention encourages alcohol misusers to identify their particular pattern of relapse and to recognise when they are beginning to indulge in a pattern of behaviour that can be a warning sign of impending relapse. The therapy also encourages alcohol misusers to develop a healthy approach to personal development that would make a sober lifestyle more attractive and fulfilling (see Chapter 23).

Motivational Enhancement Therapy

The premise of this therapy is that the alcohol misuser needs to grasp that there is a need for them to change.

In order to change their attitude and actions regarding their addiction, the alcohol misuser needs to go through a number of stages:

1. *Precontemplation* is the equivalent of denial. In this stage, the alcohol misuser simply has not addressed their issues about alcohol at all and remains ignorant of the problems associated with it

2. *Contemplation* is the stage when the alcohol misuser begins to think they might have a problem and begins to look at what the problems and benefits of changing their behaviour might be

3. *Resolution*, the third stage, is when the alcohol misuser has decided they must do something about their problem, but hasn't done anything about it yet. It is no secret that the move from the second to the third stage is the most important one in the treatment of alcoholism

4. The *action* stage is when words and good intentions result in the alcohol misuser actually initiating change by going to an AA meeting, going to a counsellor, entering rehabilitation or simply not buying and consuming alcohol

5. The next stage is *maintenance,* when the alcohol misuser engages in activity that is designed to help sustain the decisions taken and acted on in the previous stage. This stage can last for a number of years

Another stage to note is *relapse,* where an alcohol misuser slips backwards, drinks and enters the cycle again. It may mean that they re-enter the cycle quickly at the stage of action, but it may also mean going right back to the start again (see Chapter 21).

This theory of stages of change is all very well, but how does it help an alcohol misuser to actually move from stage to stage and not stay stuck in contemplation or, worse, in precontemplation, while all hell breaks loose around them?

This type of therapy is nonconfrontational. It involves gentle feedback, based on the ideas and expressions that the alcohol misuser themselves has about the whole issue of drinking. The therapist expresses sympathy for and empathy with the alcohol misuser's view of the world. The alcohol misuser is asked to take charge and to take control of their own life. They are asked to make personal choices regarding their future use of alcohol. They are asked if there is a difference between where they are regarding their alcohol use and where they would like to be in the future. This concept is called the development of discrepancy. It is the focus on this difference or discrepancy that is the core of motivational enhancement therapy.

If the alcohol misuser resists the idea of change, he or she is asked to reflect on this and is not directly confronted about it. The solutions to the problems do not come from the therapist. Any advice given is advice to change, not direct advice about what exactly to do in practical terms. Occasionally the therapist can offer a menu of things the alcohol misuser might do, but not point them in any specific direction. There is no emphasis on confronting denial or telling the alcohol misuser what they must do. There is no training, modeling or practice sessions. Clearly, it is a very gentle form of therapy.

Twelve-Step Therapy

This type of therapy is based very strongly on AA's twelve-step programme. It is the therapy most routinely practised by addiction counsellors. It is also practised in most traditional rehabilitation centres.

The AA theory of alcoholism is presented very strongly by the therapist to the alcohol misuser and they are asked to accept the AA programme for recovery. The first goal of the therapy is for the alcohol misuser to accept that they have the disease of alcoholism, that they can't control it and that there is no 'cure' for it. The second goal is for the alcohol misuser to surrender to a higher power to help gain the will to establish control over drinking.

The twelve-step method asks the alcohol misuser to reflect on the number of ways in which alcohol has come to dominate their life. They are asked to understand how their thinking about alcohol may reflect denial, and they are urged to think about the negative consequences of that denial. They are asked to explore the emotions they have regarding alcohol and how those emotional states can make them drink. They are asked about their behaviours and habits that support their drinking, and what changes in behaviour they need to make in order to stop drinking. They are asked to focus social activity on their recovery and to engage socially with AA members, individually and at meetings, in order to achieve sobriety. Finally, they are asked to develop a spiritual life, give up control of their lives to a higher power and acknowledge the harm they have done through alcohol.

The whole process is facilitated through the maintenance of journals: writing reflections on what led the alcohol misuser to drink in the first place and making plans to lead a sober life on completion of therapy.

Part of the therapeutic process involves confronting the alcohol misuser about denial, using various techniques to break through their denial barrier. These techniques can include the use of AA material such as books and pamphlets, as well as significant encouragement from family and loved ones to attend AA meetings.

Finding a Therapy that Works for You

It is a common phenomenon for someone to attend a therapist once, go to an AA meeting or attend an addiction group therapy session and not find it satisfactory. Comments, such as 'I didn't like their attitude,' 'There were too many middle-aged men there,' 'We just didn't click,' are very frequent after a single encounter.

What happens next is very important. The slightly negative experience can be used as a justification to dump any addiction therapeutic activity. On the other hand, a more compatible setting can be sought. A different therapist, a different programme, a different AA meeting, another support structure, a trial of medication – these are all alternative options. By the third try, however, if an alcohol misuser finds fault with yet another person, programme or structure, then it is clear that the problem does not lie with the therapist, programme or therapeutic setting. The problem lies with the alcohol misuser, who is not sincere in seeking help and is making excuses to avoid treatment. Then it is a matter of deciding what the least offensive option is and sticking with it, whether it is truly compatible or not.

What Does the Research Say?

The most important thing to ask about any form of therapy is 'Does it work?' Each of the above therapies developed from very different theories and traditions, and each form of therapy has its advocates in the treatment community. The really important questions about whether they actually work, and what therapy works in particular circumstances or on particular people, have actually been answered by a series of research studies carried out in the US.

Project MATCH was the name given to this major research, which examined 952 outpatients who were being treated for a

3-month period. Each attended a weekly therapy session over that time, except those who attended motivational therapy, which only involved four sessions. The patients were followed up one year and three years after the study.

Results of Project MATCH

- All types of therapy were helpful, and the majority of patients got significant benefits from each

- Those who engaged in therapy and stuck with it did better than those who did not

- There was a significant fall in the number of drinking days and the number of drinks per drinking day, and a significant increase in overall abstinence at the end of year one, and these benefits carried on to the three-year mark, with some fall off

- There were no major differences in outcome between any of the types of therapy: all types of therapy were effective

- There was some evidence that patients who came from a rehabilitation centre did somewhat better than those who didn't. There was also evidence that twelve-step therapy was better for those alcohol misusers who had to deal with drinkers in their environment and that those who had a lot of anger did better with motivational enhancement therapy

Conclusion

There is no doubt that therapy is helpful, in any format, as long as it is carried out by a competent professional. Engaging with any of the therapies outlined above makes a real difference in outcome. As mentioned, finding the right therapy for you or a loved one may involve trying out different kinds to see what works. Those who stay in whatever form of therapy works for them fare better overall. It bears repeating: treatment retention equals treatment benefit.

> A willingness to engage in therapy is a major boost to its
> effectiveness.

Case Study: The Troubled Alcohol Misuser

Joan was a troubled young woman. She had suffered episodes of sexual abuse as teenager and had felt unable to disclose this to anyone because of the threats that the abuser had made to her. He threatened to kill her pets, and to tell everyone that it was her fault it happened and that she enjoyed the sexual encounters. Joan felt trapped, depressed and guilty, and hated herself as a result.

A few years after the abuse ended, she got drunk at Christmas time and enjoyed the feeling of oblivion it gave to her. She took to drinking regularly, every weekend and during the week as well. By the time she was eighteen, she was a habitual drinker and was known locally as a wild girl. She often went out and got drunk, sometimes ending up with some man she hardly knew for the night. She began drinking every weekend and then started drinking during the week as well.

Despite her problem and an erratic attendance record, she managed to complete a teaching degree. She started work, but found herself becoming more addicted to alcohol.

Around this time, she began experimenting with drugs such as marijuana and ecstasy. She found that the drugs provided what alcohol could no longer provide in terms of escape. She spent all of her money on alcohol and drugs, and eventually was suspended from her job because of her erratic behaviour. She was found to be drunk at a parent–teacher meeting and, not surprisingly, her employers found this unacceptable.

After one year of unemployment and drinking, she reluctantly entered into treatment. She found the strictures of a treatment centre difficult to cope with and left after three days. She returned three months' later and resumed her treatment where she had left off. However, despite remaining sober during treatment, she relapsed almost immediately afterwards.

It took a second full stay in rehabilitation to help stabilise her addiction. She found AA difficult to attend, but found solace in a woman-only group. When she had achieved a number of months' sobriety with the help of an individual addiction therapist together with anti-craving medication, she then decided to try and come to terms with the suffering she had endured many years' previously.

She told her story of abuse to her counsellor and this led to her entering a full course of additional therapy. Despite real effort at the therapy, she never felt she resolved the issue of abuse fully, though she felt less depressed than before her therapy. She had a number of short relapses while in therapy, but it was only after the therapy ended that she felt she was able to focus completely on her addiction and maintain her sobriety.

She took a job as a special needs teacher, where she only had a small number of pupils to cope with. She gradually became more independent, and saw her therapist and counsellor less. She achieved the milestone of one year's complete sobriety and then came off her medication. She was slowly entering a full recovery, but was left with a vague sense of unease, even though she felt much better overall. She eventually found a gentle boyfriend, and this helped her become more content with herself and significantly increased her self-esteem.

Joe's Story: Day 17

Joe felt no better in the morning after another very poor night's sleep. He had a small breakfast and then met the doctor for a review. The doctor asked him about his overall mood, as well as how the therapy was going and how the situation was with his wife. On listening to Joe's description of the past number of days, the doctor stated that he felt Joe had actually become depressed and should consider taking an antidepressant.

Joe was surprised. Sure, he felt low and, indeed, as he thought about it, he had felt low many times in the past. However, he didn't think he suffered from depression. He recalled that his mother had suffered from depression and had required psychiatric treatment as an inpatient, and he didn't see himself in the same category as her. He admitted to himself that he felt sad, miserable even, and that he really could see no way out at times. He told the doctor he would think about it for a few days and let him know. The doctor wanted him not to take too much time as an antidepressant would take some time to kick in. Joe promised to give it careful consideration.

For the rest of the day, Joe went around like a kind of zombie. He did what was expected of him, but he really wasn't there. He was low and totally preoccupied by thoughts of what was happening to his marriage. He was angry at times, both at his wife and himself for getting into this mess. He found it very hard to blame himself for everything. At other times, he felt totally responsible and felt miserable about it. He felt he was a screw-up and had been for his entire life; he felt he had been found out as a kind of fraud.

He suffered waves of guilt, which came and receded over the course of the evening and the night. He was very low.

18

AA – God, Recovery and New Social Activity

> AA has been a powerful tool in helping many people to recover from alcohol misuse.

Alcoholics Anonymous (AA) was founded in the 1930s in the US. It is an unashamedly religious organisation and cites acceptance of a higher power as a prerequisite for achievement of true sobriety. Its philosophical origins relate to a movement in Christianity in the late nineteenth and early twentieth century. This philosophical movement believed that the pathway to spiritual enlightenment was through humble acceptance of and subjugation to a higher power, and emphasised the importance of self-imposed spiritual exercises and making reparation to those injured by the individual over the years prior to acceptance of God.

This approach underlies the twelve steps of AA, which have become so familiar in recovery literature. They are listed below. As alcoholics, the founders of AA adopted a spiritual pathway to their own recovery and found redemption.

AA has spread worldwide, and many millions of people have achieved sobriety though its pathways. Its message of hope, acceptance and unconditional support for the person underneath the disease of alcoholism means that it facilitates a transformation for many millions of its members. The organisation's rapid spread throughout the Western World and beyond was facilitated by its message, and through the support of churches and community organisations that facilitated its operation.

The twelve steps of AA are:

1. We admitted we were powerless over alcohol – that our lives had become unmanageable

2. Came to believe that a Power greater than ourselves could restore us to sanity

3. Made a decision to turn our will and our lives over to the care of God *as we understood Him*

4. Made a searching and fearless moral inventory of ourselves

5. Admitted to God, to ourselves and to another human being the exact nature of our wrongs

6. Were entirely ready to have God remove all these defects of character

7. Humbly asked Him to remove our shortcomings

8. Made a list of all persons we had harmed and became willing to make amends to them all

9. Made direct amends to such people wherever possible, except when to do so would injure them or others

10. Continued to take personal inventory and, when we were wrong, promptly admitted it

11. Sought through prayer and meditation to improve our conscious contact with God *as we understood Him*, praying only

for knowledge of His will for us and the power to carry that out

12. Having had a spiritual awakening as a result of these Steps, we tried to carry this message to alcoholics and to practise these principles in all our affairs

How Successful Is AA?

AA is the most successful self-help organisation in the world. It has allowed terms like 'recovery', 'twelve-step programme', 'sponsor' and 'sharing' to enter the general parlance, and to survive. It is the model for any self-help movement and has spawned offshoots and clone organisations, such as Narcotics Anonymous, Gamblers Anonymous, Al-Anon, Alateen, Dual Recovery Anonymous (see Appendix) and many others.

AA has been a wonderful success for many reasons:

- Its treatment method was a first in the treatment of alcoholism. Previously, no real treatment programmes were available, and sufferers and families had to rely on their own resources

- The principles and purpose of the organisation are explicit: to facilitate the achievement of sobriety and to support those trying to achieve it. It does not support or endorse any other organisation or principle

- AA encourages anonymity, and allows someone to get treatment without payment or prerequisites

- It is self-perpetuating, and encourages participants to facilitate the development and running of the individual meetings

- It uses the experience of older and more established members (sponsors) to facilitate the treatment of newer or younger members. It encourages the adoption of a new member by a sponsor, who, through selfless provision of constant support and guidance, can facilitate the ongoing sobriety of newer members

- It asks nothing of its participants beyond constant effort and offering of their support to others

- It is a nonjudgmental organisation and never criticises a person who is going through difficulties. It encourages patrons who relapse to come back into the fold, and offers them ongoing affirmation in their quest for sobriety

- Its methodology has been adopted by many mainstream treatment centres such as Hazelden in the US, and this has also facilitated its spread around the world

Reasons for Success

Independent research suggests that there are two major factors in the success of AA. This research states that the very act of showing up and making the effort to attend is helpful to the alcohol misuser of itself, and is a powerful indication of their inclination for recovery. It also states that one of the most powerful tools is the sense of support from the established members that each person feels upon entering AA. That sense of unconditional support, even affection, is one of the most powerful tools available to help an addict into recovery. It is reported so often by attendees that it has to be true. It makes the organisation stand out in relation to almost any other organisation around in its altruism, its singular focus, and the transmission of its message of support for the addict and its hatred of the disease of alcoholism.

Participation in AA may be gradual. It may mean that, for the first week, the patient sits at the back and says nothing. A few meetings later, that patient might say a few words about themselves. After that, the patient might start to participate more fully in the recovery process and embrace it more enthusiastically. As with anything in life, those who put the most into it are those who get the most out of it. Those who not only adhere to the process but who take it on board as a new purpose and a new way of life are those who will likely get the most lasting benefit from it.

Apart from turning up, the first challenge is speaking up. The speaking up bit, the simple statement 'My name is John, and I am an alcoholic' means giving up what may be years of denial. Using the word 'alcoholic' means that you are admitting the extent of your problem. That is the difficult thing for a lot of people, and the reason why many fail at the first hurdle. It is important to speak at AA meetings, even if only for a few seconds. It means embracing the possibility of change.

The latest research available shows that even low attendance rates in AA can actually be beneficial, and that, contrary to popular belief, drifting away from AA does not necessarily mean a return to alcoholic drinking. Overall, those who attend AA frequently do better than those who have never attended or have done so infrequently. Certainly, those who attend have a much better response to treatment in the beginning, but by the end of a long period of treatment many other factors also determine outcome. The most important factor is, of course, personal motivation. If you have a strong desire to remain sober then you are more likely to achieve long-term sobriety than if your motivation is less intense.

Long-term research within AA suggests that giving back to AA, in the form of active participation in the AA model, engaging with a sponsor and then maybe becoming a sponsor, is a helpful long-term thing to do. Becoming involved in the organisation in another way, such as becoming a group secretary, is also of long-term benefit.

Comparing AA to Other Therapy

When AA-type therapy is compared to non-AA types of therapy, an approximate evaluation of the benefits of AA can be obtained. Some years ago, a large number of outpatient alcohol misusers in early recovery were entered into a treatment trial whereby they used three types of therapy over the course of one year. AA therapy, based on engaging individuals in a twelve-step facilitation therapy, was performed weekly for twelve weeks. The other therapies were relapse prevention therapy and motivational enhancement therapy (see Chapter 17). This research showed that patients did very well in all the different types of therapy and, by and large, stayed sober during the treatment period. Those who engaged with the therapy longer did best and those who engaged closely with their therapist also did very well. In AA research, those who feel a degree of warmth and empathy from the AA group do well, while those who feel less of a connection drift away. As with AA groups, those patients who felt the therapist sympathetic and who felt that they were getting support did well.

Overall, the research showed that it apparently didn't matter what type of therapy people engaged in; whether they liked their therapist or group was more important. And, of course, whether or not they showed up for their therapy was also vitally important, but that was also related to how much they liked their therapist, among other factors.

Other research suggests that, if a patient emerges from rehabilitation and then attends AA straight away, this approach to treatment is more successful than coming out of rehabilitation and starting to attend AA about six months later. The delay appears to augur badly from a long-term prognosis perspective. Of course, any delay is a sign that someone's motivation may be lacking.

Criticism of AA

Yet, the organisation has its critics. It has received bad press because of the policy of not advocating any other therapy or programme apart from itself. Some people report that they find the religious associations off-putting, and that these distract from the purpose of achieving and maintaining sobriety. Some report that they find the methods generally used to encourage sobriety, namely, speaking up at meetings, telling a little bit about yourself and your recovery journey, and listening to others detailing their life stories, difficult to get used to. Some report they find that some members don't tolerate new members taking other prescription medications for problems such as depression, and let them know it. Indeed, others report that they find the whole group setting uncomfortable and would rather cover the same territory with an individual therapist. Others report that they don't find the gender mix easy and would prefer to get help in a single-sex setting. Some people say they simply don't like the organisation, they don't appreciate its format and they don't think it will help them to achieve sobriety.

When considering the benefits versus the problems associated with any one treatment methodology, it is vital to consider what the alternatives are and what might be the right method for you or your loved one. AA is only one of many treatment methods available for the treatment of alcoholism; if it does not suit you, there are plenty of options out there. It is vital, however, that you engage in some form of addiction treatment.

Different treatment methods can be helpful at different times in your recovery. AA can be helpful on one occasion, but may not be quite as helpful again. However, it is good to stick with a particular method of treatment for a suitable period before writing it off. You may not embrace AA sufficiently the first time around for it to have its benefit. You may be on your second or third programme before you find that you are engaging with it adequately and it has any lasting benefit.

Many millions of people have gotten sober through AA, and you can't argue with that. Its advantages greatly outnumber its disadvantages and there is no other form of treatment as available, free and supportive almost anywhere in the world. It may not work for everybody, but a significant number of people find it a success, even the second, third or nth time around.

Summary

Benefits of AA:

- It is available almost anywhere in the world
- Its supportive membership provides empathy and guidance
- It is free
- It has the single agenda of helping alcoholics become sober
- It has a proven track record of effectiveness
- It welcomes returning patients, even those in relapse
- It can offer individual support via a sponsor
- It offers support even when family and friends abandon patients
- It can enhance many aspects of life as part of recovery

Problems of AA:

- Its religious orientation can alienate some people
- Membership can be predominantly male and middle aged, which may discourage some people
- It is not always supportive of medication treatments for depression and psychiatric disorders
- It can be abused by people with agendas, e.g. those seeking someone of the opposite sex for a relationship
- It can become an alternative way of life, instead of a means to an end
- Anonymity is not always preserved in local settings
- Not all groups are able to handle drug addiction as well as alcohol addiction

- Absence of a professional means that other related disorders including depression are not always picked up on

> **AA is one of many treatment methods; it is not the only one.**

Case Study: The Self-Made Alcohol Misuser

Peter was a 45-year-old self-made millionaire. He came from a farming background, but went into construction at an early age. He enjoyed the active outdoor 'can do' lifestyle.

He founded his own construction supply company and went from being a small cement supplier to being a major player in the evolving construction boom that took place over a ten-year period. During that time, he built his company up to two hundred employees. He was also building up his drinking habit from drinking five pints of beer only at weekends to drinking a bottle of neat whiskey almost every day, on his own, with maybe a couple of glasses of wine at dinner as well.

His marriage went from an initially happy mixture of hard work and mutual support to angry, bitter confrontations about the degree of the problem he had with alcohol. His wife threatened to walk and ordered him out of the house of a number of occasions.

His company began to fail, in part due to his lack of attention to it and his failure to monitor all the deals his managers were making on his behalf. When the inevitable downturn happened, he was badly placed to deal with it, and his company shrank almost overnight to one-tenth of its size the previous year. His drinking escalated and he ended up in A&E on two separate occasions with alcohol-related minor injuries, sustained after falling on his face while drunk.

After a final confrontation with his wife, in which she seriously threatened to walk out for good and take the children with her, he decided he had to do something about it. He was initially very skeptical about AA, having gone once or twice previously and not enjoyed the experience. He decided to go again, this time with a number of days' sobriety behind him. And this time it began to make sense.

While not accepting all of the steps, he was able to focus on the main question, namely, 'What does it take for me to remain sober?' He found alcohol far more difficult to give up than he had envisaged. He had successfully given up cigarettes the previous year and had reckoned that all he had to do was make his mind up and things would fall into place naturally, without much effort. He found the concept of making an all-or-nothing decision at an early stage very difficult and he relapsed a number of times, sometimes on a grand scale, before finally deciding that the only way forward was complete abstinence.

Unfortunately, his wife was not prepared to wait that long and, after a particularly bitter confrontation, he was asked to leave the family home, which he reluctantly did. Also, his financial circumstances changed and, because his company was in financial difficulty, he had to sell his family home to pay off some of his company debt. By the time he was completely sober, about six months after his initial efforts, he had lost his family, his home and most of his business. On the surface, he was a broken man, but he had a fierce determination to succeed and was aiming for a reconciliation with his wife and children on the basis of his ongoing sobriety.

Joe's Story: Day 18

After another rough night's sleep, Joe decided to talk to one of the nurses. He told her how he was feeling and asked her about this antidepressant the doctor was talking about. She reassured him about how safe the medication was and gave him an information sheet about it.

He read the sheet and found out about the benefits and the potential side effects of the medication. He talked to other patients about the medication and their responses to it. He told the nurse at lunchtime that he would agree to a trial of the medication and asked that the doctor prescribe it right away. He was told he could start on it the next morning.

Joe brightened up a bit after that decision. He was able to participate in the group that afternoon, where he told people about his decision. The group approved and some of them told him about their own experiences on antidepressants. He told them about his relief at making the decision and that he hoped the medication would work soon.

The group moved on to talk about other treatment options and Joe felt a surge of joy at their approval of his decision. Maybe he wasn't such a screw-up after all; maybe he could do things right.

Afterwards, he phoned his wife and told her of his decision. She wasn't very warm over the phone, but at least she didn't cut him off or give out to him. Joe felt a little better about himself.

19

The Use of Medication in Treatment

> Medication can be very helpful in the treatment of alcoholism. It is not a cure.

Until now I have looked at addiction, alcoholism and recovery as purely personal processes. The descent into alcoholism is the ultimate personal nightmare, and entry into the recovery process is the most important and often the most difficult decision that an alcohol misuser can make in their lifetime. I haven't yet looked at the concept of alcoholism as a disease, beyond acknowledging that it is a highly genetic disorder which ultimately must have a significant biological basis.

Biology can be explored and experimented on by scientists (myself included), with the object of understanding the various biological and neurochemical mechanisms, and ultimately developing potentially useful chemical compounds. These chemical compounds, what will become the medication, are then tested in laboratories to see if they may be useful in cutting alcohol consumption in laboratory animals. They are then tested on humans to see if what works in theory actually works in practice. These compounds should help alcohol misusers to cut down their use of alcohol in a variety of ways, including decreasing their cravings for alcohol. This should allow the alcohol misuser to achieve full recovery through a psychotherapeutic or a self-help course.

Alcohol addiction is both a physical and psychological problem. Alcohol is an extraordinarily addictive substance, and dealing with the physical or chemical side of the addiction may take months or even years. Medication helps the alcohol misuser to deal with this part of recovery, thus facilitating overall recovery. Finding a successful medication to treat alcoholism is half the battle.

The Doctor

Olivier Ameisen is a French cardiologist. He trained as a doctor in France and moved to the US to complete his training. He then took up private practice as a cardiologist in a respected treatment centre. He had, on the surface, a complete and fulfilling life. He suffered, however, from a significant degree of anxiety. Over the years he used alcohol to treat his anxiety. He eventually descended into full alcoholism and found it impossible to continue his professional life.

While trying to find a cure for his addiction, he discovered reports about a medication called baclofen, which he thought sounded promising. He self-medicated with this treatment until he felt he became 'cured' of his alcoholism. He felt he could start living his life again and that he no longer had the need for alcohol. He kept on the medication because he felt it vital to his well-being and to his sobriety.

He detailed his life story in a bestselling book, *The End of My Addiction*, which has given courage to thousands of sufferers from alcoholism and their families. His message is simple: there is a possible cure for this disease of alcoholism.

The medication Olivier Ameisen prescribed himself, baclofen, has been used for years to treat muscle spasms and contractions in such disorders as multiple sclerosis. A small number of clinical trials using baclofen in cases of alcoholism were completed in the past few years in the US and Europe. The results indicate some promise, with the medication causing few tolerance problems and bringing quite reasonable benefits.

While this medication has yet to be fully researched and approved for treatment, there are a number of medications out there that have been fully researched and are proven to be of significant benefit. These fall broadly into two categories: anti-craving and aversive medications.

Anti-Craving Medications

Naltrexone and Nalmefene

The most prominent of the established anti-craving medication is naltrexone, and its chemical first cousin, nalmefene. Naltrexone has been around for many years and was initially developed as a treatment for heroin addiction. It works by blocking the body's natural opiate chemicals: the endorphins, dynorphins and enkephalins. These chemical compounds, which work by stimulating the brain's natural opiate receptors, play a vital role in the body's 'reward' system. It is thought that alcohol partially exerts its addictive potential by stimulating those natural opiates and giving the brain a sense of pleasure and reward for drinking. Naltrexone blocks that alcohol-induced rise in natural opiates and blocks the brain's feeling of the need for more and more alcohol. It doesn't stop a person from getting intoxicated from alcohol; it just stops their sense of a 'need for more'. While it can be difficult to tease out the exact reasons for someone drinking, it appears that the desire for alcohol, especially in alcohol misusers, is chemically driven. It makes sense that, once one of the chemicals associated with that need for alcohol is identified, blocking it leads to a decrease in desire for alcohol.

Naltrexone does work. Since the research into naltrexone and alcohol in humans was first published in 1992, there have been many carefully carried out placebo-controlled trials that have shown that naltrexone and its associated compound nalmefene effectively decrease craving for alcohol, cut the amount of alcohol consumed and reduce the rate of relapse to heavy drinking. Unfortunately it does not work for everyone and its beneficial effects appear to last for a number of months rather than a number of years. It appears to work best in conjunction with various types of psychotherapy, either individual or group. It can work well in conjunction with other anti-craving medication. It does not appear to work particularly well on specific subgroups such as US veterans and women with eating disorders.

Naltrexone is generally taken in tablet form, at a dose of 50 mg. It can cause some minor side effects such as nausea and headache, and may cause a rise in liver functions in a minority of people. In recent years, it has been developed in injectable form at a dose of 380 mg, and this has proven as effective as the tablet form. If anything, the results from injectable naltrexone suggest a major increase in complete abstinence and a significant reduction in heavy drinking. The benefits from the injection appear to start as early as the second day of treatment. The injectable form is given monthly, thus eliminating the need for daily administration. Its major drawback appears to be an occasional problem with soreness and muscle shrinkage at the injection site.

Nalmefene is very similar to naltrexone, both in its way of working and in its profile of effectiveness. It has been researched less than naltrexone and is not available in injectable form. It appears very promising and to be well tolerated and effective over a six-month period. It is generally used in combination with types of therapy.

Acamprosate

This medication has been available in Europe for the past fifteen years. It has yet to gain approval in the US. It works on a chemical system in the brain called the excitatory amino acid system. There is a theory that alcohol misusers, when they stop drinking alcohol, go through a protracted form of withdrawal that can last for a long time. Acamprosate helps to shorten that withdrawal.

It is generally taken at a dose of 2 g per day and is very well tolerated, with virtually no side effects apart from a rare dose of diarrhea. It has a modest anti-craving function, but does diminish actual alcohol consumption when used over a long time, such as six or twelve months, or even up to two years. It does not need to be used with psychotherapy to be effective. It has been combined with naltrexone and this was successful when studied in Europe, less so when studied in the US. It has gained modest support in the treatment community and some patients find it very helpful. Partly because it appears to work without a large reduction in craving, some patients don't feel they gain benefit, even if, overall, they are drinking less.

Topiramate

This is an anti-epileptic medication which was found to have significant anti-craving activity in alcohol misusers. It is being extensively researched and a number of large, multi-site studies have shown it to be very effective. It appears to work by calming down an excitatory amino acid system (glutamate) and enhancing GABA, a neurochemical in the brain that dampens down feelings of excitement. It has yet to gain approval in the US or in Europe, but that is largely a matter of time as the results are so impressive. It can sometimes be hard to tolerate, with some people finding it causes poor appetite, poor concentration and tingling feelings. Thus, it will not be for everybody. For that reason, the dose is escalated slowly over a period of weeks until an adequate dose is built up.

Topiramate is built up to a 300 mg daily dose. It is effective at reducing craving for alcohol and it decreases obsessive thoughts about alcohol. It also reduces alcohol consumption. It can improve liver function and overall health and well-being, including blood pressure. It has been studied in conjunction with a gentle form of therapy, which is mainly focused on monitoring the medication and encouraging compliance with the medication, so does not appear to require the addition of full psychotherapy for it to be effective.

Aversive Medication: Antabuse

Antabuse (disulfiram) has been used in the treatment of alcoholism for at least fifty years. It works in an unusual way for a treatment medication. When combined with alcohol, it blocks the breakdown of a chemical in the bloodstream called acetaldehyde. This blockade produces a strong reaction in the majority of people. The reaction includes flushing, a rash, nausea, occasional vomiting and an intense feeling of discomfort. This reaction can last for a number of hours.

The knowledge that the reaction will occur is the deterring effect of the treatment. When large studies have been done comparing the outcome of treatment with Antabuse relative to a placebo, there tends to be a good result overall and not mainly in those taking the active medication. Therefore, it is the fear of having a reaction that makes the alcohol misuser stop drinking, rather than the reaction itself.

Antabuse is taken at a dose of up to 400 mg daily and may have the effect of slight drowsiness, so it is often taken at night. Rarely, it can cause a change in liver function and a tingling in the hands or feet. It lasts in the system for four or five days. The alcohol misuser may not drink for that time, even after ceasing to take Antabuse. It is possible for an alcohol misuser on Antabuse to get a reaction to taking alcohol through eating food cooked with alcohol or ingesting an alcoholic mouthwash, or even having a blood sample taken with an alcohol-soaked skin swab. It has to be said, though, that these reactions are extremely rare and the most common cause of an Antabuse reaction is an alcohol misuser giving in to temptation, chancing their arm and having a drink. If the alcohol misuser drinks right through the reaction, and drinks very heavily, they can get an even more severe reaction and end up in hospital with a potentially very serious rise in blood pressure.

The most important thing about taking Antabuse is continued compliance. Thus, anything that keeps an alcohol misuser taking his or her Antabuse can be very helpful for continued abstinence. A spouse or family member helping to monitor the taking of Antabuse on a daily or nightly basis can double the compliance rate, and thus double the abstinence rate. The compliance rate at the end of one year is about 20 per cent only; however, with the involvement of a spouse, it goes up to 40 per cent.

It is occasionally possible for the alcohol misuser to get totally caught up in the process of taking the Antabuse and to ignore any potential therapeutic advance during their abstinence. They might refuse to go to AA or any form of therapy and end up relapsing the first time they stop taking their Antabuse. The purpose of taking Antabuse is to facilitate the recovery process, not to become an end in itself.

Many years ago it was common for some treatment facilities to give their clients Antabuse and a drink on the day before they left, so they might find out what an Antabuse reaction was actually like. Fortunately that practice has long since stopped, and most alcohol misusers, even those who have taken it for a considerable period, do not know what the reaction is like. However, the fear of the reaction is still enough to give them a considerable period of sobriety and that is no bad thing.

Benefits and Disadvantages of Medication

Positive aspects of medication:

- It is another tool to help in the battle for sobriety
- There are a number of different medications available with different modes of action
- Individuals may respond to one medication and not another
- Combinations of medication may be used
- Some medication can be successfully combined with therapy or can be taken alone
- Promising medications are in the pipeline, including injections

- The medications are non-addictive and do not make the situation worse

Negative aspects of medication:

- Some people think that medication is a cure; it is not
- The benefits of some medication seem to diminish with time
- Medication does not take the place of huge personal effort
- No long-term effectiveness (i.e. over many years) studies have been done yet
- Medications are not yet widely prescribed, despite research evidence
- Benefits are present but modest only

Resistance to the Use of Medication in the Treatment Community

It will probably take many years before the use of medication for alcoholism becomes as widespread as the use of antidepressants in depression. The research evidence would suggest that the use of medication should be promoted by psychiatrists, addiction counsellors and general practitioners. Even AA members should be encouraging the use of medication (at least in the short term) as it increases the chance of success, which is what AA is all about.

Unfortunately it looks as if it will take years before the use of medication in alcoholism really takes off. While the amount of research is impressive, resistance within the treatment community is significant. Education is required to overcome this block. It looks as if government agencies will not take up the banner of treatment medication. It may actually take the pharmaceutical industry to effectively create the market, and to educate doctors, therapists and, indeed, alcohol misusers themselves about the potential major benefits of medication. Unfortunately this will be a slow process, and many alcoholics will die before the use of medication is commonly accepted and prescriptions routinely given out.

It took many years before treatment for depression moved from theoretical discussions to the use of available effective medication. Hopefully it won't take as long for the treatment of alcoholism to make the same shift.

> **Alcohol misusers may get benefits from various medications at different times in their treatment, according to what they or a professional feels may be helpful.**

Case Study: Drinking to Cope with Stress and Depression

Theresa was a 53-year-old married woman who worked as a secretary. She was in her second marriage and had two children from her first. She had an on-and-off relationship with alcohol, having developed a binge drinking pattern in her thirties.

She grew up in a happy household, in which alcohol played little part. She first began drinking at college in her early twenties, but she only drank socially with friends at the weekend.

However, as time went on, she found herself drinking to excess to cope with negative emotions and stresses.

By the time she was in her forties she was drinking a half bottle of vodka every evening. Her life was revolving around alcohol. She had to cope with a lot of stresses, including the break-up of her first marriage, the loss of her job and personal bankruptcy. At that time she also become depressed and had significant suicidal ideation. She required treatment with an antidepressant to get her through this period. She responded well to both the antidepressant and the therapy and stopped both after about a year.

When she came for treatment the second time, she felt she had become dependent on alcohol and wanted to stop. She was mildly depressed and apprehensive about the future, but not hopeless. She agreed to enter a treatment programme for alcohol dependence that involved both therapy and the anti-craving medication naltrexone. She took the medication, entered the weekly therapy and reported a decrease in craving for alcohol within one week.

She did well in treatment until she suddenly became depressed six weeks in. She reported becoming tearful, and feeling hopeless, lethargic and irritable. Her craving for alcohol increased, despite her being on naltrexone. She agreed to treatment with an antidepressant and, within three weeks, her mood lifted and her craving diminished. She felt so well that she stopped her antidepressant ten weeks after that.

However, she became depressed about a month later, but this time described no increase in craving. She readily agreed to go back on the antidepressant and her mood improved again. She finished treatment after a period of nine months' complete abstinence.

At the end of treatment, she decided to stay on both the antidepressant and the naltrexone in order to help her long-term sobriety. She felt better and healthier than she had in years. (See Farren and O'Malley, 1999)

Joe's Story: Day 19

Joe started the antidepressant medication this morning. He awoke to find himself quite down, and felt hopeless and inadequate again. The mild euphoria at making a good decision yesterday had evaporated by today. He took the medication, and, apart from feeling a bit bloated, he felt physically fine. Psychologically he still felt down in the dumps, and questioned the purpose of his being in treatment at all. He managed little of his food at lunch, but almost none of his tea.

Worse still was what was going on in the group sessions. His counsellor was making everyone recount their worse experiences with alcohol and Joe simply didn't want to know. As he heard tales of selfishness and misery, of foolishness and embarrassment because of alcohol, Joe felt distant and removed from the proceedings. When asked to participate, Joe refused, stating he felt that he was being forced into stuff he didn't agree with and that, in reality, his problems were more likely related to depression and not alcohol.

He recalled that when he was sober he could handle things just fine and he really didn't have too many problems. His drinking was fuelled by his depression, and all he had to do was get his depression treated and he would be fine. Although he could relate to some of the stories being told in the group, he really hadn't the problems that these people seemed to have, and he mainly needed treatment for his mood.

In fact, there were times when Joe felt that talking with the group could make things worse. He found that, after group sessions, he couldn't get alcohol out of his head and he wanted a drink quite badly. It hadn't happened after every group, but it happened enough. Too much talk about drink set off cravings in him and Joe felt that he

could get more effective treatment through more counselling and less talk about drink.

Joe felt that no one was listening to him. By the end of
the day, he felt exhausted, depressed and had a residual
craving for alcohol.

20

Relapse – Causes and
What to Do about It

> Relapse is quite likely to occur during treatment for addiction.

Relapse to alcohol is one of the accompaniments to the disorder. It is not inevitable, but I've seen it occur frequently. To never experience relapse during treatment is wonderful. A number of alcohol misusers enter recovery and never look back. They keep to their chosen method of successful sobriety and maintain it for a significant period of time. After a long period, they might cut down their addiction-related activity, for example, they reduce their AA meetings from three per week to one per week, but keep up with something else to help manage their addiction. By and large, they are proud of their achievement, and will tell all and sundry that they are in recovery. They are often able to quote the amount of time they have been in recovery to the day.

The majority of alcohol misusers who enter recovery do go back to drinking alcohol at some time in their addiction career. It may be a lapse, where they only consume one to two drinks, or it may be a full relapse, where they return to heavy drinking for a time. They may resume and, indeed, embrace sobriety immediately after their lapse and never drink again, or they may continue their drinking as if they had never achieved sobriety at all. Like everything to do with addiction, the outcome is immensely variable. Like everything to do with addiction, the outcome is solely dependent on the motivation and intent of the addict.

It is estimated that up to 80 per cent of alcohol misusers lapse or relapse to drinking at some stage in their disorder, although this figure is very difficult to verify. Relapses are more frequent early in recovery rather than late. The biggest danger period is the first three to six months. The best studies based on long-term research suggest that, after a period of three to four years of sobriety, almost all alcohol misusers are unlikely to relapse again. Every day of sobriety is a day further away from the likelihood of relapse.

How an addict manages relapse will determine the outcome of their long-term addiction. Relapse is both the biggest danger point and the biggest learning point in an addiction.

The Difference between a Lapse and a Relapse

A lapse is the first drink after a period of sobriety. If an alcohol misuser drinks almost immediately after a period of sobriety, say, within the first month, they simply are not yet ready or motivated for sobriety. Intense craving, a significant degree of anxiety or depression, and a high degree of turmoil in the initial stages of sober life are simply overwhelming for them and they turn to alcohol to cope.

By far the most common reason for early lapse is a poor degree of motivation and an inadequate desire for sobriety. For a large number of people in this situation, the benefits of sobriety simply do not yet add up to a commitment to it. Recovery may be desired in the same way that someone may want to play football for Manchester United, become a pop star, own a Bentley or to be on the front cover of *Hello!* It's not that it is impossible, but it is seen as beyond current capability, and the person either feels that it is not worth the effort or doesn't believe that the effort will pay off. A lapse is a sign of addiction despair and a return to the belief that your addiction is more powerful than you. A lapse means giving up self-belief. Unfortunately, it may also be a sign that the alcohol misuser has no motivation at all and that efforts made were a sham for some other short-term goal. So, clearly, a lapse means different things to different people.

A lapse does not necessarily mean that you return to stage one of recovery. It can be dealt with quickly – the person stops drinking and resumes treatment. This may be difficult, but it is by no means impossible. The most common outcome of a lapse is a return to treatment. Thus, in the majority of cases, a lapse is actually quite useful and it helps reveal the dangers associated with the addiction. It is frequent for an alcohol misuser to challenge their diagnosis with a quick test of drinking and to make the discovery at the point of lapse that, in fact, everything the doctors and counsellors are saying is true, and they are actually addicted to alcohol. It can be the last item of the jigsaw that falls into place and they finally accept their diagnosis. In this case, practical acceptance, in the form of returning to treatment with a committed attitude, is the next stage.

Of course, with a lapse comes danger; this is a vulnerable point in time when the addict can go on to relapse fully. An alcohol misuser may have originally somewhat reluctantly accepted their family's or counsellor's perspective that they had to aim for full abstinence, but a lapse may give them 'permission' to happily settle for the aim of 'moderation' in drinking. What constitutes moderate drinking can vary from person to person, and generally changes to mean increased volumes of alcohol as time goes by and the alcohol misuser gets away with it.

Intervention at the point of lapse can be of major help. A call from an AA member, a chat with a sympathetic family member or a visit to the doctor can all help the addict at a time of lapse. Gentle support and advice at this time can be crucial in determining the outcome of the lapse. There is no one intervention that is recommended, but communication is essential and the alcohol misuser must reach out for or accept help to prevent deterioration.

Unfortunately not every lapse has such a good outcome. A significant minority of lapses lead to a full relapse to heavy drinking. This can take place at once, where a lapse turns into a relapse on the same day, or it can take days or even weeks.

Despite lots of warnings and a fear of potential consequences, a lapse can lurk in the back of the mind as a negative force pulling the alcohol misuser towards another drink and a full relapse to heavy drinking. The sore can fester for days, even weeks, and has to be fought aggressively before it can be overcome. Leaving a lapse alone is giving it permission to grow. In itself it may not cause craving, but it can have the same effect as a bout of craving.

Some addicts find themselves using a lapse as a test. If they are able to tolerate a lapse, and they get away with it in terms of nothing too severe happening, they give themselves the message that drinking isn't too bad. It is a kind of Russian roulette: they have just fired a blank cylinder and they feel they can get away with drinking again. If there were immediate consequences of a lapse, for example, a bad reaction to medication, their partner walking away from the relationship or a loss of employment, then they would probably not relapse. The alcohol misuser should see a lapse as signifying a need for extra vigilance, not a lessening of vigilance.

While a lapse may or may not be manageable, a relapse to heavy drinking can be devastating for the alcohol misuser and those around them. A spouse may have decided to give the alcohol misuser 'one more chance', and when a relapse occurs can decide to give up on the relationship. An employer who had been supportive through the initial treatment phase may decide that they can never depend on the alcohol misuser again and terminate employment. A liver, just beginning to recover from many years of addiction, might finally enter into acute liver failure after a bad bout of heavy drinking. In short, a relapse may leave the alcohol misuser worse off than if they had never stopped drinking at all.

What Can Be Done to Prevent a Lapse Turning into a Relapse?

To prevent a lapse turning into a relapse, it may not be necessary for you to start the journey into recovery again. It may not be necessary to re-enter the treatment programme or revisit the doctor or counsellor, and it may not be necessary to feel that nothing has been achieved.

What is important is an action plan. The solution is to restart the action plan that was established at the end of a treatment programme and to re-engage with the advice given by the counsellor. It is necessary to take the helpful treatment steps that proved successful first time around all over again. If that means returning to an AA group more frequently, so be it. If it is necessary to re-engage with an aftercare programme or a treatment counsellor, so be it. If it is necessary to resume some sort of medication, so be it. If it is necessary to re-do a computerised addiction course, so be it. If it is necessary to drop all the places and people associated with your drinking – those associated with your original journey into addiction and those associated with your lapse – so be it.

The optimum time to take action is immediately after the lapse. The quicker action is taken, the more likely it is to be successful. Any delay allows the desire to fester and makes a relapse to heavy drinking more likely.

A lapse may be a vital call to action. It might convey the message that half measures are inadequate and it might turn a reluctant journeyman on the road to recovery into a fully-fledged convert. It can help dispel, for the alcohol misuser, the lurking doubts about their diagnosis and the methods of recovery. The point of vulnerability immediately after a lapse may be the optimum time for an intervention to be effective, and it may be the best time for a family member, friend or professional to get a difficult but hopeful message across.

In a study of post-rehabilitation dually diagnosed alcohol misusers, that is, those with both an alcohol dependence and a mood disorder such as depression, the group that relapsed to alcohol and followed this up with an immediate extra short stay in hospital for brief rehabilitation did significantly better overall over the next number of months than the group that relapsed to alcohol and didn't return to hospital. So intervention in the form of hospitalisation can be effective, even with a particularly challenging group of patients.

Some medication (see Chapter 19) can be particularly helpful at this time. The aversive medication disulfiram (Antabuse) can be used as a way of helping to focus attention on the relapse and its dangers. Naltrexone is also particularly helpful at a time of lapse; its probable primary benefit is that it prevents a lapse becoming a relapse. Research (see Chapter 27) shows that naltrexone decreases the chances of an alcohol misuser continuing to drink after having one drink.

Intervention in the period immediately following a lapse can be effective, and probably more effective the quicker it is delivered. With no time to think and no time to delay, just doing something to help break the cycle can make it quite possible that there will be a good outcome.

If an original plan of action was only partially successful, then further steps should be taken to prevent a full relapse to heavy drinking. A lot of people are surprised that they return to drinking so quickly, and this surprise can be useful at emphasising just how big their problem actually is. Thus, not only should the action plan encompass what had originally been drawn up, but it should go one step further and the alcohol misuser should be encouraged to do more: to attend more AA meetings, to banish all activities associated with alcohol and to absolutely embrace sobriety as the only goal.

A lapse is not the end of the world and should be understood as part of the learning curve of alcohol addiction. It's how you use it that counts.

> Relapse is a place of learning, not a place of despair.

Case Study: A Successfully Managed Relapse

Jemma was a 45-year-old single woman who developed a fondness for alcohol at a young age. She enjoyed her single life and she liked to go out and party. In particular, when she was in training college as a teacher, she loved going out with her friends at the weekend and 'getting smashed'. She didn't enjoy the recovery process the next day, but that was the price to be paid for a good time and she didn't question her own habits.

She soon qualified as a teacher, but kept up her hard drinking habits while a lot of her friends moved on. She found that she would often end up going out alone, drinking herself to intoxication, maybe meeting up with someone and maybe not, and spending all of the next day in a trance. Eventually, in her mid-thirties, she realised that she was drinking a lot more than her now sober friends and that she had developed a problem.

She entered a rehabilitation course and came out at the other end in much better form, mentally and physically. As she embraced her recovery, she took up yoga as well as significant exercise in the gym twice a week. She felt and looked good and, although her life didn't change that much, she was glad that she had recognised her problem and had successfully done something about it.

One Monday, six months into sobriety, she simply bought a bottle of wine in a supermarket and drank it that evening when she went home. She had no intention of doing it, she had not preplanned it; it was simply an opportunity that presented itself to her and she took it.

The day after she drank, she was crippled with an awful guilt about her drinking. She couldn't get out of bed she was so embarrassed. However, despite her physical and psychological distress, she decided to tell her sponsor in AA, and distracted herself with an immediate regime of walking the dogs and going to see a film, a favourite pastime. She decided to do thirty meetings in thirty days and made a special effort over the subsequent months to break her habit.

Two months later, she recognised that she was craving alcohol in response to cues such as TV ads for alcohol and easily available alcohol in supermarket aisles. She decided to change supermarkets to one that did not sell large amounts of alcohol and she limited her TV viewing to her favourite programmes only so that she wouldn't be flicking from channel to channel and seeing ads for alcohol. She regarded her relapse as a learning curve for her, educating her that there might be danger lurking in the background, that she was indeed an alcoholic (which she knew anyway) and she had to be vigilant for years to come.

She felt that the secret to her successful management of her relapse was the quick action she took to deal with it. She knew that if she had hesitated, she would have gone out and bought another two bottles of wine and would have ended up lost for six months. She also felt that telling her sponsor and telling the truth at the next AA meeting was very helpful as well as being excruciatingly embarrassing. She got over it, but she recalls that AA meeting as being one of the most difficult episodes of her life. She was very proud of the fact that she did confess to her drinking when she really had to, and felt that this led to her continued sobriety.

Joe's Story: Day 20

Joe felt no better when he woke up in the morning. He felt no relief from the antidepressant yet. He was low, hopeless, and thought that the entire programme was a waste of time. He didn't want to go to talk to his counsellor and he didn't want to attend his group sessions.

However, he felt pressurised by the nurses to go, and he went reluctantly and resentfully. He didn't talk in the groups unless he was asked something directly, and then he answered only what he was asked, nothing more. He felt an inner tension and didn't really know how to deal with it.

That afternoon, Joe decided 'to heck with it'. He had had enough of all this endless talk and self-blame. He knew how he had dealt with tension in the past – he gone to the pub. He walked out of the treatment centre in the early afternoon, after the lunchtime roll call, and went straight to the nearest pub. He ordered a pint, and it was the most glorious pint he had tasted in ages.

Within minutes, all the stress and emotions of the previous few weeks disappeared. He ordered another pint, and then another. He hadn't had too much to eat that day or, indeed, over the previous few days, and so he felt the alcohol go to his head. He decided he would just have one more pint and then slip back to the treatment centre. If he was careful enough, no one would notice that he had anything to drink. He was a past master at hiding alcohol consumption and he felt confident that he could get past a few nurses.

He got back to the treatment centre just in time for tea. He was pulled aside by one of the nurses and was confronted about his absence. To Joe's horror, she produced a breathalyser. When he blew a positive reading on the meter, he admitted he had been drinking. He was

211

then sent to an observation bed and the doctor was called to examine him. He felt humiliated, and angry at himself for drinking and at getting caught.

He knew he was in for it. Hopefully his wife wouldn't find out about it because that would mean trouble. He slept the alcohol off, but awoke sweaty and anxious in the middle of the night and didn't get any rest afterwards.

21

Relapse – Prevention

> It is easier to prevent than to recover from an
> episode of relapse.

Recovering from a relapse is not an easy process. It can be painful physically if there is a significant withdrawal to cope with. It can be painful financially if there are direct costs associated with the significant amount of alcohol consumed, or if the relapse leads to missing work or losing clients or customers and there is a loss of direct earnings as a result. It can prove financially disastrous in the long term if the relapse leads to the final straw for a boss or an employer and they decide that they can no longer employ someone who is a potential problem or simply undependable. It can prove emotionally distressing both for the alcohol misuser and especially for their immediate family, who have to endure a round of dashed hopes, recriminations and blame. That emotional turmoil can resolve itself quite quickly if the alcohol misuser settles down to a sober lifestyle.

How to Identify an Impending Relapse

Relapse is an identifiable risk of an addictive disorder. With any disorder, noticing warning signs and symptoms can allow a spouse, family member, friend or employer the opportunity to intervene and prevent the addiction taking a downward spiral. The signs can also be noticed by the alcohol misuser themselves, allowing them the opportunity to reverse things. Beating the addiction and preventing the relapse may be regarded as a team effort, with spouse, family and alcohol misuser all united by the common purpose of preventing a relapse. Of course, if an alcohol misuser makes a decision to drink then ultimately nothing can stop them. But, as is more likely, the alcohol misuser is wavering slightly on the way to recovery. In this case, it is likely that some intervention or call to account is all that is required to diminish the chance of relapse. Relapse is not inevitable, even in the indecisive. Not everyone who wavers actually relapses and there is no such thing as a predetermined outcome.

Warning Signs before a Relapse

These are too numerous to detail comprehensively. However, here is a list of items that can indicate that an alcohol misuser is wavering on their pathway to abstinence and recovery:

- Failure to attend AA meetings
- Failure to visit a counsellor or therapist, or attend an after-care programme
- Failure to take Antabuse or other prescribed addiction medication
- Craving responses to alcohol cues such as adverts
- Going back to places where alcohol is available – pubs, clubs, sports venues
- Meeting up with old drinking friends

- Alcoholic dreams

- Noticing alcohol everywhere

- Wanting to try out alcohol-associated drinks like non-alcoholic beer

- Concealing emotionally charged issues from spouses and family members

- Picking unnecessary arguments with family members to invent an excuse to drink

- Failure to include abstinence plans (such as AA meetings) for periods such as Christmas and holidays, and around events such as celebrations

There are many other warning signs and each individual should compile a list of their own. This can be done in anticipation, which is preferable, or in retrospect, which represents an initial failure in planning.

There is no benefit to challenging an original diagnosis. There is no point in proving that a disorder 'doesn't exist' by drinking. There is no point in 'white knuckling' the addiction, that is, trying it out against the disorder at every available opportunity. Relapse prevention is often a strategic battle, with a series of potential relapses prevented by forethought, awareness and planning. Rarely is it a battle to fight occasional irrational impulses, which can arise for no good reason.

There may be no reason for a relapse, so endless recriminations and searches for meaning in urges to relapse are generally useless. Unless a person has a co-morbid significant psychiatric disorder, then their urge to relapse is mainly present because the addiction is present. Alcohol dependence is a 'friend' for life; the original diagnosis does not go away but is just managed out of prominence. Thus, relapse is part and parcel of the disorder, although it is by no means inevitable.

What to Do to Prevent Relapse

So, if an alcohol misuser decides that they have achieved sobriety and that they would like to avoid relapse in the future, what can they do?

The list of things that can be done is endless, but the list for any one individual may not need to be. However, for everyone, prevention of relapse involves three things:

1. Change in attitude
2. Change in effort
3. Change in action

A change in attitude and a change in effort need to be universal to all those wanting to achieve sobriety. The alcohol misuser must change their *attitude* from being that of the victim or sufferer to one of acceptance and appreciation of their own creation of the situation. They must be willing to take on board other people's perspectives and to surrender long-held singular opinions. They must make a fundamental decision to change, but it may not be necessary to embrace change on day one. Like a young adult leaving home for the first time, they must desire to grow up, and growing up is all about accepting responsibility.

It is unrealistic to hope that a change in attitude is enough. The second thing that must occur to prevent relapse is a change in the level of *effort*. A genuine alteration in attitude is wonderful and hopefully a first step on the road to recovery, but this must be backed up by effort to be successful. A philosophical change alone is an inadequate change; it fails the litmus test of 'intent'. The alcohol misuser must decide that they want to make a genuine effort to change. Sometimes efforts can be made that are deliberately designed to fail: 'I tried, but I knew it would never work.' There is no point in effort without success. And efforts made need to be continuous in order for the addiction to be successfully managed.

The changes in effort and in attitude must be directed in order for them to be effective. This is where we move from universal principles to individual plans. What I will now do is suggest what *actions* can be taken by individuals, according to their drinking pattern and 'type' (these were discussed in Chapter 9).

If you are an *emotional* type of drinker, and your relapse is driven by a significant downturn in mood, then that downturn in mood needs to be treated as well as the relapse itself. At the very least, your relapse needs to be treated with a return to AA and reconnection with an AA sponsor or an addiction counsellor. You also need to receive a degree of mood treatment, with a focus on planning and structuring the day to keep the mind occupied, and it is very helpful to engage in vigorous physical exercise. It may be helpful to attend a meeting of Dual Recovery Anonymous (DRA) (see Appendix). You should avoid any situations or persons that cause emotional stress or that you associate with drinking. Seeing a doctor, therapist or psychiatrist who might advise you about the appropriate treatment for your downturn in mood may be important; if you feel any degree of hopelessness, it may be vital.

If you are a *social* type of drinker, and your relapse is accompanied by a significant degree of anxiety, then some of the above advice applies. At a minimum, your relapse needs to be treated with a return to AA and a reconnection with an AA sponsor or addiction counsellor. The anxiety itself may need to be treated, either with medication or therapy. Engaging in some form of 'distraction therapy' is useful, which is basically keeping busy to avoid drinking or thoughts of drink.

If your drink problem is identified as having its origins in *testing personal control*, then the advice is universal as well as personal. Liaison with AA, perhaps for the first time, is very helpful, as is sharing your thoughts on the reasons for your relapse with a trained addiction counsellor. Keeping a careful plan of each day's activities and scheduling in advance to ensure your avoidance of alcohol-related activities and people is vital.

If you have an *interpersonal-conflict* pattern of drinking, then attendance at AA or a helpful alternative is also vital as a first step. Increasing your insight, which includes admitting to an alcohol counsellor or sponsor that this is your drinking pattern, is also helpful. You should avoid patterns of conflict, such as with a spouse or work colleague, which formerly led you to drink. Engaging in various physical activities, such as swimming or working out in a gym, can be an effective method of getting rid of the stress of interpersonal conflict, without resorting to drinking.

If you are described as a *dedicated* type of drinker, then you must use a lot of effort to prevent a relapse. You should try to redirect your dedication to focus on AA, where attendance at ninety meetings in ninety days may be required. A daily connection with either AA literature or other addiction and abstinence-oriented literature is also helpful. Dedicated drinkers need to fill their time, so filling what was previously drinking time with other activities is important. Dealing with craving, by avoiding both drink-related activities and drink-related friends, as well as developing distraction techniques for combating craving should it arise, is also essential. Anti-craving medication can also be considered in many situations where craving is an issue.

Prevention of relapse by and large means engaging in some form of essential maintenance programme. Not everyone who maintains involvement in a treatment regime actually manages to maintain complete sobriety, but the majority of them do. Not everyone who drops out of a structured programme, be it AA, counselling, rehabilitation or aftercare, is guaranteed an immediate relapse; it's just that they are more likely to relapse.

In terms of treatment, hospital inpatient treatment programmes allow space for physical recovery from withdrawal symptoms, and hopefully allow the alcohol misuser the time, space and encouragement to re-engage in a recovery process. It is vital that the transition from inpatient treatment to outpatient support be managed successfully. The first month after discharge from an inpatient programme is the most dangerous period in terms of relapse. This is when the principles learnt in the programme are put into practice. All the efforts of patient, family, therapists and doctors come to nil if the personal development and recovery guidelines developed while on the programme are not put into practice on departure.

The first month of abstinence is critical. Those who engage with an addiction professional or an addiction programme are far more likely to succeed than those who try to do it themselves. The success rate for those who engage with a recovery group such as AA is between two and five times greater than those who don't seek help, or those who seek help six or more months after the initiation of sobriety. So, in a nutshell, help and support cannot be started early enough.

Each choice in life, but particularly in recovery, is a matter of balancing the negatives and positives with an awareness of the outcomes and consequences of each decision. Relapses occur when either a choice to drink has already been made or there is an impulsive response to a craving-inducing situation. A (deliberate) lack of awareness of the negative consequences of choosing to drink can also lead to relapse. Therapists, doctors and concerned loved ones can help the drinker to become aware of the fact that relapse is a choice and is not inevitable. This makes up a lot of the work in relapse prevention, and emphasis is placed on helping the alcohol misuser to focus on the negative consequences of the decision to drink. The choice not to drink can be made on a daily or hourly basis, and sometimes it is made on a moment-by-moment basis. In these situations, with that degree of indecision and that degree of stress and craving, it is vital for the alcohol misuser to have outside support.

> **It is not easy to learn how to be constantly vigilant; it requires constant effort and constant learning. You can never know enough.**

Case Study: The Princess

Joan could have been regarded as spoilt. She grew up with a loving family and was the eldest of just two children. She was loved by her parents, especially by her father, a charming extravert politician. She got on really well with her younger brother and he loved her back. She went to a religious boarding school and loved it, getting on famously with the other girls and playing sports for the school. She had a rebellious streak, but kept it in check in the constricted atmosphere of the school.

Once she passed her final exams, she was awarded a scholarship to study abroad and persuaded her parents to let her study in California in the US. There, she had a wonderful time and was known as a party girl. She was pretty and she knew it. She began to drink a lot socially. In her college, if you wanted to, there was a party to go to every night. She got in with the social crowd in her class, and she dated the popular boys and the athletes. She had quite a few relationships and got pregnant by one of her boyfriends. She decided to have an abortion and carried on with her partying lifestyle.

After college, she came back home and took up the same lifestyle again. She got a secretarial job and socialised heavily. She met and married a lawyer and set up home in an affluent suburb. She had two children in quick succession. Although she gave up drinking for the first pregnancy, during the second she didn't manage it. She hid her drinking from her hardworking spouse.

With nothing to do except look after the two babies, she began drinking during the day and still drank with her meal in the evenings. Eventually she was drinking from 10.00 a.m. until 6.00 p.m. everyday, but managed to keep it secret. She was careful to purchase her drink from a variety of different off-licences. After the children were sent to school, she had more time on her hands and took up with her former school friends to socialise during the day.

Eventually her relationship with her husband got into trouble as he realised what was going on behind his back. He separated from her and their children were sent to boarding school. He had enough money to support her in a well-off lifestyle and she continued to drink using her allowance money. She began to suffer significant mood swings, and became irritable and depressed at times. She resented her ex-husband's stability after their split.

She was eventually brought into rehabilitation by her friends and her brother, who felt she would soon lose custody of her children altogether if she didn't straighten up. While in treatment, she discovered she had an underlying depression that fuelled her drinking and that required treatment with an antidepressant.

After discharge she relapsed within one month and came off her antidepressant medication. She was re-admitted six months later, and this time engaged with the treatment more intensively. She stuck with her medication, which dealt effectively with her depression. At the time of discharge, however, her husband decided to sue for custody of the children and she was obliged to get into a royal battle with him, which soured their cordial relationship.

She reluctantly engaged with AA, but did not like following the twelve steps. She found the sober lifestyle boring and longed for more excitement. Her counsellor feared for her and eventually she relapsed and required another admission before embracing recovery fully. She eventually achieved recovery, but lost her children along the way. It was a painful price to pay.

Joe's Story: Day 21

This was a tough day. Of course, the staff all knew about his drinking and he was confronted about it immediately after breakfast.

As it was the weekend, he was reviewed by the doctor on call, who felt that he wouldn't go into withdrawal and so he was not confined to bed. He felt awful – hungover, depressed and guilty. He was able to drink some water and get some food into his stomach. He was automatically suspended from the treatment programme and was strongly encouraged by the staff to tell his wife what had happened.

He was told that there would be a full review of his case by the treatment team that afternoon. He was aware that, in general, those who were caught drinking were asked to leave the treatment centre. He desperately didn't want that to happen. He felt he was on his last chance. He drummed up the courage and called his wife to tell her what had happened. She was very upset but, instead of giving out to him, she cried down the phone and hung up. From Joe's point of view, this was worse than if she had lost her temper.

He spent the afternoon in a haze of depression and guilt. He asked himself continuously why he had given in and drank the previous day. He was inclined to blame his depression. But then, a minute later, it occurred to him that he was copping out; in fact, he had drank simply because he wanted to.

He spent the afternoon in alternating states of guilt about his drinking and sheer terror about what would happen if he was thrown off the programme. He was certain that if he was discharged, his marriage and, indeed, his life would be over. Why had he done it? He was standing with one foot over a cliff. He decided that if he got one more chance, he wouldn't ruin it; he would absolutely give up alcohol for life.

He spent the night in a restless state, tormenting himself about his bad decisions and hoping against hope that he would get another chance.

22

Craving – What It Is and How to Fight It

> Craving is a dominant cause of relapse.

What is craving? Craving is one of the worst threats to recovery from the disease of alcohol addiction and can be a significant factor in an alcohol misuser relapsing to alcohol after a period of sobriety.

To crave alcohol is to be obsessed with it. When someone craves alcohol, they think about it constantly, they imagine the effects of alcohol on them and they feel a compulsion to drink. It is the great deception of craving that drinking alcohol will relieve craving for it. Of course, drinking alcohol does relieve craving, but the craving will return later, and be stronger and more overwhelming.

Craving for alcohol is more than a simple low-key desire for alcohol. Many people without a drinking problem will say, 'I'd love a glass of wine' or 'Isn't it pleasant to have a beer on a summer's day.' That isn't craving; that is simply an anticipated pleasure. There is a vast difference between a desire for alcohol and a need for it.

In alcohol misusers, what is experienced as a desire for alcohol is in fact a need for alcohol, appropriately masked. The disease of alcoholism is like a snake slithering silently in the long grass, waiting for the unguarded moment to strike and inject its venom into the victim. While that might seem melo-dramatic, this represents the experience of a lot of alcohol misusers; they can relapse to alcohol at any unguarded and unpredictable moment.

Craving is the mechanism through which alcoholism catches its victims, and, just like snake venom, its strike can be fatal.

How Do You Gauge Craving?

Craving can be assessed, partly by a questionnaire. In the last fifteen years, craving has been assessed in alcohol misusers through the use of the Obsessive-Compulsive Drinking Scale. This scale focuses on the degree of thinking an alcohol misuser engages in regarding alcohol and the degree of compulsion to drink that he or she feels.

It is a very useful scale, but it only assesses the conscious, and not the unconscious, aspect of craving. Craving can be uncon-scious as well as conscious, and both aspects can be prominent in causing a person to relapse to drinking after achieving sobri-ety, and, indeed, in their inability to give up drink in the first place.

Unconscious Craving

A number of years ago, I conducted an experiment on a group of long-term abstinent alcohol misusers. I was attempting to characterise the area of the brain responsible for craving. I devel-oped a craving framework to apply to alcohol misusers while they underwent a brain scan called a functional Magnetic Reso-nance Imaging (fMRI) scan. Each subject was asked to look at two different sets of video images while undergoing the scan, one set being of neutral images unrelated to alcohol and the other being related to drinking and alcohol. They were asked to rate their subjective feelings of craving for alcohol while look-ing at the videos.

When the scans were analysed, I found that almost all of the subjects' brains 'lit up' in the areas of the brain related to emotions as they watched the alcohol-related images, and didn't light up when watching the neutral images. However, only half of the alcohol misusers identified any sensation of craving when looking at the alcohol-related images. That would suggest that the other half had the brain reaction to the images of alcohol, but didn't have the feeling of craving. The craving in these individuals was unconscious.

Many alcohol misusers have stated to me that sometimes they slip without warning. They may be just walking past a pub and they just 'end up' inside. They end up drinking a beer before they know what they are doing. If they pass an off-licence, they find themselves buying a bottle of vodka and drinking it even before they realise what they are doing. They report no sensation of craving, but they end up acting as if they have severe craving.

Either all of them are lying, or else they genuinely have no sensation of craving before they relapse. In other words, 'It just happens.' I have heard that so many times that I believe it has to be true for those people at that time. But clearly something is happening unconsciously, or else people wouldn't end up drinking despite their professed desire not to drink. So there must be some sort of internal division, a tension between unconscious forces driving them to drink and conscious forces trying to make them stop.

The aim of the battle with an unconscious force is to make it conscious. The battle with unconscious craving is to increase your awareness of it and then to fight it. I'll deal with how to battle conscious craving later on this chapter, but first it is important to understand the circumstances that bring craving on. That way, it becomes easier to recognise.

What Brings on Craving?

Craving can be brought on by many different events or thoughts. First, craving is brought on by drinking. The closer an alcohol misuser is to their last drink, the higher the amount of craving they have to deal with. The opposite is also true – the longer ago an alcohol misuser had their last drink, the lesser the craving. The level of craving falls over time, even if it falls at a different pace for each person. That is why relapse is most common in the first period post withdrawal. Craving eventually fades altogether and a lot of alcohol misusers find they don't have to deal with craving if they have achieved a significant period of abstinence. This can be weeks or months, but it eventually happens for every drinker, however long the duration of addiction.

Craving can be brought on by 'sensational cues' or reminders of alcohol. It can be brought on by the sensation of alcohol, that is, by the taste, smell, sound, sight or touch of alcohol. A drop of wine on the tongue can trigger a craving; the smell of alcohol in a pub can set it off; the sounds associated with drinking, such as beer being poured into a glass, can trigger craving; and the sight of an alcohol advertisement can cause a relapse.

Craving can be brought on by 'internal cues' or reminders. The desire for alcohol can be stimulated by asking an alcohol misuser to recall their last most enjoyable drinking episode and to describe it in loving detail. It is not too difficult to get an alcohol misuser to describe the various sensations they had when last drinking, and that internal reminder can be enough to promote a significant bout of craving.

Craving can be brought on by stress. Alcohol researchers can induce craving by placing volunteers in a stressful situation such as asking them to make a speech or placing them in an exam situation. Eliciting a stress reaction, which can be assessed by various techniques such as measuring the extent of sweating, often generates a significant desire to drink in alcohol misusers, even abstinent ones.

Craving can be brought on by emotions, especially negative ones. These emotions can be feelings of depression, feelings of anxiety, anger at individuals in a conflict situation or occasionally even positive feelings like satisfaction and even joy. Many people drink on their emotions, and it is no surprise that these emotions can induce craving, even in abstinent alcohol misusers.

AA makes reference to 'people, places and things' associated with alcohol, which cause relapse to alcohol. In fact, particular people, places or things don't cause relapse; craving, either conscious or unconscious, induced by those associations, causes the relapse.

It is certainly possible to avoid all the sensational associations with alcohol. It may involve not going near friends who drink, avoiding pubs, avoiding advertisements associated with alcohol and staying away from any alcohol-related situations. It may be necessary to consciously strive not to think about alcohol and not to remember any of the thoughts associated with drinking. While it may not be possible to avoid any negative emotions or stress, it may be necessary to learn how to deal with stress in a more positive way, and not to drink on it.

Craving Presenting as Something Else

Not every feeling of craving is explicit or even clear. There are many feelings, situations and actions which the alcohol misuser might not associate with craving, but which are evidence of craving at some level. It is often only in retrospect that the influence of craving can be identified, and only in retrospect that feelings once thought to be something else can truly be understood as craving.

Craving Can Present as Depression

A patient of mine described a feeling that he had one month after achieving sobriety. He was in a pub with a friend after work on a Friday. His friend had a few beers, while my patient had a mineral water. The next morning he woke up and had a strong sensation of depression. He felt low and hopeless, and felt a tremendous drop in his energy. It took him a few days to shake off the feeling and he felt very uncertain about what it was all about.

On reflection, and after discussion, he came to the conclusion that he had had a bout of craving, and that it was too early in his sobriety for him to spend time with someone who was drinking in a pub. He, however, denied having any sensation of desire for alcohol and denied that he was in danger of relapse. There was nothing else going on his life that would have justified him suffering a bout of depression. At this time he was focusing on his recovery only.

Craving Can Present as Irritability

A lot of people in recovery will note their own irritability. They, and especially those around them, will see a tendency to pick arguments or to turn a difference of opinion into an argument. They will show a desire to enter into conflict about the smallest of things. It is quite possible for the conflict to escalate into a full blazing row, and the row ending with the alcohol misuser walking out and going off to have a drink to 'settle their nerves'.

While a family member may state that it was obvious that the alcohol misuser wanted a drink and was provoking the row in order to justify that to themselves, this is not how the alcohol misuser views it. The alcohol misuser has an intense personal feeling of justifiable anger and that they have a right to express their feelings, despite the outcome. It can be difficult, when in the grip of a strong emotion, to step outside the feeling and understand its origin.

The origin of the anger and the irritability is a craving for alcohol. If an emotion ends up as a 'cause' of alcohol consumption, you can bet that the desire for alcohol underlies that emotion.

While many alcohol misusers would disagree, it is only with constant repetition of particular episodes that they may be able to see the pattern for themselves. It is often worth giving feedback to the alcohol misuser about what the cause of their irritability is, because they may simply not be able to see it for themselves.

Craving Can Present as Anxiety

Anxiety can manifest itself in many forms. I have already discussed anxiety as a component of withdrawal, and it can be very powerful. But post-withdrawal craving for alcohol can present as anxiety. The desire for alcohol can present as a strong sense of fear coupled with a feeling of acute distress, leading to knots in the stomach, sweating, tightness in the chest and a feeling of needing to 'get out of here'. These feelings can result in a relapse to alcohol. Obviously the return to drinking is justified along the lines that it was the only way to get rid of the feeling, if only for a short while.

It is difficult to say with this degree of anxiety whether the independent anxiety or the desire for alcohol comes first. It is also difficult to say which has influenced the other and which has caused the other. However, whether the anxiety or the craving comes first, the outcome is the same: the alcohol misuser drinks again.

How to Deal with Craving

Clearly, in order to decrease conscious or unconscious craving, all senses must be deprived of alcohol-related cues, preferably for a very long time. All tastes (for example, sherry trifle), all smells (for example, a friend's glass of wine), all sounds (such as a music jingle from a beer advertisement), all sights (for example, the arrangement of bottles behind a bar), and all touches (such as touching a beer label on the bottle) must be removed from the alcohol misuser's world. While this may prove practically impossible, it can be partially achieved with some planning and many potential relapses can be prevented.

There are a number of ways to deal with conscious craving, once it is identified as such. Here is a list of possible interventions:

- Distraction: TV, Radio, music, games, conversation, change of activity

- Relaxation: tai chi, yoga, muscle relaxation, deep breathing, meditation, massage

- Reaching out for help: calling a hotline, using an online addiction chat room

- Going to an AA meeting

- Exercise: going to the gym, walking, competitive sport, cycling, swimming

- Talking to a personal friend, sponsor or therapist

- Guided imagery: thinking of the negative consequences of drinking and where drinking led you

- Contradiction of automatic thoughts: identifying the thoughts underlying the craving – 'What thoughts are going through my head right now?' – and fighting them rationally

- Coping flashcards: preparing craving cards in advance, with affirmations written on them such as 'This will pass if I give it time.' Then reading them at times of craving

> **Understanding and fighting craving can be a major part of recovery.**

Case Study: The Anxious, Craving Alcohol Misuser

Max was a 39-year-old plumber and he had been an alcohol misuser for at least ten years. He was an only child and, despite being indulged by his caring parents, he grew up shy and insecure. He left home and set up his own household and business, but kept in close contact with his extended family. He had few friends outside the family and, because of his shyness, he found it difficult to get to know women.

His drinking escalated during his twenties and he found he couldn't socialise without alcohol. When he did meet a woman in whom he was interested he had to get drunk to talk to her. Even if he started a relationship with someone, he would feel too insecure to handle it when he was sober and would usually end it after a short time.

Eventually his drinking escalated to the point where he was drinking a bottle of spirits every two days, and he was permanently drunk at weekends. He recognised his difficulties and entered into AA to get help. He would achieve sobriety for a week or two, but never for any length of time. He went into rehabilitation on one occasion and stayed for two weeks, but he found the atmosphere too difficult to handle because he got anxious in group situations. He relapsed soon after discharge.

He went through one further failed rehab before entering a different rehabilitation programme with proper psychiatric backup. Once there, his psychiatrist diagnosed an anxiety disorder as well as alcoholism, and he was given appropriate medication for it. Gradually he began to experience the benefits of the treatment and, although he believed he really didn't have full alcohol dependence, he began to feel the benefits of the overall treatment. After discharge, he reluctantly returned to AA and agreed to remain sober because a relapse to alcohol might interfere with his anti-anxiety medication. He had terrible bouts of craving, particularly in early abstinence. He would sit out the episodes of craving with his dog for company. He would occasionally call his AA sponsor for help, but, by and large, he did it by himself.

He improved sufficiently over two years that I was able to get him off the anti-anxiety medication. At the same time, he adopted a healthier lifestyle and took up walking as a form of exercise and therapy. He decided to remain sober for the foreseeable future in order to prevent a return of his anxiety symptoms, which he recognised as being behind the alcohol problem in the first place. He refused to consider giving up alcohol for life, but, after having dealt with very bad bouts of craving and anxiety, he decided to stay off alcohol for the present. He realised he was much happier sober than drunk.

Joe's Story: Day 22

This was decision day. After breakfast, Joe had a meeting with the doctor. He was asked about his motivation to stop drinking. He stated that he really wanted to stop drinking, that he absolutely realised just what was at stake. He admitted he had felt depressed the day he drank, but that he didn't want to use that as an excuse.

The doctor told him that he was getting one more chance and that, if he gave a guarantee not to drink and if he would take the medication Antabuse, he could resume participation in the programme. The doctor stated that he felt that Joe was still depressed and this may have contributed to his relapse.

Joe was overjoyed at being given another chance. He thanked the doctor and resolved once and for all to put alcohol behind him. He still felt down, but also felt an immense sense of relief and actually burst into tears. He hadn't cried properly in years and this was a surprise to him.

He attended a group session and was somewhat surprised at the group's attitude. He expected that they would feel pleased for him about being let stay on the programme, but he learned that a lot of the group felt that he should have been discharged to teach him a lesson. While they acknowledged that he was feeling depressed, they did not absolve him from responsibility for his drinking. They gave him a hard time about some of his attitudes and said that, instead of looking to blame others, he needed to look a lot more at himself.

He came out of the group session quite depressed and wondering what lay in store for him with his wife. She still hadn't called or visited him.

23

Recovery Means a New Life

> Recovery is a completely new life; a rebirth.

It is very easy for an outsider to say, 'Just give up drinking.' And it's very easy for an outsider to say that that's all there is to it. But anyone who has ever tried to give up drinking will tell you that it isn't as simple as that; it is much bigger and much more complicated than that. The struggle to give up alcohol starts with the initiation and maintenance of sobriety. That is extremely difficult in itself, as the preceding chapters detail. But, as recovery progresses, as the period of sobriety extends from hours into days and even into weeks, it becomes clear that sobriety is simply not enough. While sobriety is vital for the start of recovery, true recovery means:

1. A complete reassessment of all your priorities in life

2. A complete re-evaluation of all your relationships in life

3. A complete reinvestment in your primary occupation in life

4. A complete rediscovery of all your goals in life

Your Priorities in Life

What are your priorities in life? If you take a pen and paper and write down what you try to prioritise in your life, you might come up with something like this:

1. My family life

2. My work life

3. My social and recreational life

4. My spiritual life

But if you look at what a drinker has in fact been prioritising prior to recovery, the truth looks something like this:

1. My drinking life

2. My family life, my work life and my recreational life all feed into the above, and I try not to let them interfere too much with priority one (and I don't have much of a spiritual life)

As the period of sobriety extends, it becomes clearer to the drinker that they really got their priorities screwed up during their years of drinking. It becomes more and more obvious to them that they had allowed alcohol to take over their lives. The longer this has gone on, the longer it can take for them to get their sense of direction back. With sobriety, that direction and purpose should be thought through and should become a new blueprint for life.

It is quite possible to sit down with a pen and paper, and write down just what your new priorities in life are. Start with the idea that there are only so many hundred or so many thousand days left in life (unfortunately true), and ask yourself how you might wish to spend those few hundred or few thousand days. What is the portion of time you would like to spend on each of the major areas of life: family, work, social and spiritual? If we hold on to the concept that our time on earth is indeed limited, then it is easier to establish the need to prioritise aspects of our lives.

I have wandered around graveyards looking at the inscriptions on the gravestones. I have seen many tributes along the lines of 'Loving spouse, caring father, affectionate grandfather' and occasionally a reference to an enduring life interest or profession such as sportsman or doctor. I have never seen a reference on a gravestone to 'Lifelong drinker' or 'Unredeemable alcoholic', even if that were the truth. I can't believe that is how anyone would like to be remembered.

It is not easy to come up with definitive priorities in life; things are rarely straightforward and careful thought is often required. If you prioritise playing golf and getting your handicap down to single figures, does this have an impact on how much time you might be able to spend with your children? If you choose to prioritise work achievements and becoming the CEO of a company, what impact might this have on your marriage and your spouse? As we establish what our priorities are in life, we need to keep the needs of those close to us in mind.

Your Relationships

It is true to say that relationships in life are everything. It only takes the loss of a relationship, either through death, separation or drifting apart, for us to appreciate the depth of this statement. It is not easy to prioritise relationships when alcohol is your real priority. Thus, on achieving sobriety, the main goal should be the revival of any relationships that had been disrupted because of drink. Of course, if relationships have been lost for good, your priority shifts to making amends for past deficiencies and to ensuring that future relationships don't suffer the same problems.

Relationships often heal when the cause of the hurt is gone. It is still amazing to me how many seemingly broken marriages and family relationships actually heal with sobriety, time and good intentions. The first six months of sobriety are often telling in terms of relationship outcomes, and things tend to sink or swim in early recovery. The clear majority of relationships survive and thrive, and a significant minority fail. In the latter situations the damage done is too great.

It is vital in recovery to focus on relationships and ensure that development and enrichment of relationships is your first priority. This will not come as easily as it sounds on paper, and family and spousal relationships may need time to deal with a lot of anger and recrimination before balance and harmony can be restored.

It is not adequate to simply restore personal and family relationships, and to aim to have things exactly as they used to be. It is important to focus on ways to enhance relationships and to develop them in ways that were not considered even prior to the addiction. In recovery, while the first question to ask yourself everyday is 'What can I do for my recovery today?', the second should be 'What can I do for those around me today?', and you should work from there. This is not simply a matter of spending money on or time with people, though that is of course appreciated. It is a matter of deciding that the betterment of your interpersonal relationships is the best way to enhance your life in recovery.

Ten ways to enhance family relationships:

1. Think of your family deliberately first thing every morning

2. Make sure to do one specific thing per day for your family members

3. Surprise your family members with a gift or present each week

4. Organise a family outing at least once a month

5. Talk about individual birthdays in advance of the day, and plan for them

6. Tell each family member that you love them, every day

7. If you get extra money, ask the family what they would like to spend it on

8. Make sure there is one special family meal every week

9. At the end of each day, ask each family member how their day was

10. If possible, go on at least one family holiday together every year

If your immediate family consists of a spouse or partner only, then the same effort should apply. You need to demonstrate beyond words that alcohol is no longer your priority and that the changes you are making are intended to be permanent.

The advantage of prioritising relationships is that it not only assures family members about the genuineness your recovery, it also enhances everyone's quality of life. If a family or a relationship is not damaged beyond repair, then that family or relationship cannot fail to respond to your efforts. Initially your efforts may be met with a negative response, for example, 'I don't see this going anywhere' or 'How many times have I heard this before?' If you are met with this kind of response, you can react in one of two ways: by accepting defeat and saying, 'It's not worth the effort; see how everything I suggest is rebuffed' or by seeing it as a challenge worth taking – 'This only goes to show how much work I have to put in.' It may take a significant amount of time and enthusiasm before a positive response is achieved, but a positive response is guaranteed if your efforts are sustained and genuine. Any resistance to your efforts may be seen as the price to be paid for all the problems, hurt and anger that you caused through your addiction.

Improved relationships will sustain recovery and make it worthwhile. But if the structures don't hold, if your primary relationship breaks up or if your relationship with your children is damaged beyond repair, then other priorities need to be established.

Your Primary Occupation

As mentioned in previous chapters, a job often defines your self-regard, and social and economic status. The majority of people care about the jobs they do, and want to be good at their job and to be recognised for that.

In the context of alcoholism, a person's primary occupation can be lost. It can be put under threat, it can be taken away fully or an entire professional avenue can be destroyed for life. Often, as your alcohol addiction grows, your job is replaced by alcohol as a priority and your job performance inevitably slips.

Often it takes a serious threat to an alcohol misuser's job before he or she takes notice. A client might have to complain about a bad job performance to get the alcohol misuser to see beyond their addiction and appreciate that something is wrong. A boss may have to haul the alcohol misuser over the coals and state that they will be held accountable for the poor performance before the alcohol misuser realises that there is a problem. The alcohol misuser may lose a significant number of customers and suffer a big drop in income before they see that they have an addiction. For some, it may take being fired from a job, or even multiple jobs, before they truly understand their problem.

So, in recovery, a job can assume more importance than before. An alcohol misuser may need the income more then ever to help with the losses incurred during their drinking years. A job may provide significant daily distraction and occupation during periods of craving. Work colleagues can provide emotional support and understanding. An occupation may provide the person in recovery with crucial self-esteem at difficult times, and enable them to regain a sense of purpose in life and a reason to maintain sobriety.

Not everyone decides that their job is the most important thing in their life. It is quite possible to turn around after a period of addiction and realise that it is time to give up work and discover other aspects of life. You may realise that it is time to get away from the boss, the deadlines, the projects, the office politics, the stresses and the daily grind, and to simply quit.

It may be essential for a significant period, say, six months, that you attend AA every day and that a return to full-time employment is postponed for that time. A volunteer job, such as helping the homeless, engaging in charity work or helping with animal welfare, may provide the correct balance of distraction, emotional return and increase in feelings of self-worth, as well as time-out to engage in the recovery process. This can be followed by a return to original employment, hopefully with a renewed interest and zest for the job.

What can be disastrous is a return to work too soon in the recovery process. If work was a considerable source of tension and if work stress or circumstances encouraged drinking in the first place, then a premature return to work could lead to a quick relapse to alcohol. Quite apart from possibly not having enough time to attend counsellors, aftercare programmes or even AA meetings, a premature return to work might lead to disillusionment on the part of the alcohol misuser and disappointment on the employer's side. That disappointment could stem from the alcohol misuser's early relapse to alcohol or a simple lack of interest in or enthusiasm for the job. The alcohol misuser's disillusionment can stem from realising the difficulties they might have caused at work because of their addiction and the concern that they might not be as interested in their job as they hoped.

Of course, time out from an occupation to recover from an addiction may not be possible because of economic pressure. Quite simply, it is better to be quietly dissatisfied in a reasonably paid job than satisfied in an unpaid job, if the household depends on it for income.

The decision to quit a job and move on should really be made after a significant number of months in recovery, maybe even a year or two. Early recovery (the first three to six months) is not the time to make serious life-changing decisions about where to live and where to work because the primary focus of early recovery should be on recovery itself and nothing more. Major life decisions, particularly in relation to work and significant relationships, need to be thought through and arrived at over a long period of time. Impulsive decisions are generally wrong ones and impulsivity is one of the hallmarks of addiction. Simply put, don't quit a job or quit working during early recovery because change at this time is a distraction from the only business in town: recovery.

Your Aims and Goals in Life

Having established your priorities, laid the foundation for focusing on your relationships and (hopefully) re-established the importance of your occupation, it is time to make a list of your aims and goals in life. In order to find out what your aims and goals in life are, it is helpful to put them down on paper. However, your list should consist of what your goals were, what they have changed into in the recovery process and how you might go about achieving them. A simple list might be drawn up under the following headings: original aims, recovery aims and achievable goals.

A goal is a plan to change an aim into reality. The aim is the ambition and the goal is the direction. It is vital to have aims because, if there are no aims, there is just drift. It is very common in the period of immediate sobriety to feel lost to a degree, uncertain and insecure about the future. So, in a situation of change, developing aims allows you a degree of control over your long-term future which might not have been present previously. Ultimately, your aims determine your course in life.

Members of AA can accuse others in the group of being 'dry drunks'. I have often asked what that term means. Sometimes it means that the accuser simply doesn't like the person he or she is referring to. Sometimes, however, the term means that a person has entered into sobriety and is no longer drinking, but acts, feels and thinks like an alcohol misuser. The recovery process is in stagnation and the subject never moves on.

One of the ways to move on is to *write it all down*. Writing it down means that the back of the brain is engaged in the process and it is harder to get away with half truths and evasions. The capacity for self-delusion is limited when things are in writing. It is vital to focus on the changes in thinking that must occur because of the recovery process. If each aspect of life is examined, and aspirations relating to that area re-evaluated in the light of recovery, it is inevitably altered. By examining all areas of your life and constantly asking yourself, 'Is this good for my recovery?' it is possible to identify strategies that are good and ones that are not.

It is important to recognise that recovery is not just about giving up alcohol; it is a systematic revolution in thinking and outlook. Finding ways to translate the change in thinking into practical benefits is vital. Most people in recovery only begin to change their way of thinking late into the recovery process, perhaps because the whole process of sobriety and recovery is enough for them to be thinking about. However, recovery is a process that should begin with sobriety and end in a completely different way of life.

How to translate general aims in life into achievable goals requires significant effort and concentration. After writing down your aims, recovery aims and achievable goals, it is a matter of constantly referring back to them, and constantly updating and modifying them.

If the new life ain't better than the old life, it won't last.

Case Study: The Hardworking Alcohol Misuser

Peter was a pharmaceutical company engineer, who worked in a large local factory. He had a working wife who was in another branch of the same company, and two children who attended boarding school.

He was essentially a pleasant man and somewhat of a loner. Over the years, he became isolated from the day-to-day running of his household. He played golf, a major distraction, and was absent from the house over most weekends. He drank socially, with his golfing friends at the weekends and with his friends on Saturdays. He got into the habit of drinking alone in the evenings while going over his work papers. He also drank wine with his evening meals.

After ten or so years, he was drinking a full bottle of wine by himself each evening and he was drinking up to eight pints of lager with his friends on both days of the weekend. He became increasingly estranged from his family and a series of family arguments began, mainly as a result of his irritable behaviour towards his children and his inability to focus on family needs with his wife.

After a particularly aggressive argument with his wife, and after he had threatened to put his eldest child out of the house for a trivial offence, he agreed to seek treatment. He entered into rehabilitation with a significant hangover, having gone on a bender the night before to 'ease the pain' of entry into treatment.

He fought against the concept of having an alcohol problem initially, but gradually began to agree with the family that he had a problem with alcohol, not just with tensions in the household. After a particularly clear and lucid family meeting, where he began to perceive just how bad things had gotten at home, he resolved to attempt to address his problem.

He began to attend AA meetings and to share at the meetings. He explored his relationships with his wife and his two children, and found himself wanting in relation to his behaviour. He resolved to work on his relationships within the family and humbly apologised for his previous behaviour. He found he had to deal with very significant cravings for alcohol, and asked his wife for help in getting rid of the available alcohol in their home.

One month after leaving treatment, he was made redundant in the recession. He coped very well with it and didn't relapse to alcohol. He spent time with his family. He decided to go in a completely different direction and went back to night school to study social work. His wife was very supportive of this move.

His family, while never being like the Waltons, settled into a new routine, with Peter spending much more time at home and less time out with his friends. He progressed well in his recovery and was still attending AA regularly six months later. His golf handicap had gotten a lot worse. He also was a lot happier.

Joe's Story: Day 23

Today Joe had a meeting with his counsellor and his wife joined them at the meeting. She told of her disappointment at his relapse. However, after talking with the doctor, who had some understanding about how depression could affect Joe's thinking, she said she was willing to give him another chance when he was discharged. However, he would have to live by himself for a period of three months before she would let him back into the family home. He could come and go as he pleased, but he would have to spend the nights outside the home.

Joe was enormously relieved that she still wanted anything to do with him, but he was also hurt and angry that she wanted him to move out, even temporarily. However, he decided to keep his mouth shut and agree with the plan, despite his disappointment. They spent the rest of the meeting planning just what he would do on his discharge from the treatment centre, as his time here was coming to an end.

He felt daunted at the prospect of moving out of home and of starting to live on his own. He wondered whether he could remain sober on his own. He resolved to do whatever he could, including going to AA meetings or to any other recovery programme, to get back into the family home. He would do whatever it took to prove to everyone, his family, his wife and himself, that he could do it.

Despite feeling down, Joe began for the first time in a long time to feel a sense of hope about his own situation. He had a course of action planned and, if he kept to that plan, he could get out of the rut he was in.

24

Making Amends

> It is necessary to review yourself in the cold light of sobriety.

Sobriety is just the beginning of recovery. It may be necessary to spend a lifetime in recovery and never quite get there, wherever 'there' is. I have already mentioned that there is no real end point. The main thing is that the journey through life is a sober one. No alcohol misuser ever achieves true recovery; that would mean they never had an addiction in the first place. So, true and complete recovery is an aspiration, not a destination.

With a disease like cancer, a 'cure' is defined as non-relapse to the cancer within five years of diagnosis. In the world of alcoholism, no one ever achieves a 'cure', even though they might be ten years into recovery. The very threat of relapse is the threat that keeps the alcohol misuser on the straight and narrow. As mentioned in Chapter 1, the instant an alcohol misuser proclaims themselves 'cured', they sow the seeds of their next relapse.

I have met alcohol misusers who have relapsed after achieving up to twenty-three years of sobriety, although I have to say it is a very unusual thing for someone to relapse after such a long time in recovery. It is far more common for an alcohol misuser to relapse in their first month of recovery rather than in their 486th! Some long-term research into alcoholism has suggested that after achieving, say, four years of sobriety the chances of relapse are very slim. My own research and experience are in agreement with this. After a while, the majority of alcohol misusers who achieve a significant degree of sobriety also reach a reasonable state of recovery, and then manage to keep their sobriety going. But how do you change sobriety into recovery?

Making a Moral Inventory

Let's take a look at two important steps in the AA twelve-step process:

- Step 4: Made a searching and fearless moral inventory of ourselves

- Step 8: Made a list of all persons we have harmed, and became willing to make amends to them all

It is very unusual for any person to 'make a searching and fearless moral inventory' of themselves. We, as humans, are generally selfish. We often act in our own best interests, even if this is at the expense of others. We think of ourselves first and then of those around us. We are frequently capable of acts of kindness, and of helping others, but often only when we have looked after ourselves first. It is possible to argue that selfishness is necessary for survival as individuals and, indeed, as a species.

Thus, the idea of making a searching and fearless moral inventory of ourselves is not a pleasant one. It requires a significant degree of effort and an even greater degree of self-understanding and self-criticism. Not only is it an embarrassing task, it is actually a very difficult task or set of tasks. It involves stripping away all the layers of self-delusion that underlie a large amount of our thoughts and actions, and then judging ourselves accordingly: 'Did she leave me because she was an obnoxious b**** or did she leave me because I was not trying hard enough in the relationship?'; 'Did I agree to meet my old friend because it was a nice thing to do or because I thought he might help me up in my career?'; 'Did I refuse to go out to dinner with my spouse in order to make her angry and disappointed at me, and then use her anger as another excuse to drink?'; 'Is it possible I am that selfish and manipulative?'

How do you go about making a moral inventory? One simple way to start would be to write down a description of the worst thing that you did while intoxicated. It is probably not that difficult for you to identify what that thing was. What is significantly more difficult is to take the time to think about it while sober and then to write down a description of it. In order to complete the exercise, you should ask yourself the following questions: 'What was my real motivation in doing what I did?'; 'Was my motivation related to trying my hardest to get a drink or was it less selfish than that?'

Another way to make a moral inventory is to look at the major areas of your life and ask:

1. What percentage of your life is focused on your primary and family relationships, and what percentage is focused on alcohol?

2. What percentage of your life is focused on your occupation and what percentage is focused on alcohol?

3. What percentage of your life is focused on your social and recreational life, and what percentage is focused on alcohol?

In summary, how much time do you spend thinking about drinking alcohol, drinking alcohol and recovering from drinking alcohol instead of spending time with your family and friends, on other hobbies or on your work?

Here are other ways that you can take a moral inventory of yourself:

- By asking a close family member, work colleague or friend to assess your answers to the three questions detailed above, and to answer the three questions on your behalf

- By asking yourself the three questions last thing at night in relation to the focus of that day's activities

- By asking yourself about the most offensive acts you have committed that have hurt loved ones. The very act of listing those offences and realising their negative impact on your loved ones should be enough to bolster your commitment to sobriety

Gaining perspective is the most difficult thing of all. Understanding that there may be an alternative view to your long-held view is a difficult and tortuous process. While some alcohol misusers are lucky, and their shift in perspective is achieved through a one-off process of listening to others and appreciating that their perspective is the correct one, most alcohol misusers do not gain such a degree of insight that quickly. It is the repetition of the above process of self-analysis, daily, weekly, monthly, that achieves the shift in perception. Empathy with others and gaining understanding of your own condition will allow you to move from sobriety into recovery.

While sobriety must come first, as the above process cannot work on an intoxicated mind, it can only be sustained through constantly reviewing and updating your moral inventory.

The Next Stage: Making Amends

The next stage involves going beyond a fearless self-examination and identifying all those people you have offended over the years, becoming willing to make amends and then actually making amends (without doing harm). That is a tall order.

To approach this, it can help to draw up a list of those people you have hurt through your alcoholism. Next to the name of each person, write down just how they were offended or list the offences caused to that person. The next step is to go and apologise to each person individually, a humiliating but necessary process. You may need to go one step further and spend time with a particular person or make financial reparation. It may involve asking someone what he or she would feel to be an adequate way of making a true apology.

While in the midst of your addiction, you probably developed a sixth sense when dealing with others, and that sixth sense told you just how far you could push other people in order to feed your addiction. Unfortunately, at this stage, you have probably pushed other people about as far as they can be pushed and further. So, when making amends, you have to appreciate that you have probably pushed people beyond the limit.

You must now use your ability to read other people in order to make it work for the other person this time. You must get past the layers of mistrust that you have created and show your sincere commitment to change. It is worth remembering, as you approach others to make amends, that sometimes relationships have been destroyed beyond repair and this must be accepted.

To make amends, you will have to approach people sensitively. If your apology will only serve to make an offended person more upset, the apology shouldn't be performed. An apology is not a matter of words; it is a matter of finding a way to apologise that is appropriate to the person offended or the offence committed. Making amends is not a matter of making promises for the future, but a matter of demonstrating that changes have been and will be made.

Ways to make amends to an offended person:

1. Make a verbal or written apology

2. Let them know what you have done to achieve sobriety and to try to make amends

3. Let them know what changes you have made in other aspects of your life

4. Make an offer to make amends in whatever way the other person wants

5. If necessary, offer cash; do not make an offer of cash if it is not available

6. Offer to make a donation to a charity they nominate; do not offer if it can't be done

7. Offer to spend time with them, if they would like that

8. Offer to do some work for them, if that would be helpful

9. Let them know how to establish contact with you and let them make the choice whether to contact you or not

10. If you are in regular contact with the offended person (e.g. a spouse with regard to legal or child care issues), demonstration of change is more powerful than a promise to make amends

11. Never underestimate the capacity of people to forgive, but only if the apology is sincere

During their drinking years, an alcohol misuser does not mature. An addiction prevents the normal process of growing up from taking place. Maturation is what takes place through interaction with the world, and through coming up against problems and finding ways to deal with them. As an addiction develops, precisely because it is so demanding it makes the alcohol misuser turn away from other people and forces them to act in a more selfish way. If an addiction has to be fed, it means that other people will have to be put to one side to serve that addiction.

If the process of dealing with an addiction is the process of maturation, then making amends is certainly one way to mature. If, as part of achieving genuine sobriety, it becomes necessary to change from being a taker to a being a giver, then that is no bad thing. Again, as sobriety continues, the question 'What can I do to help my recovery today?' should change to 'What can I do to help others today?'

Some alcohol misusers in recovery believe they can best serve others by helping the recovery of others. They can act as chairman of the local AA group and take on the responsibility of helping others in the same situation as themselves. They can become sponsors and aim to be there for others battling through the initial stages of recovery. I have met alcohol misusers in recovery who have used the process to explore how they can combine the ability to make radical changes with the desire to help others, and, as a result, have made truly radical changes in their lives. I have met priests who entered the priesthood as part of the recovery process. I have met charity workers who dedicate their lives to helping the poor and suffering as part of their recovery process.

True recovery is true selflessness. Instead of giving to the addiction, you give to others. And, in that process, you find redemption.

> **It is necessary to look at your morality and make amends to others on a continuous basis.**

Case Study: The Religious Alcohol Misuser

Cornelius had a strong family background of alcoholism. His father owned a public house, and Cornelius spent his youth tending the bar and looking after drinkers. He watched his father's drinking take its toll on his mother, his family and himself. When his father died of a severe liver disorder brought on by his alcoholism, this had a profound effect on Cornelius and he resolved not to let the same thing happen to him.

As he grew up, he studied hard and became an accountant, all while helping his mother manage her roles of breadwinner and sole parent to a family of seven children. Gradually he moved away from the family and forged a successful career. Initially he stayed in his home country, but then moved abroad as a partner in one of the large international accountancy firms. He specialised in tax affairs, and was a sought-after specialist in offshore tax havens.

Over the years, his mother initially thrived in her role as major provider for the family, but then succumbed to her own addictive tendencies. Her son, who was now working abroad, watched helplessly as she gradually sank into alcoholism. He tried unsuccessfully to help her stop.

He, himself, began to drink too much. Business lunches turned into afternoon binges and then lonely night-times with bottles of whiskey. He was never able to sustain a permanent relationship, despite the outward trappings of success – his own house, sports car and wealthy bachelor lifestyle.

He entered into recovery through AA, found it helpful and tried to encourage his mother into recovery herself. While he battled his demons, he could do nothing to help his mother battle her own. It was his mother's death from an alcohol-related disorder at the age of fifty-nine that led him to make the ultimate decision, and he decided to give up his thriving accountancy partnership and enter a seminary.

He was ordained seven years later, but never gave up on the process of learning through AA. He still doesn't understand the addictive process that destroyed his parents and almost ruined his own life, but believes that the only way for him to progress is to keep his life dedicated to serving others as a priest. It was, he felt, the ultimate recovery.

Joe's Story: Day 24

This was only an okay day for Joe. He had seen his counsellor and he had begun planning exactly what to do when he was out in the real world on his own.

He determined that he would have to test the waters and he went out to meet a group of his friends for lunch. They chose to go to the pub for lunch, and Joe went with them. He decided that he wasn't going to drink in view of what had happened over the previous few days, and so just had a mineral water while his three friends had a few pints. It wasn't too bad. Joe enjoyed the conversation and the fun, and he felt alright going back to the treatment centre.

However, that evening he didn't feel well. He felt down, he felt upset and he felt somewhat hopeless about his prospects for recovery. He couldn't put his finger on it, but he certainly felt worse about the situation than he had the previous day.

He went to an AA meeting that evening and told the others there about his feelings. 'It's probably craving,' was one of the responses to his story. Joe found that difficult to believe, but others in the fellowship recounted details of their own experiences and convinced Joe that he was going through a bout of craving. Armed with that information, Joe decided that he just wasn't ready to fight any cravings he might feel as a result of being in a pub or being in any other drinking situation.

He thought that it would be easier to give up drinking if he wasn't around drink or anything associated with drink at all. He would take a look at his recovery lifestyle and eliminate anything alcohol-related. He was going to make his recovery easier.

25

Never Forgetting I – Long-Term Motivation

> The struggle for motivation is constant.

So, how do you ensure long-term recovery? Does it have to be regarded as a long haul; after all, AA talks about taking 'one day at a time'. Are the processes that work in the short term the same as those that work in the long term? Is there a major change that takes place during the process of recovery that allows you to progress into thinking about the long term.

There are a whole series of events that take place during abstinence that are either essential or very helpful to long-term recovery. In terms of long-term motivation (discussed in this chapter), these include:

1. Developing persistence

2. Drawing up a personal development plan

3. Using your time well as opposed to filling the time

4. Broadening your interests

I will discuss the helpful or, indeed, essential conditions for long-term recovery in the next chapter.

1. Developing Persistence

Persistence is the cornerstone of any great achievement in life. Becoming a doctor takes many years of study, first, to get into medical school, then to get through years of preparatory studies and then often spending five to ten years in postgraduate studies while also earning a living. Achieving an Olympic medal often takes many years of extraordinarily focused training in one discipline to become the best in the world. Anything worthwhile takes a long time and takes dedication and persistence.

Recovery from dependence on alcohol is also a great achievement. It can take many years to accomplish and is just as solid an achievement as a medical licence or an Olympic medal. Persistence is the ability to place long-term objectives in the forefront of the mind and, more importantly, to act on those objectives.

Recovery is the ultimate long-term objective. However, it must be a priority each day, as if it were a short-term objective for that particular day. As a result of your focus on sobriety, lots of everyday things don't get done. Work hours may need to be shortened to attend AA meetings or counselling sessions. Spending time with children, occasions with friends, hobbies and interests may have to be postponed to focus on sobriety. Giving in to short-term priorities and forgetting the negative effects of drinking can often lead to an early relapse.

In research, the one characteristic shown as demonstrably effective in all forms of treatment is persistence. As mentioned, those who stick with treatment do immeasurably better than those who drop out. That is not a guarantee that those who drop out will do badly; it is just significantly more likely. Unfortunately, there is no guarantee that those who stick with a treatment programme will not relapse, but, if they do, they are more likely to re-engage with the treatment sooner and effectively.

One of the major reasons that some people persist in treatment and others drop out is that some people forget and others don't. The trick of persistence is that you must never forget: never forget the journey into addiction, never forget the pain and never forget the effects the addiction had on others. If that means placing a list of negative consequences of your drinking beside the bedside locker and reading it every night, so be it. If that doesn't work, making a habit of revising your list every week might do the trick. There are many ways of not forgetting and constant effort is required. This is the key to persistence in treatment.

There has to be a constant attempt at personal improvement in order to achieve a full recovery. The person in recovery should feel a constant niggle inside, a restlessness. They must be constantly aware that they are striving for something. While it is difficult to say what that 'something' is, the trick is to use that feeling to struggle for improvement. Nobody can ever know enough, and thus nobody should be fully content and at ease. Recovery means never giving up, and recovery means constantly striving for perfection.

2. Drawing Up a Personal Development Plan

A development plan consists of a number of ideas about the possible future. As mentioned in Chapter 23, it is helpful to write down your aims and goals for the future. It may take a considerable amount of time to put these ideas on paper. It may take days or even weeks of effort to decide what actually makes up your set of aims, and how they are altered through the recovery process. Of course, the majority of people don't make a conscious choice about their aims and goals, and indeed never realise that a true recovery altered those aims and goals at all. Most people rely on instinct or social pressure to make major life choices, and never quite get around to thinking about them in a formal sense or committing them to paper.

The ideas should be simply listed as they occur to the planner, and not necessarily in any order. They do not have to be well thought through, but they have to be specific. 'I want to become a better educated person' may look good to someone reading a development plan, but 'I want to learn how to type' is far more practical and more likely to take place. 'I want to travel' should be written more specifically as 'I want to go to China.' The plan doesn't need to have a series of headings or a series of deadlines; it just needs to go down on paper and to be kept in a place where it can be reviewed and updated regularly.

There are numerous things that can be put into a personal development plan. It can be divided into different sections, including:

• Relationship development

• Occupational development

• Social development

I dealt with relationship development and occupational development in detail in Chapter 23. Relationship development needs to be a priority for all of us, but especially for anyone in recovery. The developments that can be put down in a plan should be specific, for example, 'I need to build a good relationship with my daughter and engage in at least two activities with her each week' or 'I need to go on a date with my partner at least once a week.' It needs to be more specific than 'I would like to get on better with everyone.'

The easiest way to specify the details of a positive development plan is to identify the negative things that require attention. It is easy to identify relationship goals when relationship difficulties are listed. If you describe one of your major problems in life as 'My relationship with my partner has gotten very bad,' then it is easy to prioritise a development plan that involves going on a date with your partner every week.

Occupational development may mean changing your career and choosing a whole new way of life. It may simply mean refocusing on career goals and establishing a set of ideal achievements for the future. Or it may simply mean working hard to save yourself from being fired or getting another job because you have been fired. It does mean giving attention and focus to a job or career that may have been neglected over many years of addiction. It is difficult to state what any one person's career development plan should be. However, it is taken as given that such a plan should be an integral part of a personal development plan.

Social development is more important than it sounds. It really means a significant focus on engaging in healthy outward-looking activities. I will talk about some of the more important elements of this later on in this chapter. Simply put, it means choosing and then engaging in at least one non-alcohol-related pastime. It may mean reviving a pastime or sport that was neglected due to alcohol. It may mean finding a new social activity that abstinence will permit you to focus on. It may mean revival of old non-drinking friendships that were sadly neglected during the drinking years. It should be much more specific than 'I need to get out more.' New life means doing new things or doing old things that were put into mothballs while drinking.

3. Using Your Time Well as Opposed to Filling in the Time

It is very common in the first few months of sobriety to find time lying heavy on your hands. It is common to feel bored, dissatisfied and have a feeling that you are just 'putting in the time'. There may be a sense of lethargy, that life is just to be endured and not enjoyed, and sense of 'What is the point to all this?'

It is all too common that someone in early recovery just about tolerates any sort of treatment such as AA or addiction counselling. They may not get any sense of satisfaction from that counselling or the AA meetings. They might feel that the whole recovery process is just 'substituting one addiction for another', and that recovery is simply too bothersome to be engaged in for any length of time. Effort at recovery can seem too difficult, too unrewarding and too unfulfilling.

Other activities can also feel worthless. Social activities, sport, pastimes and relaxation activities can all feel 'put on', fake or faintly ridiculous. Previously enjoyable activities – playing golf, watching a favourite TV programme or meeting friends – can all lose their lustre, and become tiring and uninteresting.

Over a period of time – and this can be many months – this feeling of disinterestedness or lethargy generally fades. Activities can seem more interesting to you and, indeed, more worthwhile. Your feelings of disinterest are replaced with significant interest and, eventually, passion. Things actually get enjoyable for you again. You can find recovery to be a nice place to be in, and the different blocks of life fit together again. You become interested in using your time well and filling it with things you want to do, rather than things that you have to do.

How can you bring about this sea change in your attitude to recovery? How do you switch from disinterestedness to being interested, from lethargy to activity and from boredom to enjoyment?

It is quite simply a matter of effort and time. If you want to get interested in a sport, for instance, first make an effort at that sport. It is important in recovery to put in the time to make things worthwhile. It is vital that disinterestedness and boredom are blown away, and that things begin to get moving. It can be that your interest returns spontaneously and that no extra effort is required. However, it is often necessary for the alcohol misuser in recovery to try and try again to return to the same level of enjoyment that they had previously. It does return, but not without a lot of effort.

Eventually, a sense of purpose returns. While it may take weeks or even months, it does return. It may be difficult to predict just when it will come back, but is it important to know that it will. Just don't expect it to be quick or easy.

4. Broadening Your Interests

One of the best ways to develop an interest in life is to broaden your interests. Instead of choosing one thing to explore, think of three. Instead of deciding to just take up golf, joining a golf club and spending lots of time watching golf on TV, think of taking up golf, joining a bridge club and taking Spanish classes. It may be difficult to predict just what will be of interest to you over time, so thinking broadly and trying different things is better than just focusing on one thing to see what will happen.

Broadening your interests will also allow you to fill your time more effectively. It will be easier to schedule events in a week and to fill in previous drinking time. You will meet different people, make appointments and enter into gentle obligations. It will become a little more difficult to avoid things and sink into old pattens of avoidance and eventual drinking. Fulfilled people often have many strings to their bow. The purpose of all of this is to make recovery fulfilling, not just a chore.

> **You may have different motivations at different points in recovery.**

Case Study: The Hardened Alcoholic

Jimmy was brought up the hard way. His father had had a drink problem and he grew up knowing the effects of alcohol on a family and how it could blight a childhood. Over the years, he began to drink, initially with his workmates in the prison service (he worked as a prison officer) and then with members of his family. In his twenties, he would only drink at weekends, but by his forties he was drinking every day, often by himself. He found his day was scheduled around his drinking, even though it didn't feel like that.

He had a reasonably successful marriage and had two children, a boy and a girl. His wife had gotten used to his daily pattern and his daily drinking habits, and had come to the conclusion that she had to raise the children by herself. He continued to work in the prison service and became increasingly bitter that he continued to be passed over for promotion.

Eventually he entered rehabilitation, mainly at the behest of his wife. He admitted he had a problem. However, he felt cheated when his wife announced she was seeking a separation while he was in treatment. His eldest daughter was getting into trouble, acting up and going missing at times, and he feared she was getting into drugs or drink. He promised to be faithful to the treatment regime set out by the counsellor, but he lost interest after a few weeks and gradually resumed his drinking.

He entered rehabilitation a second time and tried to focus on himself. His mind was elsewhere and he became obsessed with his daughter's problems. He was afraid she would end up in prison, her drink and drug addictions were getting so bad. She was caught shoplifting on a number of occasions and ended up with serious robbery charges against her. During his period in hospital he had to attend a number of hearings for his daughter, and she was sentenced to a short period in prison.

He was devastated and felt a complete failure as a parent. Fortunately his wife was very cooperative and they worked together on how to manage their daughter. He didn't manage to achieve complete sobriety the second time around, however, and gradually he slipped back into old ways.

The fear that his youngest child was turning to drink, drugs and crime finally helped him to come around. He admitted with difficulty that he felt he had reproduced his own childhood with his children, and they were heading the same way, only worse. He eventually embraced AA, which he did not truly enjoy. He continued to grapple with acceptance of his own addiction, but it was his willingness to do whatever it took to save his daughter that was his own pathway to recovery.

Joe's Story: Day 25

This day was spent gearing up for his discharge from the rehabilitation centre. Joe was told that he was being discharged from treatment and that he needed to get himself organised and to draw up a full plan of action.

Of course, he knew that this day was coming, but this made it all very real. He had to really face up to things and consider exactly where he should go and what he should do. He made a few phone calls and decided to spend some time with his brother before setting up on his own.

He met with his counsellor and went through a recovery plan, which included thinking about when he would return to work, how he would spend his time, and how he would incorporate AA meetings and participation in an aftercare programme into his lifestyle.

Joe had to admit he felt ambivalent about returning to the real world. He knew that he would no longer be protected by the four walls of the rehabilitation centre and that he really had to face up to things. However, he was looking forward to getting back to a life where he set the rules and he was his own master. He was aware that he had to set new rules for himself, which would mean a massive shift in his lifestyle.

He thought about how he would get to spend time with his children when he was living outside the family home. He considered what he would say to members of his own family, his friends and colleagues about his having to leave home. He felt daunted by the demands that his sobriety would make on him, such as making time for his out-patient therapy.

He felt he would miss drinking and all the good things that went with it. He also thought about where his drinking had left him and that was a big downer. If he hadn't been drinking, he would not be in the dreadful situation he was in now. He decided that his only hope of rebuilding a life for himself was to embrace the practical aspects of sobriety. If he wanted his wife and family back, that was simply what he had to do.

26

Never Forgetting II – Long-Term Recovery

> **Long-term recovery means self-development, not just sobriety.**

As for long-term motivation, there are certain conditions that must be taken on board for long-term recovery:

1. Tackling of long-term psychological issues like anxiety or depression

2. Attempting to settle relationship stresses, including calling a halt to non-functioning relationships

3. Maturing of character

4. Developing a sense of purpose

1. Tackling of Long-term Psychological Issues like Anxiety or Depression

It may take a significant period of sobriety for a person to realise that there are other problems at work together with addiction. The initial withdrawal period and the initial period of recovery can be stressful, both physically and psychologically. It can be difficult to get a hold of where your emotions are when they are confused and complicated by many immediate stressful issues. It can be difficult to deal with the question 'Do I suffer from anxiety?' when you are fighting to keep sober in the face of craving. The initial period of self-congratulation, achievement and successful wrestling with the demons of addiction can give way to a sense of questioning and emptiness.

Over the course of weeks and even months of sobriety, underlying significant mood and anxiety issues can emerge. If there is a strong sense of depression and sadness after weeks of no alcohol, then depression may be an issue. If a person is restless, has butterflies in their stomach or suffers from panic attacks after a while, they may have an underlying problem with anxiety. These symptoms will eventually emerge if already present or implicit in the addiction in the first place.

It may be difficult to recognise these symptoms for what they are. If your feelings have been long suppressed by alcohol and if there is a disconnection between your behaviour and your inner feelings, it will often take time for the symptoms to emerge. There are no rules about when feelings of sadness and stress cross into the realm of anxiety and depression, but such feelings are often stronger than first thought and should be explored, understood and, if necessary, treated. There is no point in discovering that depression or an anxiety disorder underlies your addiction, and then doing nothing about it. When unpleasant feelings arise, and last longer than one or two days, they need to be assessed and, if necessary, treated.

Treatment may involve engaging in discussions about anxiety and depression with fellow sufferers in a self-help organisation. You may need to see a counsellor or therapist to help you talk these feelings through. Anxiety and depression may need to be assessed and treated by a family doctor to decrease their intensity, and may even need treatment by a psychiatrist.

The bottom line is: if anxiety or depression emerges, *get it treated*.

2. Settling Relationship Stresses and Calling Halt to Non-functioning Relationships

As we know, when an addiction demands top billing in the theatre of life, personal relationships can falter, break down and cease, during or in the immediate aftermath of an active addiction. It can take many months or even years to assess the damage to a relationship caused by the addiction. In my experience, between one third and one half of people entering treatment do so either at the prompting of a spouse or partner or in order to save a relationship.

The surprising thing is that, at the end of a treatment period, the vast majority of spouses and partners actually take the addict back into their homes and hearts. Only a minority of partnerships end just at the turning point of entering recovery, though, for some relationships, the point of entry into recovery comes too late and the relationship has already died.

It is often impossible to tell at the point of entry into recovery just what will happen with a person's relationship. If a relationship is going to end, there is little the alcohol misuser can do about it; it simply isn't their call. No amount of pleading and no new set of promises will work when the hurt and anger are too large. If the relationship is dead, the best that both sides can do is to recognise that and to find a way to move on as amicably as possible. Many a spouse has said to me that there comes a time when it is simply too late and they can't do anything to save the relationship any more than the alcohol misuser can. It is the absence of hope that kills most relationships in an addictive situation, when a person feels that either there is no hope for their partner's addiction or no hope for the relationship. The alcohol misuser can often instinctively realise that this time the partner is for real, that they've pushed him or her too far. This realisation can often be the key turning point in an alcohol misuser's recovery. By then, of course, it may be too late.

The ending of a relationship in an addictive situation means that both partners can move on. The alcohol misuser can try to maintain sobriety and get his or her own life back. They can try to re-engage with their children or aim to establish another relationship over time. The spouse can put the difficult years behind them and also try to move on.

3. Maturing of Character

I looked at this briefly in Chapter 24. The one benefit of growing older is that we mature (if anyone knows of any other benefit of growing older, I would be delighted to know it!). In life we meet and cope with all sorts of stresses, ups and downs. As we deal with them, we learn. We learn about ourselves and other people, and we develop an ability to deal with the world. Maturity means assessing a situation thoroughly and finding the ideal way of dealing with it. Maturity means knowing where you want to go in life and then working to get on the right path.

Alcohol addiction is avoidance of life. When someone is an alcoholic and their life revolves around drinking, they are not learning and there is no maturation taking place. This is either because they are intoxicated too frequently to understand what is going on around them or because they lack desire to engage with the world. In general, alcohol misusers avoid dealing with emotionally charged events and they do not process their emotional reactions to events. In short, they don't grow up.

This lack of maturity makes things difficult when the alcohol misuser enters recovery. The first task of recovery is obviously to stop drinking and the second task is to stay away from alcohol. But the third task, or set of tasks, namely, to cope with the consequences of drinking, and the forth task, developing a purposeful balanced life, are not easy. It is clearly difficult to deal with tasks two, three and four while using coping skills stunted by twenty years of drinking.

The coping skills of an alcohol misuser are often rooted in the teenage years, with all the misjudgments, uncertainties and inappropriate self-understanding of that time of life. It takes most non-addicts many years to correct the mistakes and wrong evaluations made during their formative teenage years. In the same way, it takes a long time for an alcohol misuser to make corrections and adjustments once they achieve sobriety.

It is difficult to get someone who is set in their ways to develop and mature. It is difficult to ask someone who has achieved and sustained sobriety to alter their habits or attitudes in the name of achieving recovery. All you can do is gently point out to them that full recovery is about development, openness and a willingness to change. It is a task which is neverending because we are never fully mature and because the world is constantly changing around us.

4. Developing a Sense of Purpose

In the comic novel *The Hitchhiker's Guide to the Galaxy*, Douglas Adams famously answers the question 'What is the meaning of life?' with the rather flippant answer '42'. In a subtle way, he is saying that life is essentially meaningless and that a random number is as good an answer to the eternal question as any other.

I beg to differ. I cannot state with any certainty that there is a central meaning to life, but I can say that a large number of my patients, with appropriate effort and treatment, go from a period of serious addiction and often mental illness to a successful and balanced life. They develop contentment and quite often a significant sense of purpose. In short, they are happy. They are not necessarily deep thinkers or intellectually gifted, but, with sobriety, therapy, time and commitment, they get to a point where a psychiatrist is no longer useful in their lives. When I ask them what the key to their success is, they are not able to identify any single unifying theme. I have learnt no great answer from asking hundreds or, indeed, thousands of my patients as to why they have succeeded where unfortunately so many have failed. The most common answer is that they just got to a stage where they saw that the benefits of sobriety outweighed the problems associated with their addiction.

When I ask about how they moved on from addiction, how they moved forward and developed a new lease on life, and how they moved beyond their addiction into full contentment, most just shrug their shoulders and say that they simply got on with it. They got distracted by work, relationships, family and hobbies, and let their addiction fade into the past. In the absence of the negative, they got on with being positive.

It may be unpopular to state it, but a sense of life having a purpose may not be necessary to achieve sobriety and engage in successful recovery. If someone gets caught up in trying to answer the unanswerable and becomes preoccupied with trying to find the meaning of life to the detriment of day-to-day living, and spends a significant amount of time trying to find 'the answer', it may mean they are suffering from a significant degree of depression or anxiety and need help with that. In the absence of the psychological symptoms of anxiety, depression or, indeed, addiction, a natural human state of reasonable contentment can take over. It may not be amazingly 'purposeful', but it ain't too bad.

> **Recovery means personal growth in numerous different areas, not just one.**

Case Study: The Alcohol Misuser Who Didn't See Himself as an Addict

Shane was a 28-year-old plasterer from the inner city. Popular and gregarious, he enjoyed going out for a drink with his friends and socialising at weekends. He played football and he also used to go for a drink after a match and, indeed, after the training sessions two times a week. On the weekends he let rip and got very drunk, and, in the recent past, he started trying other recreational drugs, including ecstasy.

He came in for treatment after he was arrested by the police for breaking a number of ship windows while intoxicated. He was both incensed at being arrested and also ashamed at what he did, as he and his family had never had any dealings with the police in the past. He found it difficult to come to terms with the fact that he had an addiction problem. He saw himself as drinking in the same pattern as his friends and could not see himself as different to them.

However, he began to see similarities between his pattern of drinking and that of older men who had gone on from his type of drinking to 'full blast alcoholism', as Shane saw it. He began to engage in group therapy, individual sessions and even in AA groups with a view to seeing what he could do about his addiction problem. He resolved to aim for abstinence and began to plan for a recreational life without alcohol.

After he was discharged from the programme, Shane did well initially. He tried to take up hobbies that didn't involve alcohol and this was initially successful. However, within a few months, he got tired of 'being good' and one weekend he got very drunk. Unfortunately, on this occasion, he tried some cocaine and found that he enjoyed the effects. He resumed drinking, but started using cocaine on a regular basis also. He dropped playing sports, stopped seeing most of his friends and, after another few months, was fired from his job for being unreliable.

He found that he had moved from being what he viewed as an occasional problematic drinker to being an abuser of cocaine in a very short space of time. He didn't know what had happened to himself. He re-engaged in therapy on an outpatient basis, but found it very hard to accept that he truly had a full addictive disorder. He did not enter recovery for a very long time.

Joe's Story: Day 26

Joe knew this was going to be a difficult day.

He got up and, after breakfast, he started saying good-bye to all of the people at the treatment centre. He found it more difficult than he imagined and he felt quite emotional about his departure. By now, he felt very much a part of the group. The group had gone through a lot together and had made quite a series of emotional journeys. He would miss the camaraderie of therapy, but promised to see his colleagues in the aftercare programme and at AA meetings. He thanked his nurse and his doctor, and simply left.

He had arranged to spend the next while with his brother and to have some of his stuff sent on there later. He wasn't starting work again for a week or two and so he had some time to kill. He passed a number of pubs with people outside drinking larger and cider in the sunshine, but didn't feel tempted to join them. There were simply too many consequences.

He didn't have anything planned, so, after walking around town for a half hour, he decided to go to an AA meeting. He knew where to find one, and soon found himself in the now familiar situation of telling his life story to a group of complete strangers. The meeting went well, and he stayed on afterwards for a cup of coffee and an informal chat. He found the group so warm and welcoming that he resolved to use this group as a mainstay of his treatment.

He got to his brother's house and settled in for the evening, having been given the guest room. He appreciated his brother's kindness, but resolved that it would be a brief stay. Tomorrow he would find a place to live, move in and start his new life in recovery. It would be a big task.

27

Treatment in the Future – What Can Research Teach Us?

> Information from research can help us to understand the nature of addiction and alcoholism.

As always with the world of research, there is good news and bad news from the frontline. The bad news, as we know, is that there is no simple 'cure' for addiction to alcohol. Every victim of addiction has to do hard work and a lot of heavy lifting to engage in sobriety and enter into a full recovery. The good news is that, in terms of understanding the nature of addiction, the genetics of addiction and the causes of alcoholism, and, most importantly, in terms of developing newer and better treatments for alcoholism, there is a large and growing literature and there are genuine improvements being made all the time.

In this book, I can only take a snapshot of the state of play in the research world at present. The research articles I am choosing to emphasise are examples of important research done over the last ten years in particular. Each piece of research stands by itself as important work, but all of the articles cite in their references the work of researchers in the field that have gone before them.

Genetics of Addiction

Because of the concern that the age at which someone starts drinking can influence whether they become an alcoholic or not, researchers in Washington University in St Louis (Agrawal et al., 2009) took a group of 6,000 sets of twins from an Australian sample and examined the relationship between the age at which these individuals had their first drink and the number of resultant alcohol dependence symptoms. They found that the earlier an individual had their first drink, the more they were at risk of developing alcohol dependence. In fact, this has now been a long-established fact in research. However, they found if someone drank before the age of thirteen then genetic family history had a major influence on outcome. If someone began drinking later on, environmental influences (culture, occupation, exposure to peer drinking) were more important than genetic factors in determining whether they went on to become alcohol dependent.

One of the most important objects of genetic studies is to identify any potential areas of genes that might be associated with alcohol dependence. Through the identification of areas of genes, proteins and enzymes associated with alcoholism can be identified. The identification of these molecules could lead to the development of new medication useful in the treatment of alcoholism, to the identification of those at risk of alcoholism who might respond to early intervention and, indeed, to the identification of subgroups of alcohol misusers that might respond to one particular medication over another.

A group of researchers in Germany (Treutlein et al., 2009) studied 500 alcohol misusers who had an early onset of the disorder and compared their complete genetic profile with 1,400 non-alcoholic outpatients. They also studied another 1,000 alcohol misusers and compared them with 1,000 non-alcoholics in a follow-up study. The researchers identified many genetic 'areas of interest' in the alcohol misusers and identified two significant areas that appeared to be close together on chromosome 2. These areas have been previously identified in smaller studies and even in animal genetic studies, and suggest that they are of major significance in the development of alcohol dependence. This study is important because it surveyed the whole human genome, not just one part, in order to detect this potentially important finding.

Prediction of Development of Alcohol Abuse

An innate high degree of tolerance for alcohol has been found in some people. This is called a low level of response to alcohol. Of course, some people develop a high degree of tolerance for alcohol through heavy drinking over years, and indeed this can be one of the cardinal symptoms of alcohol dependence.

A group of researchers in San Diego (Trim et al., 2009) have investigated this innate low level of response to alcohol in 300 young people and followed them over 25 years to find out what happened to them. They also explored the individuals' family history, their alcohol consumption, the age they started drinking and other alcohol-related matters.

They found that this low level of response to alcohol, when found at an early age, predicted the development of alcohol disorders over the course of adulthood. This risk was present independently of other risk factors, including family history or early-age drinking. Of course, not everybody with an innate high tolerance for alcohol developed problems, but there was a significant correlation.

What this means is that a test of response to alcohol could be used as a screening test for young people to help identify those at risk from alcohol problems in later life. Unfortunately, because alcohol dependence has many causes, it would not be a complete risk assessment, but it could be a significant predictor.

Treatment Research

There have been tremendous advances in treatment research over the past ten years. This research has demonstrated that newer treatments are being developed all the time and that some of them offer improvements over previous treatments. These treatments involve new medications, new combinations of medications, new psychotherapies and new settings for treatment delivery. Below are a number of interesting studies to highlight these developments.

A group of researchers from Pennsylvania published a study on a combination of medications that can be used in alcohol dependence with depression. Pettinati et al. (2010) studied 170 depressed alcohol misusers in an outpatient setting who were taking the anti-craving agent naltrexone or the antidepressant sertraline, or both medications together. The patients were studied for a period of three months on a combination of medications and all received weekly group cognitive behavioural psychotherapy. The researchers found that the sertraline plus naltrexone combination produced a higher alcohol abstinence rate (53.7 per cent) and demonstrated a longer delay before relapse to heavy drinking than the naltrexone-alone group (21.3 per cent), the sertraline-alone group (27.5 per cent) or the placebo group (23.1 per cent). The percentage of patients who were not depressed in the combination group at the end of the trial was 83.3 per cent, and this appeared to be an improvement relative to the other treatment groups. The results suggest that it is worth combining an anti-craving agent with an antidepressant together with good psychotherapy in the treatment of alcoholism with depression. It is difficult to say if this applies to treatment spanning longer than three months, but it is a promising study.

Bankole Johnson (2010) in Virginia has made a number of treatment recommendations based on the idea that there are different types of alcoholics, and that it is important to try and match people to the appropriate subtype in order to maximise treatment efficacy. He suggests that if the drinker is a young adult man with early onset drinking, antisocial behaviour, binge drinking tendencies and emerging dependence, then oral naltrexone or perhaps low dose ondansetron with brief psycho- therapy may be the optimal therapy.

For a chronic alcoholic middle-aged male with heavy regular drinking bouts, a trial of the anti-craving agent topiramate could be considered. For elderly females who may have a significant amount of depressive symptoms, a trial of injectible naltrexone once a month for four months might be suggested. Overall, these suggestions are interesting, mainly from the point of view of matching treatment types with patient subtypes. However, the research needed to prove the existence of real clinical subtypes and the superior efficacy of one type of treatment over another for the patients in those subtypes is very much in its infancy.

A group of researchers in Holland have examined the evidence for an internet-based self-help intervention for prob- lem drinkers to see if there was any benefit (Riper, 2009). The researchers developed a programme which is based on motiva- tional and cognitive behavioural principles. It used a website that gave individuals feedback on their alcohol intake and then encouraged the participants, through a series of steps – including preparation, goal setting, behavioural change and maintenance – to significantly alter their drinking. The programme provided information, interactive exercises and a drinking diary. The course took approximately six weeks of weekly sessions.

The researchers recruited over 1,500 people for the course and then followed up on approximately 400 of them online after 6 months. They found that, after six months, there was a significant decrease in alcohol consumption in the group that participated in the programme. While there was a significant reduction in alcohol consumed, only 18 per cent achieved a reduction to previously defined limits of safe drinking. These findings matched the effectiveness for subjects who had under- gone a full randomised controlled clinical trial, and thus this research showed that this type of programme was also reason- ably effective in the real world and not just in a research laboratory. However, like with all treatments, the effects were quite modest.

My own recent research (Farren and McElroy, 2008) has focused on the importance of treating dual diagnosed alcohol misusers, those with depression and bipolar disorder as well as alcoholism, in the appropriate setting. I studied a large number of inpatients (230) who engaged in treatment on a four-week inpatient programme, designed to treat both the alcohol dependence and the mood disorder, and followed them up upon discharge for at least a six-month period. The programme was designed according to an eight-point programme called the FIRESIDE programme.

Patients were assessed for any drinking outcome, craving, anxiety, depression or bipolar symptoms during that time. Overall, there was a very significant drop in drinking behaviour in both depressed alcohol misusers and bipolar alcohol misusers in the six months after discharge from hospital. The overall complete abstinence rate was 56 per cent in the depression group and 54 per cent in the bipolar group, with the majority of others reporting a fall in alcohol consumption. All scores for craving, anxiety, depression and elation also fell. Middle-aged and older patients did better overall than younger patients. This study was important because it helped establish the basis for the successful treatment of an under-studied group of patients that were previously thought to have a poor prognosis.

> **New effective treatments are coming from research all the time.**

Case Study: The Superior Alcohol Misuser

David was an achiever. He came from a middle-class background and attended a prestigious school, where he was a very good athlete and where he excelled academically. He went to college and, with hard work, talent and the support of his tutors, he obtained a high honours degree. He also partied hard in college and got drunk with his friends at the weekend. He recalled doing various stupid things while drunk, and he could always entertain people with stories of the wild and exuberant things he and his friends did while drunk.

While at college, he met and got engaged to Patricia, an attractive brunette who was in his college class. She hung out with him and was a part of the group that partied together.

After leaving college, he decided to engage in a career in finance and joined a large bank. He started in the currency trading section, and soon made a name for himself as being knowledgeable and effective. He and Patricia got married and he remembered having a wild time at his wedding, with both him and his bride partying away into the small hours.

He was posted abroad with the bank, and spent time in the US and Japan in the same bank. He had two children, and worked very long hours at the bank to advance his career. He then changed banks to further advance his career, and this involved travelling frequently to meet clients of the bank at various places around the world. He drank alone during these visits, but this never influenced his ability to perform at client meetings and didn't interfere with his ability to entertain the clients, and get the deal done.

After many years, the post of sectional chief came up and the job was passed to a younger banker from outside the firm. David was devastated. He took this as a sign that he was never going to get promoted, and began to drink more heavily. He was then posted home and given a job based in headquarters. This involved less travel and potentially more time at home, but David saw this as a demotion. He began to drink during the week and didn't care to hide it. He drank 'secretly' at home and sometimes took a morning drink to get him into work. He had led such a charmed existence. He was convinced he was destined for great things, at least for a directorship of the bank, if not CEO, and he found his career stagnation very hard to take.

With persuasion from his wife, he agreed to an assessment of his problem. When given feedback that he was becoming an alcoholic and needed to stop drinking, he rejected the information and carried on drinking. He did agree to cut down and even maintained this for a number of months, but inevitably went back to his heavy binge drinking. He went to a few AA meetings, but couldn't relate to the people there and felt they were simply a bunch of losers who couldn't accept the facts. He spurned their advice and eventually stopped going.

After a few years, his wife asked him to leave the family home and he eventually did. He went to a few counselling sessions, but really didn't get anything out of them either. He refused to see any need for change and, even when he was asked to take some leave from the bank because of poor performance, he felt it was because he was too good for them and not because he had a problem. He did not engage in therapy and, despite lots of encouragement, he refused to eliminate his drinking; he just cut down his consumption from time to time.

Joe's Story: Day 27

As difficult as yesterday had proven to be, this day was just as tough. Joe got up and spent the morning looking for a place to stay. He answered a couple of newspaper ads and went online to find out about the range of suitable places. He found the whole thing very stressful, and almost broke down on a few occasions as the consequences of his addiction began to hit home. He was truly going to have to find a new life.

In the afternoon Joe viewed a place he found online. He found it very nice, if a little noisy. It was a single-bedroom apartment in the city centre and it was quite accessible to his work. It was also reasonably close to home and so he would be able to visit his wife and children from there. However, it did not have a second bedroom because he couldn't afford a two-bedroom apartment. So, for the moment, the kids would not be able to have sleepovers with him. Joe then called work and arranged to restart in a few days' time, though he detected a lukewarm response on the other side of the line. He knew he would have to prove his worth to his boss in the coming months, and he knew he would have to remain sober to keep his job.

In the evening, after dining alone in a café, Joe called his wife on the phone. She talked politely to him, but gave no signal that she was willing to forgive him and take him home. He talked briefly with the children and promised to meet them for a time the next day. He went home to his brother's house and went to bed. He was not happy, but at least he had made some headway with his plans for the future.

28

Bringing It All Together

Always seek help.

This book tries to do the impossible. It tries to advise someone suffering from alcohol addiction of all they need to know about the disease: how to establish an accurate diagnosis, what the complications of addiction are, how to tackle the problems that keep the addiction going and sabotage sobriety, and how to enter and maintain a complete recovery.

The book also tries to help people who have a loved one who suffers from alcohol addiction in terms of what addiction is, what effects the addiction can have on family and friends, and how they can help their loved one on their journey to sobriety. It also provides a basic set of tools for the treating professional, giving doctors, therapists and counsellors access to the important information necessary to advise, encourage and treat those suffering from this terribly disabling, and still poorly understood, disorder.

The whole book's purpose is to provide information. It is through understanding as much as possible about the processes of addiction and recovery that an addict can see just how they have gotten to where they are, and that getting out of 'there' is really a decision-making process. Essentially, the book is an urge to action. Getting away from an addiction is all about change, and action is the most powerful component of change. Unfortunately, everything is life is easy except change.

It is worth summarising here the main points to remember about change and recovery. Change necessarily involves perception that there is a need to change. Some individuals find that it is family pressure that gets them to that tipping point. That family pressure could range from gentle encouragement right through to last-chance threats. For others, it is fear of public scandal or of getting negative publicity for a drink-driving conviction. For others, it is fear of financial loss, of being under threat of losing a career that is the straw that breaks the camel's back. Occasionally, advice given at a timely moment by a counsellor, doctor or AA member can provide the catalyst for change. A significant number of people respond to the fear of health problems; an abnormal blood test or a physical health problem can be effective triggers. Sometimes it is purely an internal process of evaluation and self-exploration that creates the dynamic for change within someone. Sometimes a series of failed treatment interventions can lead to the realisation that it is do or die, that the choice is sobriety or death and that another treatment failure will be the last failure.

For a large number of people, there is no single thing that gives them the *insight* that sparks the process of change. It is triggered by a series of events, by thought processes and by a series of interventions. I believe that anyone who claims that there is only one road to success, only one pathway to recovery and only one effective philosophy is simply wrong. Each person's journey into addiction is individual, so it must follow that each journey into recovery is individual.

Once someone perceives that change is necessary and accepts that change is possible, *seeking help* is the next and most important stage. Enlisting the help of others – spouse, family, doctors, therapists, professionals, recovering alcoholics – is the most effective way of bringing about change. Seeking help can be humiliating, but very few can remain proud in the face of an addiction. Recognising the power of addiction is a revealing and humbling experience. Few, at the start of the journey, realise just how big and how powerful the addiction is.

Figuring out *how to get that help* is the next step. There are numerous ways of seeking help, most of which are outlined in this book. It essentially doesn't matter where that help is obtained from. The very act of seeking it out is in itself therapeutic and makes a successful outcome significantly more likely. There is also something very powerful in making a statement of needing help to another person. Thoughts and resolutions that are kept to oneself aren't really resolutions at all, and aren't likely to be fulfilled.

Persistence in seeking that help is vital. There are often roadblocks to recovery in situ and it takes persistence to get through them. Multiple research projects have shown that persistence is the one factor that primarily determines treatment outcome. Those who keep at it succeed; those who drift away from treatment or support can do well, but are more likely to do badly. Persistence is more important in prognosis terms than family history, personal background, trauma history, gender, amount of alcohol consumed or even family support. Persistence in engaging with treatment almost guarantees a successful outcome in a field where nothing is guaranteed. You can fail and indeed fail again, but if you keep trying you are more likely to succeed than someone who tries once, claims to know it all and then sails off to do everything by themselves. Indeed, it is true to say that a person's true intent is discovered by the degree of their persistence in treatment seeking, rather than how many words they use to tell everyone that they really 'get it'. Alcohol addiction is both a 'thinking' and a 'behavioural' disorder. For recovery to be successful, a person must change their thinking as well as their behaviour. Persistence is evidence that the change in thinking has occurred.

Adaptability is key. If the first route to sobriety appears blocked, then another proven way has to be tried. Thus, if a family practitioner recommends an addiction counsellor, an addiction counsellor should be sought. If that doesn't work out, and it is decided with the GP that another counsellor is actually more likely to be effective, then run with the idea. If the GP then suggests inpatient rehabilitation, then go with that suggestion.

Of course, adaptability is only effective if it is coupled with persistence. If treatment suggestions and promises are made to try a new method of recovery, the only way to make it work is by actually making the effort. It's no use being adaptable without doing anything. The only way to find out if a particular method will be successful for any one individual is to try it out. Statistics don't tell the whole story in terms of what might work for you. What works for you may vary over time, so your treatment may need to change over time. Someone may achieve years of recovery through one programme and then, if they lapse a significant while later, find they need a different combination of interventions to help a second time. Antabuse, with general support and health advice, may work on one occasion, while another medication along with full inpatient rehabilitation may be required on a different occasion. Some may find that AA meetings work by themselves at one stage of treatment, but they may subsequently need an antidepressant or anticraving medication in addition to AA.

Unfortunately, at this stage, it is impossible to tell at baseline what intervention will work for which individual on each occasion. Remember, there is *no one single way to sobriety and recovery*; there are multiple ones. The journey has to be the right one for you. If you find that one method of treatment does not work, then it is up to you to find out what the alternatives are. Most importantly, you need a willingness to listen and an openness to all methods of treatment. Often a refusal by an alcohol misuser to accept alternatives is really a reflection of their refusal to accept the true nature and implications of their addiction, and thus failure is on the cards. Insistence on only one method of recovery is a form of denial; and, like denial, it is often a question of inability to accept the extent of the addiction that is the problem, not the inability to accept the addiction at all. Unfortunately it may take a relapse for the alcohol misuser to gain some insight into the necessity of considering different methods of recovery.

There is no predicting what method of treatment will work for someone. However, we do know that the longer you spend in treatment, the more likely you are to be successful in your recovery. Effort triumphs over any other factor as a predictor of success. The best way of assessing if a method of recovery is working or not is to simply assess the degree of effort that the alcohol misuser is making with that method. In many years of working with alcohol misusers, I have never been able to predict who will fail. The choice of treatment may depend on what the alcohol misuser says about their degree of acceptance of the disease and their degree of recovery. There can be such an extraordinary difference between what addicts say and what they do that it is impossible to predict the most effective method of recovery in the early stages.

If there are too many people running around an alcohol misuser and too many people trying hard to make it happen, then the alcohol misuser is not doing enough. Addiction treatment demands huge input from the addict and lesser input from friends and family. If the alcohol misuser is not making any effort then failure is guaranteed.

Giving Back

Recovery often produces a major change in the amount of time available for other things. What do people do with the time they used to spend drinking? What do people who used to spend four or more hours per day drinking do with the extra time? Sure, some of that time is spent engaged in recovery activities like AA, and indeed it is possible to spend all of your time going from one AA meeting to another.

In time it may be okay to cut meetings to two or three per week and to find something to do with the other days. The safest way of maintaining sobriety is by trying to serve the broader community in some practical and, indeed, useful way. As I hope I've demonstrated in this book, 'giving back' is important for recovery. If addiction is selfish, then recovery should be unselfish. Once a person has achieved and maintained sobriety, a full recovery involves broadening his or her focus to other people.

The following ways of giving back were looked at in previous chapters:

- *Giving back to those in recovery.* This can be as simple as acting as secretary to a local AA group, acting as sponsor to others early in their recovery and committing time to serving the recovery community in an organisational capacity

- *Giving back to those offended in the past.* This can mean directly contacting them and offering a sincere apology. It can involve offering your time to them to make clear the sincerity of your apology

- *Giving back to the family.* This really means spending time with members of your family. Every hour spent drinking equals an hour spent away from the family. Recovery should mean trying to gain that time back

- *Giving back to the community.* Essentially this means finding ways to volunteer to help in the broader community. You can offer to help out in a local charity shop, coach a local sports team, volunteer on a hotline to help others in difficulty or become part of an organising committee for a charity

It is not just a matter of getting a balance in life; it is a matter of the alcohol misuser forgiving themselves. Because the alcohol misuser's journey into recovery involves an awful lot of self-criticism, it is hard to have high self-esteem in recovery. There is no better way to enhance self-esteem than by giving back in some way. So giving back is indeed another way of getting, but in way that's beneficial to others.

Giving back is a way to discover a sense of purpose that was probably lacking in the addiction years. While drinking may be an all-consuming activity, it is hardly serving any real purpose. Discovering a sense of purpose is one of the major benefits of a full recovery. That purpose may be resuming and enjoying an ordinary job; it may be rediscovering the contentment in a relationship that had gone sour or rescuing a damaged friendship. It may be finding a purpose through serving others or developing a spiritual appreciation of life. Being sober enables those different reasons to live to re-emerge.

Who Will Succeed in Recovery?

The list below is not exhaustive, nor is it in any particular order. It is based on research as well as personal experience.

The following people are more likely to succeed in recovery:

- Those who persist with treatment over time

- Those who exhibit a readiness to change

- Those who have a caring but non-enabling support group (family, friends, fellow addicts)

- Those who are a bit older; recovery is more difficult in adolescents or young adults

- Those who engage in recovery groups like AA soon after discharge from rehabilitation, rather than those who leave it for a number of months

- Those who suffer from an anxiety, depression or bipolar disorder, *where that disorder is effectively treated*

- Those without major health problems such as brain damage or liver disease

- Those who have one addiction, such as alcohol, rather than multiple addictions

- Those who relapse but *re-engage with treatment quickly*, either in rehabilitation or in supportive therapy

- Those who use sobriety to engage in a full recovery and not simply to stand still

> **You can never know enough; you have to keep continuously learning.**

Case Study: The Stubborn Alcohol Misuser

Peter was a 42-year-old successful business manager. He came from a dysfunctional family, with an alcoholic father and a depressive mother. From an early age, he had to fend for himself.

He was bright at school, easily learned his studies, especially accounting, and learned to stand up for himself whenever he got taunted or bullied. He got into more fights than average for a boy, and thus grew up respected but largely alone.

He had few friends at the bank where he ended up working and he spent the majority of his spare time studying for a degree at night time while working, as his parents could not support him through college. He drank alone late in the evenings, and sometimes went out, got drunk and had one night stands. He didn't develop any real relationships. He qualified as an accountant and, within five years, had set up his own business giving financial advice to a group of investors. He built up an excellent reputation and the business thrived.

His drinking continued to escalate, and he found he got episodes of depression on top of his drinking. He also had episodes where he got incredible bursts of energy lasting days or even weeks, and he was especially productive and effective during these periods. His depression got worse as his drinking escalated, and he wound up in hospital following a reasonably serious suicide attempt.

During the admission, he was diagnosised as having bipolar disorder with alcoholism, and he was advised to take mood stabilising medication together with addiction therapy to get better. He followed the advice, got well and then married a woman he met on a blind date after a three-month relationship.

When he relapsed again, he went for six months without seeking help and he came off his mood stabilising medication. He found he could arrange his drinking according to his moods, and he alternated between periods of drinking to relieve depression and periods of quite productive elation when he drank to get to sleep.

His marriage began to fail, and he sought help when his wife threatened to leave him if he didn't. He again took up his mood stabilising medication, but insisted he would treat his addiction his own way and refused to attend AA. He left hospital and, nine months later, the inevitable happened – he ended up drinking again. This time his wife did leave him, and his job threatened to let him go after his frequent absences due to his 'back pain'. This shook him back to compliance and he resumed his healthy ways of taking his medication and attending AA. He acknowledged his improvement during this phase and resolved to keep with the successful action plan.

However, he still had to do things his own way. He stopped going to AA meetings as he felt they were unnecessary and began to adjust his own medication. He dropped his aftercare programme and his psychiatrist. He eventually drifted away from treatment services altogether, relapsed and then inevitably lost his job. Three hospital admissions later, he was still insistent on doing things his own way, despite the best evidence of his therapists, doctors and his own life history.

He found it very difficult to change his way of thinking. Eventually he found a combination of medication he could tolerate, a counsellor he liked and an AA group he was popular in. He decided to take all the advice, stick with it all and, after two years of trials, found he was quite happy. It was a very long journey.

Joe's Story: Day 28

This was the start of a new life. Joe got up and had breakfast with his brother's family. He noted with regret the familiarity of the family banter, the rush out the door to get to work and to school, and the easy affection his brother's family had for each other. He knew that this wouldn't be part of his life any time soon.

He made plans for his day. He had arranged to meet his wife for lunch. He looked up the list of AA meetings online and decided to go to a meeting locally that evening.

He and his wife had a subdued meeting, where he outlined his plans to move out from his brother's place in a few days. He described where his new apartment would be and when he would be moving there. He talked about how he was going to focus on his recovery for the immediate future, and was making no major plans apart from living simply and staying sober. He said that he missed her and the children, but that, at the moment, his recovery came first. He told her of the support he received from the programme and from AA members, and about how he was attending meetings since he left rehabilitation and would be attending another one that night.

Apart from a few nods and a single wary smile when they separated after lunch, she demonstrated almost nothing. She did not ask him back. She didn't say anything negative either, and Joe took from that that at least she didn't hate him, that he had a chance to possibly repair their relationship.

He went to the AA meeting that evening and found it comforting. He received a lot of encouragement and support, and sympathy about his wife's attitude. Quite a few knew what he was going through and he found comfort in knowing that, despite everything, he wasn't alone. He left the meeting and made a single resolution to himself that night: he would go again.

References

Agrawal, A., Sartor, C.E. and Lynskey, M.T. et al. (2009), 'Evidence for an Interaction between Age at First Drink and Genetic Influences on DSM-IV Alcohol Dependence Symptoms', *Alcoholism: Clinical and Experimental Research*, 33(12), 2047–2056.

Ameisen, O. (2010), *The End of My Addiction: How One Man Cured Himself of Alcoholism*, London: Piatkus Books.

Cloninger, C.R. (1987), 'Neurogenetic Adaptive Mechanisms in Alcoholism', *Science*, 236, 410–416.

Farren, C.K. and McElroy, S. (2008), 'Treatment Response of Bipolar and Unipolar Alcoholics to an Inpatient Dual Diagnosis Program', *Journal of Affective Disorders*, 206, 265–272.

Farren, C.K. and O'Malley, S.S. (1999), 'Occurrence and Management of Depression in the Context of Naltrexone Treatment of Alcoholism', *American Journal of Psychiatry*, 156, 1258–1262.

Hasin, D.S., Stinson, F.S., Ogburn, E. and Grant, B.F. (2007), 'Prevalence, Correlates, Disability, and Comorbidity of DSM-IV Alcohol Abuse and Dependence in the United States', *Archives of General Psychiatry*, 64, 830–842.

Johnson, B.A. (2010), 'Medication Treatment of Different Types of Alcoholism', *American Journal of Psychiatry*, 167, 630–639.

Pettinati, H.M., Oslin, D.W. and Kampman, K.M. (2010), 'A Double-Blind, Placebo-Controlled Trial Combining Sertraline and

Naltrexone for Treating Co-occurring Depression and Alcohol Dependence', *American Journal of Psychiatry*, 167, 668–675.

Riper, H., Kramer, J., Conijn, B. and Smit, F. (2009), 'Translating Effective Web-Based Self-Help for Problem Drinking into the Real World', *Alcoholism: Clinical and Experimental Research*, 33(8), 1401–1408.

Schuckit, M.A. (2009), 'An Overview of Genetic Influences in Alcoholism', *Journal of Substance Abuse Treatment*, 36, S5–14.

Treutlein, J., Cichon, S. and Ridinger, M. et al. (2009), 'Genome-Wide Association Study of Alcohol Dependence', *Archives of General Psychiatry*, 66(7), 773–784.

Trim R.S., Schuckit, M.A. and Smith, T.L. (2009), 'The Relationships of the Level of Response to Alcohol and Additional Characteristics to Alcohol Use Disorders across Adulthood: A Discrete-Time Survival Analysis', *Alcoholism: Clinical and Experimental Research*, 33(9), 1562–1570.

Appendix

Useful Irish and International Organisations

Adult Children of Alcoholics (ACA)
Anonymous twelve-step programme for men and women who grew up in alcoholic homes.

ACA WSO
P.O. Box 3216
Torrance CA 90510
Tel: 00-1-562-595-7831
www.adultchildren.org

Al-Anon and Alateen Ireland
Al-Anon helps families and friends of alcoholics recover from the effects of living with the problem drinking of a relative or friend, in an anonymous environment. The twelve-step approach is adapted from that of AA. Alateen is for young people aged 12–17 who are affected by a problem drinker.

Information Centre
Room 5, 5 Caple Street
Dublin 1

Tel: 01-8732699
www.al-anon-ireland.org

Alcohol Action Ireland
The national charity for alcohol-related issues, which provides information on alcohol and alcohol-related harm, and potential policy solutions.

Butler Court
25 Great Strand Street, Rear,
Dublin 1
Tel: 01-8780610
www.alcoholireland.ie

Alcoholics Anonymous (AA) (see Chapter 18)
General Service Office
Unit 2, Block C
Santry Business Park
Swords Road
Dublin 9
Tel: 01-8420700
www.alcoholicsanonymous.ie

Anew
Anew is a self-help group for women who are experiencing or have experienced problems with alcohol.

Tel: 086-1024732
Email: carjay@eircom.net
www.anew.ie

Aware
Charity for helping those who suffer from depression.

National Office
72 Lower Leeson Street

Dublin 2
Tel: 01-6617211; Helpline: 1-890-303302
www.aware.ie

Childline Ireland
Part of the Irish Society for the Prevention of Cruelty to Children, Childline is for children and young people up to age eighteen who wish to communicate their problems to a trained volunteer by phone, text or through the online service.

National Helpline: 1-800-201890
www.childline.ie

College of Psychiatry of Ireland
5 Herbert St
Dublin 2
Tel: 01-6618450
www.irishpsychiatry.ie

Dual Recovery Anonymous (DRA)
A twelve-step self-help organisation to help people with a dual diagnosis, i.e. those affected by alcoholism and an emotional or psychiatric illness.

World Network Central Office
P.O. Box 8107
Prairie Village, Kansas, 6620
Tel: 00-1-913-991-2703
www.draonline.org

Irish Association of Alcohol and Addiction Counsellors
84 Drumcondra Road
Drumcondra
Dublin 9
Tel: 01-7979187
www.iaaac.org

Irish College of General Practitioners
4/5 Lincoln Place
Dublin 2
Tel: 01-6763705
www.icgp.ie

Rutland Centre
Private alcohol and drug rehabilitation centre.

Knocklyon Road
Templeogue
Dublin 16
Tel: 01-4946358
e-mail: info@rutlandcentre.ie
www.rutlandcentre.ie

Samaritans (UK and Ireland)
Long-established organisation that provides emotional support to those in distress by phone, email, letter and face-to-face communication.

PO Box 9090
Stirling FK825A
Tel: (Ireland) 1-850-609090; (UK) 08457-909090
e-mail: jo@samaritans.org
www.samaritans.org

St Patrick's University Hospital
Ireland's largest mental health service provider, with a strong addiction and mental health service.

James Street
Dublin 8
Tel: 01-2493200
www.stpatrickshospital.org

Index